Time Allocation and Gender

Time Allocation and Gender

The relationship between paid labour and household work

Edited by

Kea Tijdens
Anneke van Doorne-Huiskes
Tineke Willemsen

Tilburg University Press 1997

Text revision by The Write Company, Amsterdam
Typeset by Justus Damman, Amsterdam

© Tilburg University Press 1997

ISBN 90-361-9648-5

Acknowledgements

We are particularly indebted to the Department of Women's Studies of the Netherlands Organization for Scientific Research (NWO/WVEO) for funding 'Time allocation and gender' the research program with a five-year grant. The final research program's workshop which was held in 1995, was financially supported by the NWO (ISW and WVEO) and the Tinbergen Institute, the Netherland's Research Institute and Graduate School for Economics and Business of the Erasmus University Rotterdam, the University of Amsterdam and the Free University, Amsterdam.

Table of Content

1   Introduction

Kea Tijdens

From the 1960s on, almost all Western, industrialised countries underwent an increase in female labour force participation resulting in a larger proportion of economically independent women. However, even after more than four decades of increased participation, both rates and working hours continue to be low compared to male participation rates and working hours. These observations have highlighted the fact that the dilemmas of reconciling family life and paid employment are far from resolved. As a result, feminist scholars have recently shown a growing interest in the phenomena of time and time use.

Since 1992, a group of ten researchers from various disciplines (i.e. economics, sociology and psychology) and from four universities have been working together to articulate new, interdisciplinary viewpoints about existing theories concerning time allocation. This research program, *Time Allocation and Gender*, was stimulated by a five-year grant from the Netherlands Organisation for Scientific Research (NWO). By the end of 1995, the group organised a workshop to present the theoretical and empirical work carried out so far. The central theme of the workshop was time use and time allocation in paid labour and household work, and, specifically, the dilemmas women and men are confronted with if they try to combine domestic responsibilities and employment. The aim of the workshop was to benefit from the international experts in the field, who were invited to comment on the papers. Andrea Doucet from Saint Mary's University, Halifax (Canada), Elizabeth Harrison-Neu, from Humboldt University, Berlin (Germany) and Catherine Hakim, of the London School of Economics (United Kingdom) commented on the contributions in an intriguing and excellent way. The papers gained much from their comments. This volume contains the revised versions of most of the papers presented at the workshop, as well as some additional papers on the theme at issue. Therefore, this book offers a broad interdisciplinary perspective on theories and empirical findings concerning time allocation and gender.

The first part of the book, called *Time Allocation, Identity and Power Issues in the Family,* addresses issues concerning the value of household work, masculine and feminine identities, the role of justice in the division of household, efficient household decision making, and marital conflict. To introduce time allocation to

Time allocation and gender, Kea Tijdens, Anneke van Doorne-Huiskes & Tineke Willemsen (eds.), Tilburg University Press, 1997, © Kea G. Tijdens

unpaid work, the issue of unpaid household work is examined by Janneke Plantenga and Marieke Sloep. They explore the volume and the value of unpaid labour in the Netherlands. Different methods to measure both the volume and the value are discussed.

In their chapter on work, gender and identity Mascha Brink and Tineke Willemsen focus on masculine and feminine identities. Being a breadwinner is an important aspect of masculine identity, whereas caring is important to feminine identity. A non-traditional division of work is reported to cause a 'loss' of masculine or feminine identity. They explore the mutual influence of work roles and gender identity, and the results show that all effects went in predicted directions, but not all effects were equally strong for men and women.

Hester van der Vinne's chapter deals with the role of social justice in the division of household labour. Many European governments want men and women to share both paid and unpaid work as a matter of social justice. In this chapter implicit assumptions in this policy are addressed, such as ideas that tasks in families should be justly divided. It is argued that the concept of justice is not as simple or straightforward as it may seem. What is considered fair is different for people in varying situations and there are profound differences between men and women in their experiences of justice in the family.

Time allocation is very much related to partner bargaining power, as is argued by Susan van Velzen. Growing concern about the dominant 'common preference' approach to household decision-making recently gave rise to a new, game theory approach based on the Nash bargaining concept. This new approach modelled family decisions related to time-use as the result of a bargaining process between two individuals. Both stand to gain from co-operation but have conflicting interests with respect to the division of this gain.

The second part of the book, *Allocation of Time to Paid Work*, addresses working time issues. When do women stop working when having a child and when do they return? These questions are dealt with in the chapter by Siv Gustafsson and Cecile Wetzels. They analysed labour force transitions in Germany, Sweden and the UK. The differences between these countries can be unveiled as broad political and social patterns, which place Sweden and Germany on opposite extremes of the breadwinner versus equal role-sharing scale, with the UK in between. Using another dimension, the market versus bureaucratic solutions, the UK is placed at one extreme, i.e. relying on the market, while Sweden is positioned at the other, through its sponsored benefits and subsidies for mothers with children, with Germany occupying the middle ground.

Time allocation in households with children under the age of five is explored by Henriëtte Maassen van den Brink and Wim Groot. How do women in these households allocate their time to paid work and to the care of their children? Using survey data, they conclude that women's employment and the use of child care services has little or no effect on men's allocation of time.

Labour force participation of women in Western European countries has increased steadily over the decades. Yet, as Tanja van der Lippe argues in her chapter, the participation of women in Scandinavian countries is much higher than in other Western European countries. In Eastern European countries women's participation has been high for a long time. The authors explain the patterns of women's participation in the labour force in European countries by using individual characteristics as well as institutional characteristics like income level, tax systems and child care facilities.

The third theme, *Time Allocation and Institutional Arrangements*, relates to working time policies by institutions and organisations. Chantal Remery and Laura den Dulk analyse work-family policies by the government, in collective bargaining agreements, and in organisations. The research shows that though the number of work-family arrangements in organisations and in collective agreements is increasing, the type of arrangements remains limited. Child care and part-time work are most common. Sectors and organisations differ to the extent in which they achieve work-family policies. More arrangements were found in sectors and organisations with a comparatively high percentage of women.

In her chapter, Kea Tijdens examines the variables that may explain women's working time. As expected, the presence of a partner, the number of children, a youngest child aged 0-3 years and a youngest child aged 4-12 all influence working time negatively. Working time depends positively on both contributions to household work from either a partner or domestic help and a continuous working career. It does not relate to age and education, but depends negatively on a partner's income when this is above the minimum standard needed for living.

In chapter 11, Kea Tijdens focuses on employers' strategies on working hours over a 30-year time span. Four factors have been distinguished, i.e. bringing manpower levels in line with work supply, recruiting workers for low-paid, part-time jobs, recruiting part-time female workers in times of scarce availability of full-time female workers, and employer agreements of accommodating worker requests for reduced working hours. Although the arguments have changed considerably over the time, the latter argument has become more important.

In their conclusions, Tineke Willemsen and Anneke van Doorne-Huiskes address the following question: Is a more emancipated time allocation possible and if so, which conditions have to be fulfilled to create equal time allocation patterns between women and men? It is shown that changes in time allocation of paid work of women and men do not automatically lead to changes in their division of unpaid work. This redistribution of unpaid work, however, is the very basis of better conditions for women in the labour force. Examples from Great Britain, Italy and The

Netherlands show that, on the one hand, there is a growing consciousness that changing men's and women's behaviour by policy measures at government level is a hard job. On the other hand, this recognition gives room to very innovative and practical projects of which the Italian City Time Project is an excellent example.

2   Accounting for unpaid labour

Janneke Plantenga
Marieke Sloep

2.1   INTRODUCTION

Countless unpaid activities are performed in the Netherlands every day. Beds are made, sandwiches are prepared and children are taken to school. Shopping is done for that elderly neighbour who doesn't get out much any more, the local football club's annual accounts are readied, coffee is served at the community centre and action-group meetings against the proposed motorway extension are organised and attended. The number of hours involved in all these and other unpaid activities is considerable. An estimate based on a time use survey shows that the annual volume of informal labour in 1988 amounted to almost 9.2 million labour years. The volume of formal (paid) labour in the same year was 6.2 million labour years (CBS, 1991a). Thus, informal labour volume is one-and-a-half times as great as formal labour volume. The same survey also showed that the majority of this unpaid labour is performed by women; while men account for around 70 percent of paid labour, women perform about the same percentage of unpaid work. The importance of this work is self-evident; without these activities, society would simply cease to function. Yet, all of this work is not evaluated on its economic and social merits. It is work that just 'happens' and whose performance is automatically expected. It is work on the 'B-side' of society.

This chapter attempts to win back some of unpaid labour's ground. The common assumption is that unpaid labour is an essential binding agent in our society. Household work, care work, voluntary work, etc. - all form major mainstays in the quality of our lives, and lack of focus on unpaid labour in current socio-economic policy is inappropriate to say the least. The fixation on paid work seems to overlook relationships between the informal and formal economy and results in the danger of losing sight of the fact that a specific organisation of the formal economy always implies an equally specific organisation of the informal economy. This chapter represents a first step towards a more integrated approach to the economy.

The chapter is structured as follows. Section 2 explores the concept of productive

Time allocation and gender, Kea Tijdens, Anneke van Doorne-Huiskes & Tineke Willemsen (eds.), Tilburg University Press, 1997, © Janneke Plantenga & Marieke Sloep

labour. Section 3 examines the volume of unpaid labour in relation to the national product. Although it is not a central theme in this chapter, attention will also be given to the division of unpaid labour between men and women. The central question in section 4 is how unpaid labour can be included in national accounts and which information can be derived from it on, for example, the division of informal income and the relationships between the informal and formal economy. Finally, section 5 summarises the most important findings.

2.2   WHAT IS PRODUCTIVE LABOUR?

A more integrated approach to the economy requires first and foremost a review of the economic labour concept. De Galan and Miltenberg define labour in the economic sense as *'the human activity which leads to the production of goods and services which are useful for others, for society.'* (De Galan and Miltenberg, 1991: 13). A definition of this kind excludes labour performed only for one's own advantage; consumption and leisure are not counted as labour in the economic sense. In principle, the majority of household work, care work and voluntary work does fall under this definition, i.e. when it supplies a need, but these activities are not usually taken into account in economic analyses. Thus, the economic labour concept is, in fact, narrowed down to comprise formal, or paid, work only.

There are various reasons for leaving unpaid work out of the equation. One argument is that the volume of unpaid labour has remained the same over time. This would imply a more or less constant measurement error with regard to formal production (cf. Priemus, 1979). A second argument against the inclusion of unpaid labour is that it would upset the balance between national income and national product (cf. Pen, 1970). However, the most thorny problem is that drawing boundaries between consumptive and productive unpaid labour is not simple, and results in a situation where, for example, household work volumes cannot be determined without ambiguity. In a discussion between Pen and Bruyn-Hundt on the productive labour of housewives, Pen expresses the problems as follows: *'Cooking food is work. But is making tea? I would think so. But what about pouring tea? Stirring it to dilute the sugar? Raising the cup to one's lips? If we answer all these questions affirmatively, then only drinking remains as consumption. If we say no somewhere along the line, then we are working arbitrarily.'* (Pen, 1970: 592; cf. also Bruyn-Hundt, 1970).

The classification problems were partially solved by Hawrylyshyn's utility criterion (1977). Hawrylyshyn distinguishes between direct and indirect utility whereby the first comprises the satisfaction derived from performing an activity, such as sleeping, eating or playing the violin. Indirect utility is derived from the result of an activity; it does not concern the activity as such, but the specific

6

goods or services which are generated, such as a meal or laundered and ironed clothing (cf. Van Ours, 1986). According to the utility criterion, only those activities which produce indirect utility are counted as unpaid productive labour. Indirect utility for a household or individual emerges when a third person can perform the same activity with the same result - often known as the third-person criterion. In terms of the debate between Pen and Bruyn-Hundt, stirring sugar in tea is therefore a form of productive unpaid labour, whereas drinking, as an activity which generates direct utility, is counted as consumption.

Although this utility criterion provides some clarity, all problems have not been resolved. The main problem is that various activities within the formal economy generate both direct and indirect utility. For example, for many people cooking is both a hobby and an activity which generates direct utility, i.e. a tasty meal. Making clothes, gardening, caring for (one's own) children - all are examples of activities which combine both consumptive and productive aspects. For this reason, a market criterion is also proposed as alternative. According to this criterion, production of *'all goods and services which can be acquired via the market'* is counted as productive labour (Priemus, 1979; Van Ours, 1986). This market criterion appears more objective because only the result of an activity counts and not any intrinsic pleasure which might be derived from it; according to this criterion, gardening, cooking and making clothes are all activities which should be counted as household production, also when they are enjoyed. The disadvantage of this criterion, however, is that boundaries are now very wide because a market equivalent can be found for almost every human activity. Knulst and Schoonderwoerd (1983) note that according to this criterion, all kinds of pursuits, such as photography and cycling, should be counted as productive unpaid labour, even though intuition resists such a classification. In their view, the literature offers no criteria or definitions which (a) work selectively enough and (b) can be applied unambiguously. *'The term "unpaid labour" concerns a remainder category of occupations in which the "unpaid" but not the "labour" characteristic can be operationalised.'* (Knulst and Schoonderwoerd, 1983: 56). Thus, according to these authors, some arbitrariness cannot be avoided.

In this respect, Hill (1979) is rather more optimistic. In her view, there is a simple criterion which distinguishes productive activities from all others and that is if *'another economic unit'* can take over these activities. In fact, this brings us back to Hawrylyshyn's third-person criterion, but without the distinction between direct and indirect utility. According to Hill, such a distinction is not relevant. Many people also derive direct utility from their paid work, but this has no influence on the classification of their activities (Hill, 1979: 35). Thus, according to Hill, the difficulties caused by the utility criterion within the informal economy are also applicable to the formal economy, and she rejects it as *'quite irrelevant'*.

Against the backdrop of this discussion, this chapter reserves the term 'unpaid labour' for all those unpaid activities which can be qualified as 'productive' according to the third-person criterion. Thus, activities such as household work, shopping, caring for children, do-it-yourself and voluntary work are counted as productive unpaid labour. This definition (and classification) of productive unpaid labour is also applied in time-use surveys carried out by the Dutch Central Bureau of Statistics (CBS - cf. CBS, 1991b). The term 'informal economy' is also used in this chapter as a more abstract reference to that section of economic reality where unpaid (productive) labour is performed. To avoid misunderstandings, it should be noted that this term does not refer in any way to the so-called black circuit. Black and/or grey activities are not touched on in this study, not least because they *are* paid for.

2.3   UNPAID LABOUR AND GROSS NATIONAL PRODUCT

In determining the economic significance of unpaid labour, in principle four different methods can be used (Goldschmidt-Clermont, 1982):

- measuring input in volume units;
- measuring output in volume units;
- measuring input in value units;
- measuring output in value units.

An example of the first method is to discover the number of labour hours inputted into the informal economy and then relate this to the volume of the number of formal working hours. The second method measures the volume of informally produced goods and services in physical units, such as the number of children cared for in the home, the number of kilos of laundry, etc. and relates these volumes to the volume of comparable 'products' in the market sector. The third measures the value of the input, e.g. through valuing the number of hours spent in the informal sector at a specific price and comparing this value with market production. The fourth method, finally, attempts to determine the value of informal production by comparing and relating it to the value of market equivalents. In practice, output measurements are scarce; only a small number of studies have attempted to approach the economic significance of unpaid labour in this manner (see e.g. Clark, 1958). The input method is used far more frequently, with input usually measured in time.

2.3.1   Unpaid labour - the volume

By far the majority of studies on the volume of unpaid labour attempt to approach its (economic) significance by discovering how much time is spent on caring for children, on doing shopping, vacuuming, cleaning the windows, helping out neighbours etc. The answer to these questions is usually found in time use studies. Such studies provide an overview of the time spent on informal and formal labour, and tend to be sub-divided according to, for example, the nature of the (informal) activity, the family composition, gender and age (for the Netherlands, see e.g. CBS, 1991b; Knulst, 1975; Knulst and Schoonderwoerd, 1983; Knulst and Van Beek, 1990; De Hart, 1995).

However, time-use studies or surveys are not unproblematic. For example, participants are expected to register what they have done every 15 minutes (Knulst and Schoonderwoerd, 1983; CBS, 1991b). One activity is noted for every quarter of an hour. If more than one has been performed in those 15 minutes, participants are required to identify the main activity. This can prove to be problematic if two tasks are being carried out simultaneously, such as ironing clothing and thinking up the shopping list or telling a story to a child. The respondent then has to determine what he/she thinks is the most important. Or, as Hawrylyshyn puts it: *'How does one tally time allocation in the common circumstances of simultaneous performance of two or more duties? If over a period of two hours, one prepares and watches over the roast, loads, unloads and folds the wash, changes diapers, cleans Junior's shoes and tries to explain to a nine-year-old child what an election is and what a Prime Minister does - how is all this time to be allocated among the separate functions?'* (Hawrylyshyn, 1976: 123). A related problem is that the availability of people is not measured in time-use surveys. For example, someone can have a 'free' evening and identify 'watching television' as the primary activity, but continues to listen in case the baby wakes (again). In fact, the problem here is joint production through which an individual's available time can be 'stretched' considerably. A day in time-use surveys has only 24 hours, which means that usually only primary activities are identified. Van der Lippe and Niphuis-Nell therefore argue that time-use surveys *'possibly lead to an underestimation of time spent looking after children.'* (Van der Lippe and Niphuis-Nell, 1994: 17). Thus, some caution is necessary when interpreting time-use survey data, especially in the area of child care.

A second problem relating to time use surveys is that they only measure time spent, rather than what has been achieved; whether these hours are used efficiently is not important. With this in mind, Hawrylyshyn (1977) argues for the introduction of a certain efficiency requirement that would be based on the *'minimum time necessary'* for maintaining the household. The reason here is that full-time housewives appear to spend more time on household labour than working women. Thus, there is a danger that unpaid household work would be measured too broadly because this sector lacks *'market discipline'*. In order to resolve this problem, Hawrylyshyn suggests taking the time needed by working women for their house-keeping as a point of departure for calculating the value of unpaid labour because it is assumed they use their time more efficiently. Van der Lippe and Niphuis-Nell do not share this view. They do not believe that based on time-use surveys it can be concluded that *'housewives work more thoroughly or allow themselves more time for a specific task than women with a job outside the home.'* (Van der Lippe and Niphuis-Nell, 1994: 17). Women have very different attitudes to the importance of a clean home and household work. From their research, it appears this attitude is related to educational level and age. The higher the educational level and the lower the age, the less important a clean home and household work becomes. Moreover, the amount of time spent on household work depends on how many alternative activities and hobbies and how much paid work a person has. The greater the competition from other activities, the less time remains for house-keeping (Van der Lippe and Niphuis-Nell, 1994: 17).

With these notes in mind, an initial impression of the total volume of unpaid labour in the Netherlands performed by people over 12 years old can be derived from Table 2.1. Unpaid labour here is demarcated based on the third-person criterion, i.e. only those activities are included which could be performed with the same results by third parties. According to the table, the year volume for 1988 amounts to almost 9.2 million labour years. This would appear to indicate that the volume of unpaid labour is almost one-and-a-half times greater than that of formal, paid labour, which has been calculated at 6.2 million for the same period (CBS, 1991a: 22). A subdivision has been introduced in the table according to various forms of unpaid labour and by social framework. By far the greater part of unpaid labour is performed within one's own household: almost 8.4 million labour years, or 92 percent of total informal labour. Over 5 million labour years are spent on household work. Given this figure, the amount of time spent with/for children is relatively modest; over half a million labour years. This finding is probably due to the already noted problem that time spent with/for children is usually seen as a secondary activity alongside doing the shopping, doing the laundry, etc. The remaining 8 percent of total informal labour is used for largely unpaid work in another household or in an organisation. Of this figure, over 70 percent consists of voluntary work, often, but not necessarily, through some kind of organisation. Only 0.5 percent of the total informal labour volume is recompensed, either in money or in kind. This can be, for example, baby-sitting for neighbours or small do-it-yourself jobs or voluntary work.

Table 2.1   Annual volume informal labour according to cluster and social framework, 1988 (x 1,000 labour years).

	Own household	Other household		Organisation		Total
		Paid*	Unpaid	Paid*	Unpaid	
Household work	5,327.5	5.0	62.5	5.8	8.7	5,409.5
Shopping	1,385.3	0.4	19.4	0.8	3.7	1,409.5
For/with children	563.4	14.9	23.6	0.3	1.5	603.7
Odd jobs and creative activities	1,119.6	8.0	63.4		7.4	1,198.4
Club/voluntary work		0.9	118.4	10.6	418.9	548.9
Total	8,395.8	29.2	287.3	17.5	440.2	9,170.0

*Activities are registered as 'paid' if the respondent indicates these have been performed for financial or another kind of reward.
Source: CBS, 1991a, Table 1.

10

Table 2.2 provides a further breakdown of this voluntary work. It appears that a total of 2.7 million people are engaged in work of this kind, spending an average of around 15.5 hours per four weeks. Striking here is the large group of volunteers involved in a church or ideological organisation. Many people are also active in sports clubs; if canteen helpers are included, this produces a total of 864,000 people. Other sectors with major input from volunteers are organisations for socio-cultural and development work, nursing and caring organisations, and political parties or action groups.

Table 2.2 Volume voluntary work by the Dutch population aged 18 and above, in hours per preceding four weeks and the number of volunteers by activity in absolute figures, 1987/1988.

	Hours	Number of volunteers
Political party or action group	11.8	166,000
Trades Union or company organisation	8.4	122,000
Church or ideological organisation	10.1	753,000
Sports club	10.6	687,000
Canteen of sports club	7.2	177,000
Socio-cultural or development work	15.4	609,000
Nursing or caring organisations	11.6	210,000
Others	14.2	709,000
TOTAL	15.5	2,700,000

Source: NCV, 1993.

Time-use surveys not only provide information on the volume and composition of unpaid labour, but also on the actors. Table 2.3 collates some data which is broken down according to gender and paid and unpaid labour. The leisure time included in this table relates to productive free time. Two leisure-time activities are classified as such in the time use survey - 'giving music lessons' and 'creative activities' (CBS, 1991b: 14). Based on the data in Table 2.3, a first conclusion is that there is little gender difference in the total volume of productive labour. On average, women have a slightly longer working day; this difference emerges primarily through the longer working week of women with older children. The greatest difference between men and women is the nature of time use: women spend a larger part of their time on unpaid labour, especially when there are small children in the household. In contrast, men perform more paid labour. There is a striking element to this finding - men spend more time on paid labour, 5:50 hours per day, when there are children under five in the household. Apparently, the division of tasks between men and women is most pronounced in this type of situation. Based on the fact that children cost both time and money, the woman takes on the time and the man the monetary costs.

Table 2.3 Average productive time use per person per day in the population over 12 years, by activity and gender in 1988; hours:minutes.

Column	1		2		3		4		5	
Activity	Man	Woman	Man	Woman	Man	Woman	Man	Woman	Man	Woman
Household work	0:59	3:17	0:50	3:53	0:53	4:16	0:52	4:39	1:08	4:38
Shopping	0:26	0:41	0:18	0:47	0:25	0:47	0:20	0:51	0:29	0:46
For/with children	0:07	0:22	0:31	2:03	0:11	0:44	0:03	0:08	0:03	0:04
Odd jobs/DIY	0:36	0:09	0:34	0:06	0:43	0:09	0:58	0:13	0:52	0:08
Leisure	0:06	0:08	0:05	0:04	0:05	0:08	0:05	0:07	0:04	0:09
Club/voluntary work	0:15	0:10	0:13	0:07	0:17	0:17	0:19	0:14	0:27	0:10
Total unpaid labour	2:27	4:47	2:31	6:59	2:34	6:17	2:37	6:16	3:01	5:55
Total paid labour	3:32	1:23	5:50	0:45	4:56	0:58	5:00	1:19	3:30	1:13
Total unpaid and paid labour	5:59	6:10	8:21	7:44	7:30	7:19	7:37	7:35	6:31	7:08

Column 1:   Average productive time spent per person, by activity and gender.
Column 2:   Average productive time for couple with youngest child between 0 and 5 years, by activity and gender.
Column 3:   Average productive time for couple with youngest child between 6 and 12 years, by activity and gender.
Column 4:   Average productive time for couple with youngest child between 13 and 17 years, by activity and gender.
Column 5:   Average productive time for couple with youngest child of 18 or older, by activity and gender.

Source: CBS, 1991b.

This specialisation is further illustrated by Figure 2.1 which shows time use by men and women according to stage of life. The groups distinguished are shown in the vertical axis, while the horizontal axis reflects the number of hours spent on paid labour (left-hand side), and the number of hours used for 'household and family tasks (right-hand side). It is clear that in all stages men spend more time on paid labour and that ratios are extremely lopsided, especially in stages where there are children in the household. Children living at home and single people under 40 and over 64 have almost comparable time-use patterns. This also applies to a slightly lesser extent to cohabitants without children and under 40. However, as soon as children arrive in a family, women especially spend their time on household and family tasks, with a peak when children are under 6.

Figure 2.1 Time spent on paid and household and family tasks by stage of life and gender (in hours per week).

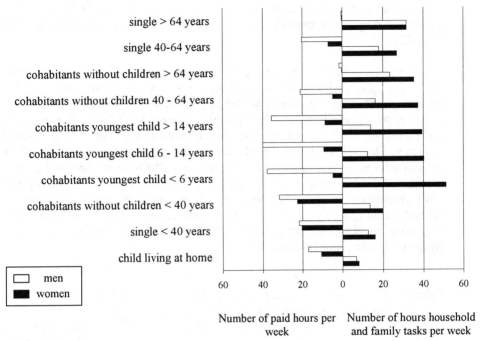

Source: Van der Lippe en Niphuis-Nell, 1994.

2.3.2   Unpaid labour - the value

Up until now, the informal economy's volume has been determined in hours. Such a physical measure is, in itself, already an important indicator of the importance of this sector. However, a lot of studies go one step further and attempt to estimate the informal economy's production by valuing these hours at a specific wage. To this end, for example, the hourly wage of a (specialised) household help can be used, or the wage of an employee with a comparable job description in the market sector, or the average hourly wage. The main problem with this approach is that the end result of a market process (wage rate) is considered applicable to a non-market sector whose ultimate structure is - in all probability - defined by very different processes. In the market, wage formation is subject to the supply and demand process. However, other laws and practices apply in the informal sector: children's clothes are home-made simply because it is great fun; an apple pie is baked at home because it is a family tradition on birthdays; small children go to kindergarten three rather than five days a week because caring for them at home as much as possible is considered very important. The added value of the informal economy cannot really be equated with the allocated market value of time spent informally, precisely because decisions in the informal sector are not only determined by economic considerations, but are also directed by social and cultural preconditions (Goldschmidt-Clermont, 1990: 291/292).

Resolving this problem is no easy task. The argument that the production-level of, for example, civil servants is approximated by equating it with wages paid is not relevant because these wages are subject, indirectly, to market forces and, directly, to budget mechanisms. The informal economy lacks both. Measuring actual output appears to be the only way to approximate the value of the informal economy. The added value of the informal economy would then be calculated by valuing informally produced goods and services at the price of comparable market articles. Such a method is also used in national accounts when an estimate of 'own production' in agriculture and horticulture has to be made. This type of method would probably also mesh with the experiences of families themselves as they often equate their own production with the (price of) market equivalents. However, to date, such research is rare.

Table 2.4 Calculations of share household labour in GNP in percentages, by method and country based on nine studies.

Study	Country	Method	Percentage household labour/GNP
Mitchell (1919)	United States	wage household help	36%
Küznets (1929)	United States	wage household help	35%
Sirageldin (1964)	United States	opportunity costs	32%
	United States	wage specialised jobs	28%
Nordhaus & Tobin (1929)	United States	opportunity costs	36%
Nordhaus & Tobin (1966)	United States	opportunity costs	34%
Walker-Gauger (1967)	United States	wage specialised jobs	31%
Weinrobe (1973)	United States	opportunity costs	39%
Colin Clark (1956)	United Kingdom	wage household help	37%
Lindahl et al. (1929)	Sweden	wage household help	32%

Source: Hawrylyshyn, 1976.

So, with the necessary reservations, Table 2.4 provides the results of nine different studies on the value of household labour, expressed as percentage of GNP and calculated via allocated market wages. In doing so, three methods are discerned: calculations based on the wages of a household help; calculations derived from wages for specialised jobs; and the opportunity costs method. In this latter method, the volume of household labour is valued at the wage base which the individual could earn on the market. As can be seen from the table, the value of household labour varies between 28 and 39 percent of GNP. Based on these results, Hawrylyshyn concludes that its value amounts to around one-third of GNP.

Bruyn-Hundt has produced various estimates of the value of household labour for the Netherlands, valuing it at minimum wage, at the average wage earned, at the wages of family helps and at collective labour agreement (CLA) rates for specialised employees. In this respect, unpaid labour is defined as: household work, shopping, child-care and other activities. Voluntary work and neighbour help are, therefore, not included in the calculations (Bruyn-Hundt, 1983). Table 2.5 summarises the results.

Table 2.5   The value of unpaid labour in households against various wage components, including employers' premiums, 1980.

	in mln. guilders	in percent NNI[*]	in percent GNP
legal minimum wage	225.037	84.08%	67.71%
average hourly wage	309.278	115.55%	93.06%
wage home help	269.221	100.58%	81.01%
CLA-wage specialised jobs	257.930	96.36%	77.61%

*Nett National Income

Source: Bruyn-Hundt, 1983.

Expressed in percentages of GNP, the results vary from 68 to 93 percent. Compared to the figures in Table 2.4, this is remarkably high. One of the causes here is the fact that Bruyn-Hundt made the calculations based on gross hourly wage including employers' premiums, while most studies exclude the latter. If employers' premiums are not included, then the value of household labour falls to 72 percent of GNP when the average (gross) hourly wage is used as benchmark and to 52 percent when it is valued against the (gross) legal minimum wage. Another explanation for this high estimate is that Dutch time-use surveys have a low age limit - the activities of children aged 12 and over are also included. A third explanation, finally, should be sought in women's low labour-market participation in the Netherlands; given this situation, high projections on informal GNP are hardly surprising. Aldershoff's calculation based on the net minimum hourly wage for married adult employees concluded that, in 1980, the value of household production in the Netherlands should be estimated at at least NLG 120 billion, or around 36 percent of GNP (Aldershoff, 1983).

2.4   UNPAID LABOUR AND THE NATIONAL ACCOUNTS

An integrated GNP, as advocated in the previous section, would, in an ideal world, be the result of an integrated system of national accounts. Moreover, such a system could chart in detail the interrelations between the formal and informal economy. However, to date this type of integrated approach has remained unusual: with only rare exceptions, unpaid labour tends to be excluded from the system of national accounts. Yet this exclusion has frequently been a point of debate and a number of attempts have already been made to incorporate unpaid labour into the system.

2.4.1 Unpaid labour in national accounts

From 1938 onwards, the Central Bureau of Statistics (CBS) compiled the Netherlands' national accounts. It goes without saying that the initial system was very simple and, since those early beginnings, accounts have been adjusted and expanded many times, both in terms of the definitions used and the classifications applied (Nooteboom, 1978: 8). The way national accounts are constructed depends greatly on the aim, which is to provide the most complete and systematic overview of the economic process. To achieve this aim, they tend to be organised based on types of transactions and sectors. At present, seven sectors are discerned - non-financial companies, banking, insurance, government and other public bodies, social insurance, households, and non-domestic. The sector accounts are constructed in such a way as to represent different types of transactions in different accounts. The sector accounts distinguish between goods and services, income, consumption, capital generation and capital transfer.

The specific organisation of national accounts is not solely a national affair. To enhance comparisons, national accounts are expected to comply with certain international guidelines which were laid down in the *System of National Accounts* (SNA) following an initiative by the United Nations (United Nations, 1953). This publication contains the agreements defined by an international commission of experts. Since the formulation in 1953, numerous discussions on the SNA have taken place, covering revisions and adaptations of the classifications used, definitions, the aim and the way national accounts are presented. The first major revision took shape in 1968 (United Nations, 1968); a second followed in 1993 (System of National Accounts, 1993). This latter version of the SNA came about following co-operation between the UN, the European Union (EU), the World Bank, the International Monetary Fund (IMF) and the Organisation for Economic Co-operation and Development (OECD).

A continual focal point in these discussions was the position of unpaid labour, and especially the fact that it was excluded from the official system of accounts (cf. also O'Brien, 1993: 10). One of the most important pioneers of modern national accounts, Küznets, indicated as early as 1947 that comparisons between countries based on national accounts and GNP were problematic because of differences between extent and organisation of household activities (in: Eisner, 1989: 3). As a result, for example, the GNP differences between developing countries and Western, industrialised countries can seem much greater than they actually are. A second problem is the comparability of GNP over time. This problem arises when a production shift occurs from non-market to market sector (and vice versa). The size of GNP can be influenced by such a shift while actual production has remained the same.

At a more abstract level, the discussion on the inclusion of unpaid labour relates to the production boundary applied in the current system of national accounts; which activities should and which should not be registered. The 1993 SNA, published in the so-called Blue Book (a reference to the cover of this weighty tome), devotes great attention to determining the production boundary. In principle, according to the compilers, household activities should be considered productive. After all, these are activities which can be performed by another person with the same results. Nevertheless, the SNA production boundary has been drawn in such a way as to exclude the production of goods and services by households for their own use (SNA, 1993: 124). Activities such as cleaning, do-it-yourself and maintenance of the home, cooking meals, caring for and raising children - all fall outside the production boundary and are thus excluded from national accounts. A number of reasons are given for this exclusion: *'namely the relative isolation and independence of these activities from markets, the extreme difficulty of making economically meaningful estimates of their values, and the adverse effects it would have on the usefulness of the accounts for policy purposes and the analysis of markets and market disequilibria - the analysis of inflation, unemployment, etc.'* (SNA, 1993: 125). Furthermore, a different production boundary would have major consequences for the labour statistics of, for example, the International Labour Organisation (ILO) because in that case *'virtually the whole population would be economically active and unemployment eliminated.'* (SNA, 1993: 125). In other words, the exclusion is the result primarily of practical objections, while the advantages of the whole operation are not perceived as positive by all parties.

The general rule of excluding unpaid labour does have some exceptions. In principle, the production of market goods for own use is counted as part of formal production and included in national accounts (SNA, 1993: 125). The best known example here is production for own use by 'professionals', i.e. the production of vegetables for home consumption by horticultural companies or growing them in allotments. This exception to the rule is especially important for less industrialised countries because a far greater proportion of production there takes place within the non-market sector than in their industrialised counterparts (SNA, 1993: 125).

Clearly, the exclusion of a lot of unpaid labour also means the exclusion of a lot of work traditionally performed by women. In her book *If women counted* (1988), Waring shows that the production boundary principle consistently excludes the work of many women. Besides the fact that no value is attributed by national accounts to peace or a clean environment, also missing from these accounts is unpaid work which, in terms of participants and hours worked, is more extensive than paid employment. She advocates the allocation of a value to productive and reproductive unpaid labour; not only to make this work visible, but also to re-evaluate fundamentally such concepts as production, income and prosperity. Waring: *'Reasons given by men for their failure to account for women's work are (1) conceptual problems and (2) the practical difficulties of collecting data. It does not seem to occur to them that if you have a conceptual problem about the activity of half the human species, you have a conceptual problem about the whole.'* (Waring, 1988: 80).

This discussion on the exclusion of unpaid labour is part of a broader-based criticism of SNA guidelines, namely that they are too inflexible to do justice to all aspects of very different national economic systems. Countries have different histories and structures, and are often in different stages of development, so a single standardised system is not always applicable. This realisation generated arguments, also from the Netherlands, favouring more flexibility (Van Bochove and Van Tuinen, 1985; Van Bochove and Bloem, 1986; Bloem, et al., 1991; Pyatt, 1991; CBS, 1993). According to Van Bochove and Van Tuinen: *'We should not attempt to construct, in a single monolithic framework, the "true" or "best" all-purpose description of national economies, simply because there is no "true" and no "best" description. Instead, there are various alternative descriptions, each useful for its own purpose, each "best" and "true" from its own underlying theoretical point of view. (...) we should cease to force our data into a single, restrictive model.'* (Van Bochove & Van Tuinen, 1985: 20).

The 1993 SNA attempts to accommodate this criticism by introducing so-called satellite accounts. Depending on the requirements and capacities of individual countries, these satellite accounts offer the option of providing a place for certain important aspects of the national economy without encroaching on the production boundaries of the SNA. In other words, the central framework remains intact; its classifications and definitions are fairly stringent, with only limited options for shifts in emphasis or sector deaggregation (SNA, 1993: 50/51). However, the satellite accounts offer the required flexibility and offer countries opportunities to test new insights. The condition of the environment especially is often mentioned as ideally suited to inclusion in satellite accounts (SNA, 1993: 508). Another option is unpaid labour.

2.4.2 Unpaid labour and a Social Accounting Matrix

In the discussions on the reform of the SNA during the 1980s, the Dutch advocated the introduction of a core-module system which can be described as a system comprising a core and various types of ancillary modules (cf. Van Bochove and Van Tuinen, 1985; Van Bochove and Bloem, 1986; Van Eck et al., 1983). To

18

some extent, the philosophy behind the core-module system is similar to that of the satellite account system which was ultimately chosen for the 1993 SNA.

A great advantage of the core-module system is that attention can be concentrated on a specific subject without reference to current classifications and conceptual frameworks. Moreover, in an experimental module data does not necessarily have to be described in terms of money. When environmental consequences of production are described in a module, then this can be done in terms of physical units, while the volume of unpaid labour can be expressed in hours. A further advantage is that modular descriptions can comprise more meso-information - for example, through further sub-division into (sub)sectors. Three frequently mentioned subjects for experimental modules are environment, research and development, and unpaid labour. As regards the latter, Van Bochove and Van Tuinen proposed shifting the production boundary to such an extent that non-marketed activities are also included among productive activities on condition that: *'their non-marketed output is substantial; the output is a close substitute for marketed goods or services (and) the sales of the marketed goods and services are substantial.'* (Van Bochove and Van Tuinen, 1985: 43). By applying a definition of this kind, it is possible to allocate a different meaning to the concept of production in different countries, thus doing justice to the specific organisation and situation inherent to a country. Furthermore, the authors argue that placing a monetary value on unpaid labour is desirable but not yet feasible; to achieve this, more information and more research on the nature and quality of these activities is essential.

An example of an experimental module which presents unpaid labour in an SNA framework is the Social Accounting Matrix (SAM) (Kazemier and Exel, 1992). The term 'SAM' refers to both the form (matrix) and the fact that the household sector especially is deaggregated (social) (SNA, 1993: 468). Thus, a SAM can be used to present national accounts in a matrix form whereby the classification is such that the household sector can be broken down according to one or more characteristics. A SAM can be part of the SNA central framework, namely in those cases where data is presented according to the 1993 guidelines. If this is not the case, then it becomes a satellite account: *'... some SAMs may incorporate adjustments which go beyond this (central framework - JP/MS), in order to serve specific analytical purposes. (...) In the SNA terminology, this means that one then enters into the realm of satellite accounting.'* (SNA, 1993: 469). As Kazemier and Exel's SAM incorporates both formal and informal production, it is an experimental representation of total the Dutch production within the framework of a satellite account of the SNA.

Achieving the inclusion of unpaid labour would require an expansion of the production boundary. Kazemier and Exel apply the third-party criterion here and interpret productive activities as all those activities which can also be performed by others with the same result. Household work, do-it-yourself jobs and neigh-

19

bour help are thus all considered informal productive activities; leisure, personal care and study are excluded. Voluntary work is allocated a somewhat separate status because it involves unpaid labour within formal production. Kazemier and Exel's arguments for this separate status are scant. However, the most important consideration appears to be that voluntary work occurs within the framework of formal production. Activities that come to mind are, for example, mothers' reading to children in primary school and coffee ladies in hospitals. The level of informal production, expressed in hours, is derived by the authors from CBS time-use surveys.

In their proposal for *'An Aggregate Social Accounting Matrix of the Formal and Informal Economy'*, they thus distinguish both formal and informal production processes, while also making a distinction between formal and informal income in income generation and appropriation. The overlaps between the formal and informal economies consist of those formal goods within production processes which are used as intermediate input for the production of informal goods and services, i.e. butter, cheese and eggs used in the production of a lunch. A further overlap between both economies is voluntary work which, as formal production, generates informal income.

The SAM *on total production* comprises no quantitative interpretation; Kazemier and Exel do not, therefore, come up with an estimated value of total production. Their main reservation concerns the valuation of informal labour which they claim is *'highly controversial'*. Instead, the SAM for the informal economy, expressed in labour years, is further elaborated. In doing so, the authors also offer some data on the total (formal and informal) use of labour. Thus, the controversy around determining the value of informal labour is side-stepped, but the model still comprises an indication of the relative importance of informal production. A number of data on this point are summarised in Table 2.6. Within informal production, distinctions are made between household work, shopping, child-care, do-it-yourself activities and travelling to and from work. Kazemier and Exel list this latter category separately because it is not immediately clear how such time use should be classified. Is, for example, travel a productive activity? And if so, should it be categorised as an independent activity, or should it be included as part of the activity for which the journey is needed? Given the third-party criterion, driving a car from point A to point B can be considered a productive informal activity because someone else could just as easily drive the car on the same journey. However, the opposing argument here would be that someone else cannot make your journey for you. These problems gave Kazemier and Exel cause to classify travel to and from (in)formal work as a productive activity but which should be treated in a different way. It should be seen as an informal service which is produced by the informal 'transport services to and from work' sector and which is consumed by the same households which generate the informal labour output 'travel' (Kazemier and Exel, 1992: 8).

Table 2.6 Formal and informal income generation in labour years, 1987 (x 1,000).

income genera-tion	formal production	informal production					total
		hh. work	Shopping	child care	DIY	travel	
formal	4,908						4,908
informal voluntary work	381						381
neighbour help		110	34	120	83		347
own house-keeping		4,581	1,103	469	928		7,080
travel time						723	723
total	5,290	4,691	1,137	589	1,011	723	13,439

Source: Kazemier en Exel (1992) based on table 3.

The volume of formal and informal production in 1987 is shown in Table 2.6. According to the table, formal production accounts for 4.9 million labour years; voluntary work represents 381,000 labour years; and informal production has a volume of 8.15 million labour years. The time spent on informal production is, therefore, more than one-and-a-half times greater than that used for formal production. If this informal labour output (excluding travel) is valued at NLG 1,000 per month (i.e. significantly lower than the current net minimum wage), then the value of informal labour can be estimated at around NLG 90 billion which is equal to about 25 percent of net national income at 1987 market prices (Kazemier and Exel, 1992: 10). From Table 2.6, it also appears that household work accounts for around 58 percent (4,691/8,150) of the total informal production and about 35 percent (4,691/13,439) of total production. Shopping takes up almost 14 percent (1,137/8,150) of informal labour. The table also shows that around 20 percent (120/589) of child-care can be classified as neighbour help. According to Kazemier and Exel, the majority of this work consists of '(unpaid) baby-sitting' (Kazemier and Exel, 1992: 11). This high share is a further indication of the underestimation of the time spent on child-care in time-use surveys.

Table 2.7 shows total generated income, again expressed in labour years, according to gender and type of household and is broken down by composition of the household and primary source of income.

Table 2.7 Income appropriation by gender and household type, in (string) percentages.

	formal		informal		travel		total	
	men	women	men	women	men	women	men	women
Composition household								
Single hh.	20	13	18	43	4	2	41	59
hh. without children	24	13	20	38	3	2	47	53
hh. with child	30	9	17	39	4	1	50	50
hh. with 2 or more children	29	7	17	42	4	1	50	50
Primary source income								
Wage	31	13	16	34	5	2	52	48
self-employed	36	16	10	34	3	2	49	51
(early) retirement pensions	6	3	25	65	1	1	32	68
other benefits	11	11	29	46	2	2	41	59
Total	25	11	18	40	4	2	47	53

Source: Kazemier en Exel (1992), Table 4.

Table 2.7, which should be read horizontally, shows string percentages so that the amount of productive time spent by women on informal activities (75%: 40/53) can be determined; for men, this percentage is not even 40 percent (18/47). It also appears that women's share of informal activities in total productive activities increases as the household becomes larger. The opposite applies for men; their share decreases. If the total labour output of men and women is examined, it appears that differences are greatest between pensioners; women in this group perform 68 percent of all productive activities. This high contribution from women is probably partly explained by the over-representation of women in this group. In addition, the fact that men's 'compensatory' formal activities have (largely) ceased also plays a role. Finally, another noteworthy point here is that men only perform more productive activities than women in households in which wages are the primary source of income.

Further elaboration and detailed breakdown of the SAM could generate a lot of information on the significance of informal labour in the economic process. For example, the input of volunteers within health care and social services could be determined. It could also be discovered in how far cuts in the care sector - expressed in working hours - are translated into an increase in voluntary work, or in an increase in informal production in one's own home, or in the form of neighbour help. Obviously, such a cutback could also translate into a changing structure of voluntary work and/or informal labour input; when the ceiling of available hours has been reached, then the essential additional input in one area will have to be compensated with a reduced input in another, less urgent, area. Such data could play an important role in the current debate on blanket care or, more generally, in the present discussion on the reorganisation of paid and unpaid care. For this reason, the Emancipation Council warns that a lack of structure in home-care policy could be at cross purposes with emancipation policy: *'on the one hand, women are stimulated to enter the labour market while, at the same time, they are perceived as automatic providers when any kind of blanket care is required.'* (ER, 1993: 6). Accurate data on the interaction between paid and unpaid labour could be the source of badly needed underpinning for the *'structurally cohesive policy'* advocated in this respect by the Emancipation Council.

A further area of application is income distribution. Based on the SAM data, formal income appropriation, expressed in money, could be supplemented by informal income appropriation, at least it could be if the informal labour input could be valued at a specific hourly rate. Based on these data, the income distribution could subsequently be calculated by correcting for income transfer and taxation and for the redistribution effects of voluntary work and neighbour help. Research by Homan (1988) on prosperity differences between single and double-earner households showed that inclusion of informal income has a levelling effect; double-earners' higher formal income is compensated by the lower informal income. More broadly-based research, in which the redistributory effect of voluntary work and neighbour help is also taken into account, could further support this finding.

In summary, it can be stated that Kazemier and Exel have added the informal sector to an already existing matrix for the formal economy. This supplies a lot of information on the relative volume of informal production (measured in labour years) and the nature of informal production. Moreover, the SAM also provides opportunities for other, extremely relevant areas of application. However, in their approach, the distinction between the formal and informal economy continues to exist; shifting the production boundary only creates the opportunity of bringing together activities under the total production umbrella.

2.5   CONCLUSIONS

A review of concepts such as production, income and prosperity begins with a review of GNP. Only a more integrated GNP, in which both the volume of paid and unpaid labour is taken into account, can be considered a real indicator of prosperity. But, the valuation of unpaid labour is no sinecure. The most frequently applied valuation method first estimates the number of informal labour hours spent and then values these at a specific market hourly wage. However, the informal economy is characterised by its own laws and practices, which complicates any comparison with the market. As a result, efficiency is not always a priority, joint production is an ordinary occurrence, and decisions on whether or not to carry out a particular activity are not always based on economic considerations alone, but also on tradition, pleasure-elements, moral and social pressure, etc. Against this background, projections like those presented in section 3 should also be seen as relatively rough approximations of the value of unpaid labour. A more adequate approach would probably be measuring output rather than the more usual input. As this would lead to extensive statistical exercises on the number of dishes washed or babies changed, Goldschmidt-Clermont offers a compromise proposal which involves calculating *the returns to labour* for a number of household goods with a reasonably well-defined market alternative. These returns to labour could be calculated by subtracting from the household product's gross value (valued at the price of the market equivalent) the value of intermediary consumption and depreciation, and then dividing this 'added value' by the number of hours spent (Goldschmidt-Clermont, 1990: 295).

It is not inconceivable in that case that the economic value of unpaid labour would prove lower than in the studies presented in section 3, simply because other productivity requirements apply in the informal economy. However, at least two notes are needed on such a low estimate. The first refers to the problem of joint production; time-use surveys measure primarily the main activity and not all secondary activities performed simultaneously. A realistic estimate of the value of household work would have to take this aspect into account and it is not impossible that the value of informal labour would, as a consequence, be higher than in the studies presented above. A second note here concerns the fact that the specific value of informal labour cannot always be defined in economic terms. Unpaid labour has a different dimension which can (with some difficulty) be described in terms of safety, attention and respect. In time-use surveys, this is reduced to an x-number of minutes 'cleaning the house' and to a y-number of minutes 'caring for baby/child'. As a result, the inherent qualities of this work are lost. However, this does not mean that economic research on the value of unpaid labour is a hopeless enterprise, destined in advance for failure. It does mean that some discretion is required here and that the real value of informal labour is hard to quantify in terms of sterile monetary units. Given this background, an estimate of its economic value should, therefore, be seen as a minimal projection of the real value of unpaid labour.

The System of National Accounts' goal is to register a nation's economic activity. The international guidelines for this registration are laid down in the 1993 SNA, which comprises a total of 711 closely printed pages. From these pages it becomes clear that not all essential data can be distilled with equal ease from empirical reality: in many cases, agreements have to guarantee consistent treatment. One of the agreements is the exclusion of unpaid (productive) labour from the system of national accounts. Concepts such as employment, production and income are thus related to the formal economy; the perception is that the informal economy has no influence on them. The fact that this is a problematic stance is recognised. The exclusion of unpaid labour is especially problematic when it comes to one of the traditional aims of national accounts, i.e. the generation of reliable information on (the growth of) GNP. However: *'National accounts serve a variety of analytical and policy purposes and are not compiled simply to produce indicators of welfare.'* (SNA, 1993: 124). Thus, resistance to a more integrated approach is based primarily on practical objections; the problems which could arise in measuring the value of unpaid labour and those which would emerge around the traditional aims of the national accounts are pointed out. The proposals for a more integrated approach advocate, on the one hand, a revision of the SNA radical enough to do more justice to the actual aim of national accounts (c.f. Waring (1988) and Eisner (1989)). On the other hand, a more pragmatic course has been chosen and options, such as satellite accounts, are sought within the SNA itself. The satellite option leaves the central SNA framework intact, but offers opportunities to examine specific aspects of an economy further in a less straight-jacketed form.

Whether such an option is considered adequate depends on aims. At the most general level, the plea for a more integrated system is inspired by the conviction that it would generate a more accurate registration of (formal and informal) economic activity, but also by the conviction that this type of approach would do more justice to the activities performed by women. Thus, it is generated by both scientific and political goals. A satellite account can, in principle, meet both goals, although the subordination to the central framework is already apparent in the title 'satellite'. Apart from this, at present only a first step has been made towards creating such satellite accounts. The significance of unpaid labour and the influence which could be exerted by a more integrated approach on socio-economic policy means the construction of such a satellite account – or module – is urgently needed. It would not only increase considerably our understanding of the current state of affairs, but would also greatly improve insight into potential effects of policy proposals.

REFERENCES

Aldershoff, D. 1983: 'Huishoudelijke produktie in 1980'. Den Haag: SWOKA.
Bloem, A.M., F. Bos, C.N. Gorter and S.J. Keuning 1991: 'Vernieuwing van de Nationale rekeningen'. *Economische Statistische Berichten*, 25 september 1991, p.957-962.
Bochove, C.A. van, and A.M. Bloem 1986: '*The structure of the next SNA: review of the basic options*'. Occasional Paper NA-009. Voorburg: Centraal Bureau voor de Statistiek.
Bochove, C.A. van, and H.K. van Tuinen 1985: '*Revision of the system of national accounts: the case for flexibility*'. Occasional Paper NA-006. Voorburg: Centraal Bureau voor de Statistiek.
Bruyn-Hundt, M. 1970: 'De huisvrouw als producente'. *Economische Statistische Berichten*, 13 mei 1970, p.470-473.
Bruyn-Hundt, M. 1983: 'De waarde van onzichtbare arbeid gemeten'. *Economische Statistische Berichten*, 27 juli 1983, p.666-669.
CBS (Centraal Bureau voor de Statistiek) 1991a: 'Omvang van informele arbeid in 1988. Jaarvolume schattingen op basis van tijdsbestedingsgegevens'. *Sociaal*

Culturele Berichten, 1991-6, Voorburg/Heerlen: Centraal Bureau voor de Statistiek.

CBS (Centraal Bureau voor de Statistiek) 1991b: '*De tijdsbesteding van de Nederlandse bevolking. Kerncijfers 1988*'. Voorburg/Heerlen: Centraal Bureau voor de Statistiek.

CBS (Centraal Bureau voor de Statistiek) 1993: '*Nationale rekeningen 1992*'. Voorburg/Heerlen: Centraal Bureau voor de Statistiek.

Clark, C. 1958: 'The economics of housework'. *Bulletin of the Oxford Institute of Statistics*, may, p.205-211.

Eck, R. van, C.N. Gorter and H.K. van Tuinen 1983: '*Flexibility in the System of National Accounts*'. Occasional Paper NA-001. Voorburg/Heerlen: Centraal Bureau voor de Statistiek.

Eisner, R. 1989: '*The total incomes system of accounts*'. Chigago: University of Chigago Press.

ER (Emancipatieraad) 1993: '*Advies vrouwenmantel èn mannetrouw in de thuiszorg*'. Den Haag: Emancipatieraad.

Galan, C. de, and A.J.M. Miltenburg 1991: '*Economie van de arbeid*'. Alphen aan den Rijn: Samson H.D.Tjeenk Willink.

Goldschmidt-Clermont, L. 1982: '*Unpaid work in the household. A review of economic evaluation methods*'. Women, Work and Development 1. Geneva: ILO.

Goldschmidt-Clermont, L. 1990: 'Economic measurement of non-market household activities. Is it useful and feasible?'. *International Labour Review*, vol.129, no.3, p.279-299.

Hart, J. de 1995: *Tijdsopnamen*, Sociale en Culturele Studies – 22. Den Haag: Sociaal en Cultureel Planbureau.

Hawrylyshyn, O. 1976: 'The value of household services: a survey of empirical estimates'. *The Review of Income and Wealth*, series 22, p.101-131.

Hawrylyshyn, O. 1977: 'Towards a definition of non-market activities'. *The Review of Income and Wealth*, series 22, p.79-96.

Hill, T.P. 1979: 'Do-it-yourself and GDP'. *The Review of Income and Wealth*, series 25, p.31-39.

Homan, M.E. 1988: '*The allocation of time and money in one-earner and two-earner families; an economic analysis*'. Alblasserdam: Kanters.

Kazemier, B. and J. Exel 1992: '*The allocation of time in the Netherlands in the context of the SNA; a module*'. Occasional Paper, nr. NA-052. Voorburg/Heerlen: Centraal Bureau voor de Statistiek.

Knulst, W.P. 1975: '*Een week tijd, rapport van een onderzoek naar de tijdsbesteding van Nederlandse bevolking in oktober 1975*'. Cahier 10. Sociaal en Cultureel Planbureau. Den Haag: Staatsuitgeverij.

Knulst, W.P. and L. Schoonderwoerd 1983: '*Waar blijft de tijd? Onderzoek naar de tijdsbesteding van Nederlanders*'. Sociale en Culturele Studie - 4. Sociaal en Cultureel Planbureau. Den Haag: Staatsuitgeverij.

Knulst, W.P. and P. van Beek 1990: '*Tijd komt met de jaren. Onderzoek naar tegenstellingen en veranderingen in dagelijkse bezigheden van Nederlanders op basis van tijdbudgetonderzoek'*. Sociale en Culturele Studie - 14. Rijswijk: Sociaal en Cultureel Planbureau.

Lippe, van der, T. and M. Niphuis-Nell 1994: *'Ontwikkelingen in de verdeling van onbetaalde arbeid over vrouwen en mannen, 1975-1990'*. Werkdocument. Rijswijk: Sociaal en Cultureel Planbureau.

NCV (Nederlands Centrum Vrijwilligerswerk) 1993: *'Cijfers en feiten'*. Brochure. Utrecht.

Nooteboom, L. 1978: 'Veertig jaar Nationale rekeningen' in: *Denken en meten. Statistische opstellen*. Den Haag: Centraal Bureau voor de Statistiek.

O'Brien, E.S. 1993: *'Putting housework in the GNP: Toward a feminist accounting?'*. Paper prepared for the Conference 'Out of the Margin - Feminist perspectives on economic theory. Amsterdam, June 2-5.

Ours, J.C. van 1986: 'Huishoudelijke produktie als economische buffer?'. *Economische Statistische Berichten*, 30 april 1986, p.424-430.

Pen, J. 1970: 'De consument als producent'. *Economische Statistische Berichten*, 17 juni 1970, p.592-593.

Priemus, H. 1979: 'Over de huishoudelijke sector'. *Economische Statistische Berichten*, 10 januari 1979, p.32-38.

Pyatt, G. 1991: 'SAM's, the SNA and national accounting capabilities'. *The Review of Income and Wealth*, series 37, p.177-198.

SNA (System of National Accounts) 1993: Prepared under the auspices of the Inter-Secretariat Working Group on National Accounts, Commission of the European Communities-Eurostat, International Monetary Fund, Organisation for Economic Co-operation and Development, United Nations, World Bank. Brussels/Luxembourg, New York, Paris, Washington D.C.

United Nations 1953: *'A System of National Accounts and supporting tables'*. Report prepared by a group of national income experts appointed by the Secretary-General. Studies in Methods, no.2. New York: Department of Economic Affairs, Statistical Office.

United Nations 1968: *'A System of National Accounts'*. Studies in Methods, Series F, no.2, rev.3. New York.

Waring, M.J. 1988: *'If women counted. A new feminist economics'*. New York: Harper San Francisco.

ACKNOWLEDGEMENTS

This chapter is part of a study commissioned by the Emancipation Council, The Hague, Holland. The study was published in May, 1995. The authors wish to thank Brugt Kazemier (CBS) for guiding them through the terrain of unpaid labour and national accounts.

BIOGRAPHICAL NOTE

Janneke Plantenga is lecturer at the Institute of Economics of the University of Utrecht. She has a PhD in Economics from the University of Groningen. Her main fields of interest are the history of women's work, changing working time patterns and social policy. She is the Dutch member of the European network of 'Gender and Employment'.

Marieke Sloep works as a researcher for research agency Regioplan Research, Advice and Information in Amsterdam. At the time of this research she was working as a research-assistant at the Economic Institute of the University of Utrecht. She has done studies on labour markets, female participation and human resource management.

Part I

Time Allocation, Identity and Power Issues in the Family

3 Work, gender and identity: An exploration of gender(ed) identities of women and men in relation to participation in paid and household work

Mascha Brink
Tineke Willemsen

3.1 INTRODUCTION

This chapter focuses on the relative influence of gender and gender(ed) identities of men and women on their participation in paid work and household tasks. Attempts at explanations of the well-known sex differences in this field often use the concept of identity as a 'black box': if other variables such as attitudes or economic reasons cannot explain why women have less paid work than men and why men spend so little time on household work, then these differences must be caused by something very deep, like identity. This chapter starts with an overview of traditional psychological research which uses gender identity as an explanation for differences in women's allocation of time to paid and unpaid work. Then the concept of gender identity as used in these studies will be elaborated towards a more diversified and social concept of gendered identity. The data derived from a study of gendered identity, in relation to time devoted to paid work and household tasks.

3.2 GENDER IDENTITY IN PSYCHOLOGICAL RESEARCH ON SEX DIFFERENCES IN TIME ALLOCATION

Since the introduction of Bems's Sex Role Inventory (Bem, 1974), psychological research has made ample use of this instrument to measure gender identity, i.e. the self concept in terms of masculine and feminine characteristics. According to Bem, masculinity and femininity are two separate and independent dimensions of gender identity. Individuals can score high or low on either or both of these dimensions. In Bem's view, gender identity is expressed in personality traits. High femininity is expressed through the self attribution of many stereotypically feminine traits and high masculinity through masculine traits. By relating gender identity to sex stereotypes, i.e. to the cultural image of men and women, gender identity expresses one's position in relation to these cultural images. Gender

Time allocation and gender, Kea Tijdens, Anneke van Doorne-Huiskes & Tineke Willemsen (eds.), Tilburg University Press, 1997, © Mascha Brink & Tineke M. Willemsen

identity is then defined as the degree of congruence (or of difference) between one's personal self image and the cultural image of men and women. Based on the scores on the masculinity and femininity subscales, four categories of individuals are distinguished. High femininity and low masculinity indicate a *feminine* personality; high masculinity and low femininity a *masculine* personality; high on both dimensions is called an *androgynous* personality; and low on both an *undifferentiated* personality (Bem, 1977). The four categories are based on the scores on the subscales only and are the same for men and women. These categories combined with biological sex lead to another division, indicating individuals' fit with the cultural image of their own sex: masculine men and feminine women are called sex typed, feminine men and masculine women cross-sex typed (in this categorisation androgynous and undifferentiated are the same as in the previous one).

The obvious hypothesis in studies which relate this type of gender identity to time allocation in paid and unpaid work is that psychological femininity is associated with the feminine role of taking care of children and household work, while psychological masculinity is associated with paid work. Overall, most of these studies indicate that partners' masculinity and femininity scores relate to the division of tasks, although sex of the subject is still the best predictor of the relative amount of time spent on household work. Results from a study by Gunter and Gunter (1990) indicate that individuals of both sexes who were classified as androgynous or feminine did more household tasks than persons of the same sex classified as masculine. The influence of gender identity was the same for men and women. Atkinson and Huston (1984) also found that highly gender-typed couples (masculine husband/feminine wife) had a traditional division of labour. Single sex studies yielded the same results (Hoffman & Fidell, 1979; Russell, 1978). But although using a related measure, Steil and Weltman (1991) did not find the predicted relationship between gender type and the division of household tasks. In other studies the expected relationship was only established for either the male or the female partner. In a study by Denmark, Shaw and Ciali (1985) masculine men did fewer household tasks than other men, but there was no difference between feminine women and other women in the amount of time spent on household work. Antill and Cotton (1988) also found different results for masculinity and femininity in men and women. Male masculinity had no influence on the division of tasks, but femininity in men was related to an increase in participation in traditionally feminine tasks. Masculinity in women increased their relative contribution to traditionally masculine tasks, but femininity in women did not raise levels of participation in feminine tasks. Contradictory results for femininity in women were found by Nyquist, Slivken, Spence and Helmreich (1985). As predicted, men who scored high on femininity did more of the routine household tasks than other men, but women scoring high on either masculinity or femininity did less household work than women scoring low on these scales. Surprisingly, there are no studies available relating masculinity and femininity scores to the division of paid work in couples.

In summary, these studies indicate that even though the subjects' sex is the best predictor of the division of household work, gender identity generally is found to correlate with the division of household work in couples, and with a few exceptions in the predicted direction that associates traditional sex typing with a traditional division of work. Unfortunately, most of the studies focus only on the division of household work and not on paid work. Paid work is sometimes included in these studies as a background variable, or as a grouping variable used to compare working mothers to housewives, or as a variable that restricts the amount of time available for other tasks.

3.3   AN EXTENSION OF THE CONCEPT OF GENDER IDENTITY

In the studies mentioned above the concept of gender identity is restricted to personality traits. However, to modern theorists identity is usually a more complex concept. Most recent definitions incorporate an element of positions in a social structure, combined with the personal meanings a person attaches to these positions (Deaux 1992, Breakwell, 1986). In the present study we will use a social psychological framework as described by Deaux (1993), who considers identity a connected set of (sub)identities. These (sub)identities are defined by the social groups or categories to which a person belongs, such as gender and ethnicity, and by a person's roles, such as parent or colleague. These identities are often called 'social identities' as they relate to positions of the individual in the social structure. Not all social positions an individual has, however, are necessarily 'claimed' as an identity by the individual. Deaux cites the example of Hispanic students, not all of whom claimed 'Hispanic' as an identity (Deaux, 1993). Social identities are imbued with a complex of meanings, i.e. are given meaning by the individual in the form of traits, roles or behaviours that an individual experiences as connected to this identity. One can distinguish between culturally shared meanings and personal meanings. The meanings people attach to a social identity can show many individual differences even if the social identity label is the same. In the present study we have extended the concept of gender identity, in accordance with Deaux' definition of identity, to include not only personality traits but also roles, gender roles in this case, and social identity, in this case one's sense of belonging to the "group" of men or women in our society.

3.4   GENDER ROLE IDENTITY

A definition of the term role in relation to gender is given by Eagly: 'Gender roles are defined as those shared expectations (about appropriate qualities and behaviours) that apply to individuals on basis of their socially defined gender.' (Eagly, 1987). Social role theorists assume that children, through identification and other learning processes, learn the roles appropriate for their gender and the qualities that belong to these roles. Gender roles are more general and cover a

33

wider domain than the roles that come with specific functions someone may have. Individuals vary in the extent to which they conform to role demands, and situations differ in the extent to which they demand compliance to specific roles (Eagly, 1987). The roles considered most typical for the sexes are the provider role for the adult man and the homemaker role for the adult woman.

There is little or no research available in which individuals' internalisation of gender roles, i.e. the degree to which the traditional gender roles are incorporated into one's self image, is studied in relation to participation in paid and unpaid work. Attitude measures, i.e. the degree to which one expects men and women in general to adhere to traditional gender roles, are usually used in this context. Based on these attitude measures individuals can vary from egalitarian, i.e. the opinion that men and women should perform more or less the same roles, to traditional, i.e. the opinion that men and women should stick to the provider/homemaker division of tasks. The hypothesis in this type of study is then that, in general, people with more egalitarian attitudes will show more sharing of both paid work and household work.

Confirming this hypothesis, a study by Stafford, Backman and Dibona (1977) among married and cohabiting men and women (students) found that division of household tasks was consistent with gender role ideology. In a study by Antill and Cotton (1988) egalitarianism of the male partner was the best predictor of the task division. Ross (1987) also found that husbands with less traditional gender role beliefs did more household work. In her study wives' attitudes did not significantly affect the division of tasks. In contrast to these findings, a study by Barnett and Baruch (1987) on determinants of fathers' participation in household and child care tasks, found the amount of household work done by the man in double-earner families depended mainly on the gender role attitudes of the wife. The gender role attitudes of the man were less important. Even reverse relations between egalitarian attitudes and task sharing are sometimes reported. Coverman (1985) found that non-traditional attitudes (as measured by only two questions) reduced male participation in household work.

The above is in no way a complete overview of studies in which the relationship between attitudes towards gender roles and the division of tasks is studied, but it forms a representative selection. In general, these studies show the predicted relationship between gender role attitudes and participation in household work. However, some studies do not support these results, and some even find contradictory results. Remarkable is that in some studies egalitarian gender role attitudes of the wife are the best predictor of an egalitarian division of work whereas in other studies attitudes of the husband are more indicative.

3.5   SOCIAL GENDER IDENTITY

Individuals can see themselves as members of various social groups. Unlike the two aspects of identity discussed in the preceding paragraphs, the application of the concept of social identity to gender issues is relatively new. The notion that part of the identity or self concept is formed by the social groups someone belongs to was formulated in social identity theory (Tajfel, 1978, Tajfel & Turner 1985). Social identity is defined as 'That part of the self concept of an individual that stems from his knowledge of his membership of a social group or groups' (Tajfel, 1978). From the wording of this definition it is obvious that Tajfel was not particularly concerned with gender identity. Originally, social identity theory was developed to explain intergroup relations and conflicts between ethnic groups. The basic assumption underlying the theory is that persons are motivated to preserve a positive self image and that they achieve this by comparing themselves to other individuals and groups. However, as a consequence of existing differences in status, these comparisons cannot be positive for everyone. Members of low status groups will therefore be motivated to change the social order through various strategies ranging from individual change of group membership to various forms of collective action. Because it theorises the link between the personal and the social, social identity theory offers the possibility to establish a connection between individual choices about work and care on the one hand, and the collective striving for equal opportunities on the other. The division of work within families is a personal decision but it is also one of the most important areas where inequalities between men and women are reproduced. Individual decisions on division of paid and household work issues can be considered strategies to change unequal (status) relations between men and women.

Only a few studies have been carried out on the role of social identity for women's decisions concerning work and family. A study by Baker (1989) on the change in social identity when a woman's first child is born is particularly relevant to the use of social identity theory for analysing the division of paid and unpaid labour. Baker used interviews in combination with the 'repertory grid' method (Kelly, 1955), a method in which the relationship with important persons and (representatives of) social groups is explicated by asking people to describe themselves in relation to the other person. Baker interviewed 53 women 11 weeks before the expected birth of their child and 16 weeks after giving birth. She assumed that mothers form a separate social group who construct their identity mainly in comparison with other women, rather than with men. Therefore, only groups of women were included as comparison groups in this study. The results indicate 'self' and 'ideal self' were most highly associated with 'a good mother', close were 'own mother' and 'a good friend'. The lowest association was with 'career woman' and 'not a good mother'. A shift in social identity from 'worker' to 'mother' could not be demonstrated, probably because of the late timing of the first interview, when the identity as a mother was already well established. Mothers with a more positive social identity had, on average, a shorter

35

work history, and were younger and less well-educated than mothers with a less positive social identity. However, the mothers who had worked longer did not identify more strongly with career women and even planned to go back to work at a later stage than mothers with a shorter work history. Their negative social identity cannot be explained by a stronger identity as a 'worker'. The two groups did differ with regard to the closeness of relatives and friends in the same situation. Therefore, the more negative social identity of these women was explained by Baker not by referring to the loss of identity as a worker or the lower status of the mother compared to a working woman, but by the fact that in general these women received less social support. Even though it is often assumed that the role of mother has a low social status (Oakley, 1980), most mothers in this study did not see their role in that way. Motherhood was valued positively, but this had nothing to do with perceived status. Baker concluded that it is more meaningful to relate social identity to previous experiences of the mother than to general notions about the status of the mother role. With regard to perception of status it is interesting to compare these findings with the study by Marshall and Wetherell (1989) in which motherhood did emerge as a low status activity that was valued negatively. In that study, however, the respondents were law students, on their way to start a career. This difference in adopting the 'mother' identity confirms the prediction by social identity theory that people will value their own group more highly than other groups.

Neither social identity theory in itself nor the studies mentioned above lead to clear predictions about the influence of social identity on the division of paid and unpaid work. However, they indicate that identification with social groups is important in these fields of life as well. They further indicate that identification with certain groups is related to the subjective status of those groups and to the evaluation of oneself as a group member. This can be an important influence on a person's motivation to change their situation, and probably influence their decisions on work patterns. Unfortunately, no research has yet been reported on the social identities of men in relation to these issues.

3.6   METHOD

Overview
The study presented here was a mail survey in which three forms of gender identity were measured: gender identity in the form of a personality characteristic, gender role identity, and social gender identity. As dependent variables participation in paid work and household work was measured. The survey took place in the summer of 1995.

Respondents
A sample of 1200 individuals, selected at random from the Dutch telephone book, were contacted by phone and asked to participate in a study on opinions on

work and the family. Individuals who agreed to participate were sent a questionnaire. This resulted in a total sample of 432 respondents (191 women and 241 men). For that part of the study described in this chapter we only included individuals who in principle could have a full time paid job, so individuals aged 65 or older, and students were excluded from the sample. The remaining sample consisted of 355 individuals, 150 men and 205 women. Ages varied from 18 to 64, with a mean age of 40.7 years. 71.6% of respondents was married; 7.5% cohabited with a partner; 6.6% was widowed or divorced; and 13.9% single or with a non cohabiting partner. 76.6% had one or more children.

Measures

To measure *gender identity in personality traits* a section of the 'Nederlandse Sekse-Identiteit Vragenlijst' (NSIV, Dutch gender identity questionnaire) was included (Willemsen & Fischer, 1997). The questionnaire consists of 30 positive or slightly negative personality traits, which were rated as stereotypically masculine or feminine by several Dutch samples. Respondents are asked to rate on a five-point scale to what extent these traits are applicable to them. The masculine and feminine traits are combined into separate masculinity and femininity trait scales. Reliabilities of these scales were alpha = .73 and alpha = .72, respectively.

To measure *gender role identity* a questionnaire was developed to measure the extent to which an individual in his or her own life is oriented towards the family and/or oriented towards paid work. The scale consists of 12 statements about personal preferences concerning work and family roles. Respondents are asked to rate on a seven-point scale to what extent they agree or disagree with these items. The items are combined to form one scale on which a low score indicates strong family-oriented preferences and a high score refers to strong work-oriented preferences. Reliability of the scale is alpha = .80.

To measure *social gender identity* an adaptation was made of the group identification scale used by Ahlers (1994). This resulted in a 12-item questionnaire with items on personal identification as a man or woman ('It is important for me to be a man'), identification with members of one's own sex ('I identify with men as a group'), and extent to which one differentiates oneself from members of the other sex ('I have much in common with women'). There were separate lists for men and women, differing only in the gender mentioned. Respondents are asked to indicate on a 7-point scale to what extent they agree with the item. The reliability of the scale is alpha = .74 for the whole group, with alpha = .73 for men and .74 for women. A low score indicates little identification with one's sex group, a high score indicates strong social gender identity.

As a measure of participation in paid work respondents were asked for their profession and the number of hours of paid work. As a measure of participation in household work the following question was asked: 'How much of your own maintenance (including preparing meals, doing the laundry, grocery shopping, cleaning etc.) do you do yourself?' Respondents could answer on a five-point scale ranging from 0-20% or almost nothing to 80-100% or almost all. Note that this general question does not ask about amount of household work for others.

The question was phrased in this way to allow also individuals living without other adults to answer it.

3.7 RESULTS

Paid work and household work
Respondents worked an average of 22.8 hours a week in a paid job. These hours of work are strongly related to sex of respondent. Men worked 36 hours on average, women 16 hours. 78.4% of the men worked full time (women 15.8 %) and 42% of the women had no paid work, compared to 12.2% of the men. A comparable difference between men and women occurs for the percentage of household work performed by an individual. The majority (71.8%) of women reported doing more than 80% of their own household work, while for men there is more variation with the largest group doing less than 40%.

Table 3.1 Percentage of their own household work, by sex of respondent.

	men (N=150) %	women (N=209) %
0-20 %	26.7	2.4
21-40%	32.0	3.8
41-60 %	16.0	5.3
61-80%	7.3	16.7
81-100%	18.0	71.8
total	100	100

Among women there is little variation with respect to the percentage of household work they perform but more variation regarding hours of paid work, with the largest group not working in a paid job. Men show little variation in hours of paid work but more on percentage of household work. Involvement in paid work and household work are inversely related. The correlation between hours of paid work and percentage of household work for the total sample is -.60 (p < .001).

Gender identity
In table 3.2 mean scores and standard deviations are shown for the gender identity scales. Scores of men and women differ significantly on all scales when compared with a t-test (p < .001), but these differences are not great. Women identify more strongly with their own gender group than men. Women score higher on feminine traits and men higher on masculine traits, as is usual. On role preference, women expressed a more family-oriented preference and men a more

work-oriented preference. On this scale, men and women also differed in variance, with men showing less than women.

Table 3.2   Mean scores and standard deviations on the gender identity measures.

	whole sample		men		women	
	mean	sd	mean	sd	mean	sd
masculine traits (1= low, 5 = high)	3.19	.43	3.31	.43	3.10	.41
feminine traits (1= low, 5 = high)	3.49	.38	3.34	.36	3.60	.36
role preference (1= family-oriented, 7 = work-oriented)	3.52	1.06	3.95	.83	3.21	1.10
social identity (1= low, 7 = high)	4.82	.75	4.58	.74	5.00	.72

Gender identity and paid work

To check the hypotheses about the relationship of work and gender identity a regression analysis was performed with hours of paid work as the dependent variable. Apart from the four identity measures, a number of respondents' background characteristics that were expected to relate to involvement in paid work were also included. These are sex, age, living situation (alone or with a partner), children (yes or no) and educational level. The background characteristics were entered in the first block, the identity variables in the second block. In this way, we can study how much variance is explained by gender identity in addition to that explained by demographic variables. The regression analysis was done for men and women together, and for men and for women separately. Results are shown in table 3.3.

Table 3.3 Regression model of paid work

	standardised regression coefficients		
	men and women (N=273)	men (N= 118)	women (N=155)
Sex	-.411***		
Age	-.155**	-.290**	-.15 *
Living situation	.136**	.333**	.00
Children	-.123*	-.009	-.27 ***
Education	.070	.053	.05
Gender identity:			
Masculine traits	.027	.060	-.00
Feminine traits	-.066	-.061	-.03
Role preferences	.320***	.123	.48 ***
Social identity	-.025	-.022	.02
R^2	.479	.106	.45
F	28.630***	2.741**	17.22 ***

$* p < .05, ** p < .01, *** p < .001.$

For the entire sample, sex of respondent is clearly the most important predictor of involvement in paid work. On its own, sex of respondent explains 30% of the variance in hours of paid work, indicating that women work fewer hours than men. The background variables together account for 40% of the variance. Apart from sex also age, living situation and presence of children contribute significantly to the equation. Older people and people with children work fewer hours and cohabiting people work more hours. When gender identity measures are added R^2 rises to .48. From the gender identity measures only role preference contributes significantly to the equation, with more work- oriented preferences relating to more hours in paid work. The analyses for men and women separately show that for men only 12% of the variance is explained and only age and living situation contribute significantly to the equation. Older men work fewer hours and cohabiting men work more hours. For women $R^2 = .45$ with age, presence of children and role preference contributing significantly to the equation. Older women and women with children work fewer hours and women with work-oriented preferences work more hours.

Gender identity and household work

The same analyses were performed for household work. In this case paid work was included as a predictor in the equation, in order to facilitate comparison of our results with existing literature on this topic. Results of the analyses are shown in table 3.4.

Table 3.4 Regression model of household work

	standardised regression coefficients		
	men and women (N=273)	men (N=118)	women (N=155)
Sex	.442***		
Age	.010	.17	-.106
Living situation	-.268***	-.54 ***	-.178*
Children	-.034	-.13	.170
Education	.035	-.07	.037
Hours paid work	-.300***	-.18 *	-.289**
Gender identity:			
Masculine traits	.051	.08	.086
Feminine traits	.039	-.00	-.032
Role preferences	-.113*	-.16 *	-.178
Social identity	.037	.00	.068
Adjusted R^2	.566	.41	.209
F	36.493***	10.13 ***	5.540***

* $p < .05$, ** $p < .01$, *** $p < .001$.

Here we see to some extent the same pattern as for paid work. For men and women together sex of respondent is the main predictor. For household work sex alone explains 40% of the variance, indicating that men do less household work. With the other demographic variables added, R^2 rises to .56, with living situation and paid work as significant contributors. Cohabitors do less household work, as do people who work more hours in paid jobs. Note that amount of household work refers to a percentage. If the gender identity variables are added, R^2 rises only slightly to .57, which indicates that these variables do not add much to the explanation of the relative contribution to household work. However, gender role preferences do contribute significantly to the equation, indicating that people with more family-oriented preferences do more household work.

41

For men separately, 43% of the variance is explained, with age, living situation, hours of paid work and gender role preference adding significantly to the equation. Older men and men with a more family-oriented role preference do relatively more household work, whereas more hours of paid work and cohabitation relate to a lower percentage of household work. For women, only 20% of the variance is explained by the variables in the equation, with only paid work and living situation contributing significantly to the equation, as they do for men.

3.8   DISCUSSION

The results show that sex of respondent is the main predictor of both hours of paid work and percentage of household work, explaining respectively 41 and 44 percent of the total variance. This means that traditional sex differences also exist in our sample. In looking for explanations for sex differences in behaviour, as we did in this study of participation in household work and paid work, the researcher is almost glad to find these sex differences indeed occur in the sample, otherwise there would not be much to explain. In the present study we could, again, demonstrate that men perform a lot more paid work and do only little household work, while women do relatively little paid work and much more household work than men. However, these same sex differences we seek to explain also lead to methodological problems in the process of explanation, especially if we want to perform the same analyses for men and women separately. Because men almost always work full-time if they are not jobless, there is hardly any variation in men's working behaviour. And where there are no individual differences there is no variation, or in terms of statistical analysis, no variance. The statistical methods we usually apply, such as analysis of variance, regression analysis, multivariate analysis, are meant to explain variance. In the case of paid work it is, therefore, to be expected that we can much better explain the differences among women than those among men, as there are far more differences in work participation within the group of women than within the group of men. This is exactly what the results of our study show. For household work it is the other way around: here, there are few differences among women whereas men show more variation in behaviour. Consequently, we did a much better job explaining men's participation in household tasks than women's participation. We cannot, therefore, attach too much importance to the fact that one model is more powerful than the other, as more than anything else this is a methodological artefact.

Within these restrictions, insofar as differences between the explanatory variables occur, some interesting results can be noted. For women there is no relationship between their participation in paid work and whether or not they live with a partner. For men, however, cohabiting is positively related to the hours of work they put in; in fact, it is the best predictor of those hours. The provider role seems the dominant guiding principle for this behaviour. That is, for men it is not important whether or not they have internalised this role into their identity, just like other aspects of identity are not important in this field. Only their actual role in life, being married or cohabiting, seems to ensure they are (at least one of) the main providers. For women, on the other hand, it is not whether or not they live with a partner but whether or not they live with children that seems the most decisive background variable for the hours of paid work they put in. Here, however, we see that gender role identity is even more important: the more a woman has incorporated an orientation towards work into her self concept, the more she will indeed participate in paid work.

As a measure of participation in household work we used a relative measure, asking how much of the household work necessary for one's own maintenance, such as cooking, doing the laundry and cleaning, one performs. It seems only logical that this share will diminish when one cohabits, for if one lives alone there is no possibility to share, except for people who can afford to have paid household help. Indeed, we see that for both sexes cohabiting means less of these household tasks. However, for men this influence of the presence of a partner is much larger than for women. For men role preference is also influential in 'determining' what percentage of household work they do, while for women their role preference does not make a difference. Taking the influence of gender role identity for paid work and household work, it seems that role preference of individuals only influences the participation in work that is not congruent with traditional gender roles and the gender-congruent work is done whether preferred or not.

Gender role identity is the only aspect of gender identity that explained significant variance in paid work and household work, after the demographic characteristics had been considered. Masculine and feminine traits, as well as social gender identity do not contribute to the explanation of how much paid work and household work individuals do.
For gender identity in terms of masculine and feminine traits the absence of a relationship is surprising, considering the results of previous studies. However, this lack of effect indicates that it is useful to take a more extended version of gender identity, which includes role preference. For social gender identity there were no hypotheses or studies to generate an expected relationship with paid or household work. However, it could very well have been that identification with one's gender group is greater when one conforms to the stereotypical roles that are attached to this group. Our results confirm the contrasting idea that social gender identity is relatively independent from the meaning that is given to it. They indicate that the attachment of men and women to their gender group neither influences nor is influenced by their participation in paid work or household work.

In the theoretical introduction to this chapter we have extended the concept of gender identity as it is usually adopted in studies of the relationship between gender identity and paid and unpaid work, i.e. as a personality characteristic, to include also gender role and social identity aspects. In all three aspects of gender identity there is a relationship between the personal self image and the social context, in the forms of cultural gender stereotypes, social roles, or the social groups of men and women. Although in our study we have, therefore, gone beyond the usual conception of gender identity in terms of only personality characteristics, the same assumption continues to underlie it as in so many other studies in this field. Gender identity is implicitly considered a stable characteristic of people, regardless of variations in time or context. Theoretical developments of the last decades have made this an improbable assumption as they indicate gender identity - or any other form of identity - is not as simple as that (Breakwell, 1992). Identity is now considered to be formed by the social context and therefore not stable but changing with different contexts. Identity can then be considered a consequence as well as a cause of social interaction. Currently, many authors agree that identity is both formed by the social context and influences it (Honess & Yardley, 1987; Deaux, 1993; Lieblich & Josselson, 1994). To see a single direction of causality is usually the effect of taking a look at a 'frozen' moment in time (Breakwell, 1986), as we also did in our cross-sectional study. We agree that the relationship between gender identity and work is best conceptualised as a process of mutual influence. The nature of the present study did not allow this. However, such an extension of research on the relationship between gendered identities and task participation is certainly advisable for future studies.

REFERENCES

Ahlers, J. 1995: *Similar differences and different similarities.* Thesis. Amsterdam: Amsterdam University press.
Antill, J. K. & Cotton, S. 1988: Factors affecting the division of labor in households. *Sex Roles*, 18, 531-553.
Atkinson, J. & Huston, T. L. 1984: Sex role orientation and division of labor in early marriage. *Journal of Personality and Social Psychology*, 46, 330-345.
Baker, D. 1989: Social identity in the transition to motherhood. In S. Skevington & D. Baker, (eds.) *The social identity of women.* London: Sage.
Barnett, R. C. & Baruch, G. K. 1987: Determinants of fathers' participation in family work. *Journal of marriage and the family*, 49, 29-40.
Bem, S. L. (1974). The measurement of psychological androgyny. *Journal of consulting and clinical Psychology*, 42, 155-162.
Bem, S. L. 1977: On the utility of alternative procedures for assessing psychological androgyny. *Journal of consulting and clinical Psychology*, 45, 196-205.
Breakwell, G 1986: *Coping with threatened identities.* London: Methuen.
Breakwell, G (ed.) Social *Psychology of the self concept.* London: Surrey University Press.

Coverman, S. 1985: Explaining husbands' participation in domestic labor. *The Sociological Quarterly*, 26, 81-97.

Denmark, E. L., Shaw, J. S. & Ciali, S. D. 1985: The relationship between sex roles, living arrangements and the division of household responsibilities. *Sex Roles*, 12, 617-625.

Deaux, K. 1992: Personalizing identity and socializing self. In G. Breakwell (ed.) Social *Psychology of the self concept.* London: Surrey University Press.

Deaux, K. 1993: Reconstructing social identity. *Personality and Social Psychology Bulletin*, 19, 4-12.

Eagly, A.H. 1987: *Sex differences in social behavior: a social role analysis.* Hillsdale, NJ: Erlbaum.

Gunter, N. C. & Gunter, B. G. 1990: Domestic division of labor among working couples: does androgyny make a difference? *Psychology of Women Quarterly*, 14, 355-370.

Hoffman, D. M. & Fidell, L. S. 1979: Characteristics of androgynous, undifferentiated, masculine and feminine middle class women. *Sex Roles*, 5, 656-663.

Honess, T. & Yardley, K.M. (eds.) 1987: *Self and Identity: perspectives across the lifespan.* London: Routledge & Kegan Paul.

Kelly, G. A. 1955: *The psychology of personal constructs.* New York: W. W. Norton & Co.

Lieblich, A. & Josselson, R. 1994: *Exploring Identity and Gender.* The narrative Study of Lives, volume 2. London: Sage.

Marshall, H. & Wetherell, M. 1989: Talking about career and gender identities. In S. Skevington & D. Baker, (eds.) *The social identity of women.* London: Sage.

Nyquist, L., Slivken, K., Spence, J. T. & Helmreich, R. L. 1985: Household responsibilities in middle class couples: the contribution of demographic and personality variables. *Sex Roles*, 12, 15-34.

Oakly, A. 1980: *Women confined.* Oxford: Martin Robertson.

Ross, C. E.1987: The division of labour at home. *Social Forces*, 65, 816-833

Russell, G. 1978: The father role and its relation to masculinity, femininity and androgyny. *Child Development*, 49, 1174-1181.

Stafford, R., Backman, E. & Dibona, P. 1977: The division of Labor among cohabiting and married couples. *Journal of Marriage and the Family*, 42-57.

Steil, J. M. & Weltman, K. 1991: Marital inequality: The importance of resources, personal attributes, and social norms on career valuing and the allocation of domestic responsibilities. *Sex Roles*, 24, 161-179.

Tajfel, H. (ed.) 1978: *Differentiation between social groups: Studies in the social psychology of intergroup relations*. London: Academic Press.

Tajfel, H. & Turner, J.C. 1985: The social identity theory of intergroup behaviour. In S. Worchel & W.G. Austin (eds.) *Psychology of intergroup relations.* Chocago: Nelson-Hall.

Willemsen, T. M. & Fischer, A. H. 1997: De Nederlandse Sekse-idnetiteit Vragenlijst (NSIV). *Nederlands Tijdschrift voor de Psychologie*, 52, 126-130.

BIOGRAPHICAL NOTE

Tineke M. Willemsen is a social psychologist. She has had academic positions in Social Psychology at Leiden University, and in Women's Studies at Amsterdam University and Tilburg University, where she now holds the Chair of Women's Studies. Her research interests concern gender stereotypes and gender identity; female managers; and the division paid and unpaid work. She is co-ordinator of a network of researchers that is doing a comparative study on the last topic, The European Network on Policies and the Division of Unpaid and Paid Work.

Mascha Brink is a social psychologist. She is works the department of women's studies at Tilburg University on her PhD thesis concerning the relationship between gendered identities and the division of paid and unpaid work in households.

4   What's fair is fair - or is it? On the role of social justice in the division of household labour

Hester van der Vinne

The Dutch government wants men and women to share both paid and unpaid work equally, because that would be fair. The division of labour between men and women is seen as a question of social justice. This paper addresses some of the implicit assumptions in this policy, such as the idea that families should be fair, that they are currently unfair and that it is the division of labour within families that makes them that way. It is further argued that the concept of justice is not as simple or as straightforward as it may seem. Justice does not mean the same thing to all people at all times; there is ample evidence to show that what is considered fair varies for different people in different situations. Fairness is a judgement rather than an objective state. There are, for example, profound differences between men and women in their experiences of justice in the family. Also, the experience of (in)justice is shaped by more than outcomes (i.e. the actual division of labour in terms of time and tasks) alone. Implications for public policy will be discussed briefly.

4.1   INTRODUCTION

This paper is about the division of household labour between men and women and, more specifically, about the concept of social justice and its place in the division of labour. First, I will discuss the concept of justice and its relevance to family life. Then the difference between criteria of fairness, preferences for and experiences of justice or injustice will be discussed. It will be argued that all are subjective perceptions rather than objective states. Individuals can differ in what they define, perceive and experience as just. Consequently, policies aimed at justice in general, gender justice or justice in the family need to take individual differences into account. It should be noted that the terms "justice" and "fairness" are used interchangeably in this paper. Although a distinction is indicated in the literature, discussion on this topic is beyond the scope of the present argument. Fairness is taken to mean the everyday-speech version of justice. As outlined in their Equal Opportunity Policy, the Dutch government wants men and women to share paid and unpaid labour equally (Tweede Kamer, 1992 /1993). Why does

Time allocation and gender, Kea Tijdens, Anneke van Doorne-Huiskes & Tineke Willemsen (eds.), Tilburg University Press, 1997, © Hester van der Vinne

the government want such a thing? It appears there are two main reasons. First, this redistribution of labour is a means to an end (the end being a larger number of women in the labour force, resulting in increased productivity, which would in turn generate increased welfare). Moreover, redistribution of labour between the sexes is also an end in itself. The Dutch government strives for equal treatment of and equal opportunities for men and women; a policy it has been pursuing in the labour market for some time. Recently, they have recognised that redistribution of paid labour cannot take place without a matching redistribution of unpaid labour. This has led to the development of policies aimed at families as well. An equitable division of housework is deemed necessary for women's participation in paid labour. The current situation, where it is almost impossible for women, but not for men with children to work has been labelled as social injustice by the government's Council for Equal Opportunities or Emancipatieraad (Noordhoff, 1996).

Accomplishing an even distribution of costs and benefits between the sexes, both in the labour market and in the household, is the goal. Policy is the means to achieve that goal. The division of labour between men and women has changed from a private matter, to be negotiated between partners in their own households, to a target for public policy.

The applicability of justice to families
The existence of a policy directed at families and fairness within families is in itself a new development. In biblical times, justice meant "getting what one deserves". It was, first and foremost, a legalistic concept that defined the punishments appropriate to committed crimes, as opposed to "mercy", which implied taking the context of the crime into account. It was not until the Middle Ages that the interpretation of justice became somewhat broader. Many church fathers wrote extensively about justice and applied it to situations other than law. Also, justice and mercy were no longer seen as opposing but, rather, mercy became incorporated into justice. Still, for the longest time, the family was not regarded as a suitable arena for fairness issues. Also, theories about justice have excluded the family - and usually ignored gender.

The arguments given for this exclusion can be classified into two categories. First category arguments idealised the family. It was regarded as a social institution for which fairness is not an appropriate virtue. Fairness was assumed to operate only when interests differ and goods being distributed are scarce. The family, on the other hand, was assumed to be an intimate group, held together by love and shared interests and governed by virtues nobler than justice; it had no need to be subjected to the tests of justice to which we subject other social institutions (Okin, 1989).

The second type of argument states that the family is not to be judged by its fairness because the hierarchical structure that exists within the family is the natural structure. This seems to be the position of (among others) the aforementioned church fathers. Thomas Aquinas, for example, defined justice as follows: "In distributive justice a person receives all the more of the common goods, according as he holds a more prominent position in the community. In other words, to each according to his or her status." This model is based upon assumed and necessary inequalities between people, including the inferiority of women (Andolsen, 1985). A division of labour based upon sex is taken for granted as well. In this view, women are perceived to be created solely to bear children and do housework. In the words of Thomas Aquinas: "Among those works that are necessary for human life some are becoming to men, others to women." (quoted in Andolsen, 1985, p. 7). This perception may be unjust according to modern standards, but - the argument goes - justice does not really apply here, because this order is grounded in nature and therefore inevitable as well as necessary. This is also the position implicitly taken by an influential justice theorist such as Rawls (1971): in spite of his gender-neutral language, the "individuals" his theory refers and applies to are really men only; they are defined as heads of households. A traditional division of labour, i.e. a wife who takes care of these heads of households, is both assumed and necessary for the rest of the theory.

Why is it important that families are just?
Although the arguments mentioned above, or at least some version of them, will sound familiar to most of us, it seems that these days fairness is generally perceived to be applicable to families. That is, families and distributions in families can be seen as more or less fair. Moreover, fairness is held to be preferable to unfairness. Now what are the reasons for wanting justice in families? Two motivations for justice in families can be identified.

First of all, the family has been recognised, even by those who do not feel that the family itself can be considered either fair or unfair, as an important locus for the development of a sense of justice. It is presumed to be the place where children learn the difference between what is just and what is not. If this is one of the major functions of the family, then it follows logically that a just family is preferable to an unjust one. For if the relationship between a child's parents does not conform to basic standards of justice, how can you expect that child to grow up with a sense of justice?

The second argument for justice in the family is even more crucial than the first. The family cannot be separated from the rest of society. In fact, a just society requires just families for a number of reasons (Okin, 1989). First, the family is the site of enormously important distributions, not only of material goods, but also of social goods, such as responsibilities, rights, favours and power. Where there are distributions, there is potential for justice and injustice. Second, the family as it exists today was shaped by political decisions. If we care about the justice of these political decisions, we should also care about the justice in families. Third, the family is not only the place where children learn about justice, it is also the

49

place where they learn about gender and become gendered. So, if we care about justice between the sexes, we should care about justice in families. The final reason for wanting justice in families has to do with the consequences the traditional division of labour has for women outside the family. The traditional division of labour, in which women perform housework and childcare raises barriers for women's participation in other spheres. These barriers are not only practical (e.g. who is going to look after children when their mother is working?), but also psychological (e.g. feelings of guilt women may experience when they are working).

4.2   WHAT IS A FAIR DIVISION OF LABOUR IN A FAMILY?

In the previous section I hope to have shown that families and their division of labour need to be just. Apparently (according to the government) they are not. The government is not the only body which thinks this division is unjust. Scientists seem to think so as well. In writing about the division of labour the words "fair" and "just" are used frequently. However, they are used in the same, unproblematic way the government uses them: the division of labour between men and women needs to be fair, period. It is held to be a "matter of simple justice" (Arts & Hermkens, 1994, p. 147). What constitutes fairness is not discussed, rather, it is assumed to be apparent to everyone.

While policy makers and scientists may agree that the current division of labour is unfair, there is one important group that does not agree. This group consists of the people who are supposedly dividing their labour unfairly, the men and women whom it concerns and at whom the policy is targeted. Although a large majority of the Dutch population subscribe to the notion that housework and childcare should be divided equally[1] between men and women (SCP, 1992) a division of this kind is hardly a reality. One would expect, then, that they feel their division of labour is unfair. But this is not the case. Both men and women feel their own unequal division of labour is fair (Arts & Hermkens, 1991; de Jong & de Olde, 1993). This finding has puzzled many (social) scientists. How can people be aware and disapprove of gender inequalities at a societal level, and simultaneously fail to recognise their occurrence in their own lives?[2] And, how is it possible that policy makers and scientists agree the situation is unfair when the men and women it concerns, who are experiencing this alleged unfairness on a daily basis, perceive the situation as fair?

Another problem with the government and scientists' calling for a fair division of labour is the fact that they are not quite clear what exactly constitutes "a fair division of labour". In all of the instances where fairness is mentioned, the focus is exclusively on factors influencing the unfairness of the current situation. Everyone seems to know exactly what "unjust" is, but nobody actually says anything about what would be just. Sometimes, rather vague descriptions are given: fairness has something to do with "sharing work" (for example Knijn, 1992 p. 508), men performing more housework and childcare especially is seen as fair. Some talk about each doing his or her fair share, equitable shares, or even equal shares. In most instances, however, no definitions are given and it is assumed to be clear and known to all what is a fair division of labour in a family. So far, no one has given us a clear fairness criterion for this particular situation.

4.3   DIFFERENT PERSPECTIVES ON THE DIVISION OF LABOUR

Most of the research that attempts to explain the division of family labour, is based on assumptions along the following lines (Thompson & Walker, 1989): housework is unpleasant work and it takes power to get out of doing it. Power in the family is affected by women's paid employment and by the resources obtained through paid employment. The more power women have in their relationships, the more housework is done by their partners. In this view, the choice for a certain division of labour is a rational one and it follows more or less automatically from a set of characteristics, such as potential earnings. Behaviour can be predicted from a specification of an individual's circumstances.

If a certain division of labour can be considered the outcome of a choice[3], there are at least three ways in which this choice can be posed: it is the choice of a rational individual; it is the choice of real people; or it is the choice that follows moral intuition. In some explanations that have been given for the division of labour all three choices coincide, whereas in others only one or two of the three options are taken into account. In this section I will consider briefly how the main theoretical perspectives that have been used to study the division of labour conceptualise this choice differently.

Economics
The field of economics is primarily concerned with the first type of choice, the choice of a rational person. The question of whether or not the choice of rational people and the choice of real people are the same thing is debatable. Some say they are, some say they are not. For the present purpose, however, this question could be answered by saying that they would be the same, if the assumption is that individuals are rational and maximise utility. The third type of choice, the moral choice, on the other hand, has not received much attention in this field. Few economists have addressed the fairness issue. In fact, the question of whether or not a social choice (or its results) is "fair" is mostly thought to be irrelevant. Applied to the division of labour, this means that the division of labour leading to the most efficient means of production and the highest level of welfare for the household is not necessarily the fairest.

Still, there are economists who worry about fairness. Kahneman, Knetsch & Thaler (1987) report a series of experiments in which it was found that people are sometimes willing to forego profit, if that means they can resist unfairness or punish an unfair actor. Kahneman et al. conclude that a realistic description of actors should include the following: "they care about being treated fairly and treating others fairly" (p. 115). Fairness criteria are not described by the standard economic model; it appears that (at least in some cases) people are willing to pay for fairness. Concerns about fairness can keep people from behaving perfectly rationally. So, considering the evidence that people do not always choose maximising behaviour but are also motivated by concerns about fairness, we might ask ourselves if maybe this holds true for the division of labour as well. Van Velzen (1994) suggests something along these lines when she says: "..it is very well possible that some members of the household would want to exchange a part of the efficiency for a fairer division of household production.." (p. 121). In any case, it seems that economic theory cannot tell us what is considered fair or unfair.

Another economist who has concerned himself with the fairness of allocations and distributions is Amartya Sen. In his view, fairness is defined by two conditions: Pareto optimality and the freedom from envy. As for the first condition: there are many possible divisions of labour that would fulfil the requirement of Pareto optimality. None are necessarily seen as fair. For that we need the second condition. Sen states there is an absence of envy when both parties are willing to trade positions. Or, in other words, when no one feels that his or her partner is better off. This, however, implies a comparison with one's spouse and, as I shall argue later, this comparison may not be one that people are likely to make.

Exchange Theory
A model that is frequently used in the social sciences (either explicitly or implicitly) to explain the division of labour in a family is exchange theory. In exchange theory, or its social-psychological derivative, equity theory, the three choices mentioned above coincide. The assumptions of rationality are there, rational people are thought to be the same as real people, and equity is defined as fairness, so the actions of these rational and real people are, by definition, fair. However, equity theory fails to describe adequately the behaviour of real people, i.e. the current division of labour between men and women in the Netherlands.

According to the exchange (or equity) model, the adults in a household compare their inputs and outcomes and strive to obtain the same input-outcome ratio for both. The result would be a situation that yields satisfaction and is perceived as fair. On the input side of this model we find the number of hours worked (paid or unpaid, inside or outside the home); on the outcome side we find the amount of pay received for working outside the home and the results of housework. The outcomes are assumed to be divided equally, so in order to obtain the same input-outcome ratio for both spouses, they will have to work an equal number of hours.

Time allocation studies of the last decades, however, have shown that women spend a disproportionate amount of time on housework and childcare, much more than can be expected on the basis of equity theory. The equity model holds true for traditional couples, where one person performs all the housework and the other is the sole provider, but their number is declining steadily. The typical, if there is such a thing, couple of today consists of a man who is employed full-time and a woman who is employed part-time and performs most, if not all, of the housework. In these couples, the total number of hours worked per week (paid and unpaid work combined) is greater for women than for men. The division of labour in these couples is clearly inequitable. At the same time, it has been found repeatedly that both men and women are satisfied with their unequal (or inequitable) division of labour and that they perceive it as fair. It seems that there is a discrepancy between what researchers, based on this type of objective model, call fair and what people perceive subjectively as fair. Defining a fair division of labour in a family is, therefore, not as easy or as straightforward as it may seem.

4.4 DIFFERENCES IN DISTRIBUTIVE JUSTICE BEHAVIOUR

In this section it will be argued that fairness is not an objective standard but a subjective judgement. The fairness of a situation cannot be determined from the outside by any objective standards; fairness cannot be calculated. A situation can be called fair by one person and unfair by another. Social-psychological research has shown that there are substantial individual and situational differences in which distributions are regarded as just. I will mention some of them in this section.

Situational differences
One important factor is the sort of relationship that is being judged. Deutsch (1985) argues that there are three different fairness criteria: equity, equality and need. Each of these principles has its own specific application: when productivity is a primary goal in the relationship, equity will be the preferred justice rule. In situations where fostering or maintaining pleasant social relations are emphasised, equality will be the preferred justice rule. And in relationships where fostering personal development or well-being is a primary goal, need will be the guiding principle. In economics, the family/household is generally seen as a productive unit, "a small factory" as it were. In research in which exchange theory is used, the family is usually seen as aimed at having a pleasant relationship. I contend that the family is not only one of the three situations described by Deutsch, but that it has characteristics of all three situations. There is no doubt that the household is a place where commodities are produced. But this is not the only function of the household. The members of the household will also attempt to maintain pleasant social relations and look out for each other's well-being. Therefore, it is hard (or perhaps even impossible) to state beforehand what the distribution principle in a family will be.

53

Gender differences
Another complicating factor is that justice appears not to mean the same thing to men and women. Relatively early on in justice research, systematic differences between the sexes were found. Kahn and Gaeddert (1985) point out that the values associated with equity theory (ambition, status, competition, to name a few) happen to coincide with the masculine stereotype. This is hardly surprising in a society where the masculine is the norm and where most researchers and their subjects are men. In a review of justice research, Major and Deaux (1982) summarise the differences between men and women in justice behaviour as follows: men seem to have a preference for equity as a justice rule, whereas women seem to prefer equality. In particular, women give themselves lower rewards than equity theory predicts and when they are distributing rewards to others, they tend to keep differences in rewards to others as small as possible. In these situations, men generally conform to the equity rule. As a heterosexual household usually consists of both men and women, again, we cannot easily tell which allocation principle will be used.

4.5   JUSTICE IS MORE THAN OUTCOMES

The above mentioned differences all refer to *distributive* justice, the way outcomes are distributed. But justice is more than a certain distribution of rewards and/or costs. Fairness judgements are not based on outcomes (the actual time allocation in a household, for example) only. Another important factor in fairness judgements is *procedural* justice (Lind & Tyler, 1988); the circumstances under which the outcomes were created. Two factors have been proposed as playing a role in fairness judgements besides the outcomes (Thompson, 1991; Major, 1993): the comparison standards used to evaluate one's own situation and the perceived legitimacy of a gap between one's own outcomes and those of others. I will discuss these factors and their meaning in the context of the division of labour in families.

4.5.1   Comparison standards

I will first describe a study from the field of economics that illustrates the importance of the comparison process. Kahneman, Knetsch & Thaler (1986) conducted an experiment in which fairness judgements about price increases were compared. Results showed that a price increase was considered fair when it was framed as maintaining one's profit. The same price increase was considered unfair when it was framed as exploiting one's market power at another's expense. Kahneman et al. conclude that outcomes are ascribed meaning relative to a point of reference, or reference state as Kahneman et al. call it. Since these reference states are subject to framing, judgements of fairness cannot be understood without considering the factors that determine the selection of a reference state.

54

This notion of a reference state has a counterpart in social psychology as well. In order to feel that a certain outcome is unfair, one has to feel entitled to another, more favourable outcome (Major, 1987). Individuals determine what they are entitled to by comparing their outcomes with other possible outcomes, so-called referent outcomes (Mark & Folger, 1984) or comparison referents (Thompson, 1991). These are the standards people use to evaluate their existing outcomes. So, to understand fully judgements of fairness about the division of labour one has to take these comparison standards into account.

Several kinds of comparisons that may contribute to the (continuing) existence of an unequal division of labour between men and women have been identified (see Thompson, 1991; Major, 1993). I will discuss two of them in some detail. First, there is the *social comparison*. It is often assumed (as, for example, in equity theory) that husbands and wives compare themselves with each other and base their fairness judgement on this comparison. However, there is strong evidence that both men and women are more likely to make comparisons within their own gender. Social comparison theory states that comparisons are made with others who are perceived to be similar with respect to relevant dimensions (Goethals & Darley, 1977). In the family, gender is obviously a highly relevant characteristic. The consequences for the perceived fairness of an unequal division of labour of these within-gender comparisons are clear: if women compare themselves with other women rather than with their partners, they are more likely to feel that the amount of work they are doing is normal and appropriate. Another comparison which is often-made in this context is with the same-sex parent (e.g. Hochschild, 1989; Van der Vinne, 1995). Husbands tend to draw comparisons between themselves and their fathers and see themselves doing more. Similarly, wives compare themselves with their mothers and see themselves doing less. Both feel that the division of labour is fair. So Sen's condition of absence of envy does not seem to be particularly appropriate in this context, for if spouses do not even compare themselves to one another, they are not likely to think of trading places.

Another type of comparison with implications for the perceived fairness of the division of labour is the *feasibility comparison*. The evaluation of a certain situation is based not only on absolute comparison standards, but also on the perceived feasibility and attractiveness of alternative arrangements. It may be the case that many women simply do not see an alternative that is better than their current situation. A suggestion made by Spitze (1988) for which I have found support in my own research is that working women compare their situation to a hypothetical situation in which they are not employed. This alternative is perceived as less attractive than their current situation. Another unattractive alternative would be the break-up of the relationship, for a divorce is usually more damaging (financially) for women than for men. In order for an alternative to be taken seriously or to be contemplated seriously, it has to be seen as feasible. The alternative of sharing work equally may not be considered feasible.

A reason why women seem to prefer to make downward comparisons (comparisons with a situation that is less favourable than their own) could be self-protection. Research on social comparison shows that individuals who are disadvantaged tend to avoid comparisons with others who are better off - especially if they feel they cannot change the situation - because such comparisons would be distressing psychologically.

4.5.2 Legitimacy

But even if women were to compare themselves with their partners and recognise the inequality of their respective workloads, they still might not feel unjustly treated. They might perceive the difference as legitimate, they might feel that there are sufficient justifications for it. Several of the justifications used in this situation have been identified (for the Dutch situation, see Komter, 1989). Furthermore, there seem to be gender-specific justifications, that is, reasons men give for not doing housework would not be acceptable from women (Thompson, 1991). Men's alleged incompetence and inexperience in housework, their dislike of it and their lack of time; these are all well-known examples of justifications that are used, by both men and women, to explain an unequal division of labour (Hochschild, 1989; Komter, 1989). These reasons would, in all likelihood, not stand for women.

Another important and often used way to justify unequal outcomes is to appeal to the application of fair procedures. Research in an organisational context shows that satisfaction with a situation depends to a large extent on the perceived fairness of the procedures used, regardless of the actual outcomes (Lind & Tyler, 1988). An important aspect of procedural fairness is having a say in the decision. Individuals who have had a say in a decision are more satisfied than those who have not, even if it had no effect on the outcomes. This might hold true for the family context as well. It might be the case that women, as long as they feel that they have chosen freely to do more of the unpaid work than their husbands, will not see their unequal division of labour as unfair.

4.6 CONCLUDING REMARKS

Fairness is a relevant topic in decision-making and the family. This conclusion is shared by both policy makers and social scientists. There cannot be justice in society without justice in families. It is not easy, however, to define what justice in families is. Indeed, I have argued that it is impossible to define what *is* just, for justice is a judgement. In order to understand a fairness judgement, comparison standards and justifications have to be taken into account. Therefore, a public policy that focuses on outcomes only (that is, on the actual division of labour in terms of who does what and how often do they do it) is, in my view, inadequate.

Simply telling people that they ought to divide tasks equally (or equitably) because it is fair is not enough. As I have argued, justice is not the same thing for all people. It can mean different things to different individuals in different situations. Dutch government policy which states that the division of labour between men and women should be more equal because that would be just does not do justice to the different conceptions of fairness that people may have. Instead, it forces one ill-defined justice rule on everyone, without taking individual experiences into account. For even if a majority of the Dutch people agree that men and women should share housework, which would mean that they support the goals of the government, they do not act on this and fail to see any injustice in their actions. They clearly have different ideas about justice. Moreover, this policy implies (but does not explicitly state) that the way tasks are currently divided is unjust. It assumes that justice is no more than the way costs and benefits are distributed and the fairness of a situation can be calculated by an objective bystander.

Furthermore, no reasons are specified for wanting justice in families. The connection between just distributions in families and justice in larger society may be obvious to policy makers and scientists, but I think a government that wants to influence what is still considered by many to be a highly personal matter, should explain *why* it is so important. It should be clear that the goal is not to intrude on people's privacy by telling them how to live their lives, but rather to make them see the consequences of a traditional division of labour. Saying that it is a matter of "simple justice" is not enough, for there is no such thing as simple justice.

The policies aimed at redistribution of labour between the sexes are not very far-reaching. Especially when they concern the division of unpaid household labour, they consist mainly of creating conditions under which different divisions would be possible, thus leaving actual decisions about the division of labour to the people sharing a household. It has to be concluded that the attitude of the Dutch government is ambivalent. They claim to want gender justice but fail to define it. Their policy is normative but, it appears, not for enforcement.

NOTES

[1] It is hard to tell whether these data refer to equality or equity. In the 1992 publication the word "equally" was used. In a publication from 1994 the phrasing had retrospectively changed to "equitably". It seems that the SCP is under the impression that these two words mean the same thing; they only mean the same thing if both spouses spend the same number of hours on paid work.

[2] This phenomenon is not exclusive to the context of division of labour. Its existence has been established in several empirical studies and has come to be known as the denial of personal disadvantage (see Crosby, Cordova & Jaskar, 1993).

57

[3] I will not address the notion of choice here, although whether or not this decision qualifies as "choice" and if it can ever be considered a completely voluntary decision is debatable.

REFERENCES

Andolsen, B.H. 1985: A woman's work is never done: unpaid household labor as a social justice issue. In B.H. Andolsen, C.E. Gudorf & M.D. Pellauer (eds.), *Women's consciousness, women's conscience*, pp. 3-18. San Francisco: Harper & Row.

Arts, W. & Hermkens, P. 1994: De eerlijke verdeling van huishoudelijke taken: percepties en oordelen. *Mens en Maatschappij, 69*, 147-168.

Crosby, F., Cordova, D. & Jaskar, K. 1993: On the failure to see oneself as disadvantaged: cognitive and emotional components. In M.A. Hogg & D. Abrams (eds.), *Group motivation: social psychological perspectives*, pp. 87-104. Hertfordshire: Harvester/Wheatsheaf.

Deutsch, M. 1985 *Distributive justice: a social-psychological approach.* New Haven: Yale University Press.

Goethals, G.R. & Darley, J. 1977: Social comparison theory: an attributional approach. In J.M. Suls & R.L. Miller (eds.), *Social comparison processes: theoretical and empirical perspectives*, pp.259-278. Washington: Hemisphere.

Hochschild, A. 1989: *The second shift: working parents and the revolution at home.* New York: Viking Press.

Jong, A. de & Olde, C. de 1994: *Hoe ouders het werk delen.* Den Haag: Ministerie van Sociale Zaken en Werkgelegenheid/VUGA.

Kahn, A.S. & Gaeddert, W.P. 1985: From theories of equity to theories of justice: the liberating consequences of studying women. In V.E. O'Leary, R.K. Unger & B.S. Wallston (eds.), *Women, gender, and social psychology*, pp. 129-148. Hillsdale: Lawrence Erlbaum.

Kahneman, D., Knetsch, J.L. & Thaler, R.H. 1986: Fairness as a constraint on profit seeking: entitlements in the market. *American Economic Review, 76*, 728-741.

Kahneman, D., Knetsch, J.L. & Thaler, R.H. 1987: Fairness and the assumptions of economics. In R.M. Hogarth & M.W. Reder (eds.), *Rational choice: the contrast between economics and psychology*, pp. 101-116. Chicago/London: The University of Chicago Press.

Knijn, T. 1992: Balanceren op ongelijke leggers; veranderingen in zorg- en arbeidsverhoudingen tussen de seksen. *Tijdschrift voor Vrouwenstudies, 13*, 497-509.

Komter, A. 1989: Hidden power in marriage. *Gender & Society, 3*, 187-216.

Lind, E.A. & Tyler, T.R. 1988: *The social psychology of procedural justice.* New York: Plenum Press.

Major, B. 1987: Gender, justice, and the psychology of entitlement. In P. Shaver & C. Hendrick (eds.), *Review of Personality and Social Psychology, vol. 1*, pp. 124-148. Newbury Park: Sage.

Major, B. 1993: Gender, entitlement, and the distribution of family labor. *Journal of Social Issues, 49*, 141-159.

Major, B. & Deaux, K. 1982: Individual differences in justice behavior. In J. Greenberg & R.L. Cohen (eds.), *Equity and justice in social behavior*, pp. 43-76. New York: Academic Press.

Mark, M.M. & Folger, R. 1984: Responses to relative deprivation: a conceptual framework. In P. Shaver (ed.), *Review of Personality and Social Psychology, vol. 5*, pp. 192-218. Newbury Park: Sage.

Noordhoff, I. 1996, September 25: Een 32-urige werkweek met een geëmancipeerd minimumloon. *Trouw*, p.9.

Okin, S.M. 1989: *Justice, gender and the family*. New York: Basic Books.

Rawls, J. 1971: *A theory of justice*. Cambridge: Harvard University Press.

Sociaal en Cultureel Planbureau 1992: *Sociaal en Cultureel Rapport 1992*. Den Haag: Sociaal en Cultureel Planbureau.

Spitze, G. 1988 Women's employment and family relations: a review. *Journal of Marriage and the Family, 50*, 595-618.

Thompson, L. 1991 Family work: women's sense of fairness. *Journal of Family Issues, 12*, 181-196.

Thompson, L. & Walker, A.J. 1989: Gender in families: women and men in marriage, work, and parenthood. *Journal of Marriage and the Family, 51*, 845-871.

Tweede Kamer 1992/1993: *Beleidsprogramma emancipatie 'Met het oog op 1995'*. Tweede Kamer Vergaderjaar 1992/1993, 22913, nrs 1-2. Den Haag: SDU.

Velzen, S. van 1994: Het huishouden: harmonieus huisgezin of arena? In H. Maassen van den Brink & K. Tijdens (eds.), *Emancipatie en economie*, pp. 109-125. Amsterdam: UvA, Faculteit Economie, Leerstoel Vergelijkende Bevolkings- en Emancipatie-economie.

Vinne, H. van der 1995: *It is fair because we both agree that housework is her job: on the division of housework and child care among dual earners in the Netherlands*. Paper presented at the Fifth International Conference on Social Justice Research, Reno, June 26-29.

ACKNOWLEDGEMENTS

The author would like to thank Elizabeth Harrison-Neu for her comments on and additions to an earlier version of this paper. The research has been made possible by NWO grant no. 717-603-613.

BIOGRAPHICAL NOTE

Hester van der Vinne is currently completing her PhD at the Faculty of Social Sciences of Tilburg University. The PhD will address the familial division of labour in connection with justice theory.

5   Economics, strategic behaviour and the intrahousehold division of labour

Susan van Velzen

5.1   INTRODUCTION

A division of labour within the family, with men specialising more in market activities and women specialising more in non-market activities, is the dominant
pattern of intrahousehold work organisation in virtually every country studied.
Within economics, there exists a sizeable body of literature which tries to formulate rationales for this intrahousehold division of labour. The explanations put for-
ward are formulated on the basis of normative, prescriptive theories, rather than on
the basis of positive, descriptive ones. The purpose of this chapter is to provide an
introduction to this normative approach. After a short first section in which some
data on the actual division of labour between men and women are presented, section 2 discusses Becker's New Home Economics approach to the division of labour within the family. In section 3 this discussion is continued, giving special attention to the assumption of an a priori agreement between household members on
how to divide the profits accruing from a particular division of labour. In section 4,
the risks associated with specialisation are discussed. It is argued that within a
New Home Economics framework, these risks cannot be incorporated satisfacto-
rily in the analysis. This can be done in bargaining approaches to the division of
labour within the family, which are explored in sections 5 and 6. This chapter concludes with a brief consideration of the usefulness of these normative models for
an understanding of the actual division of labour within the family.

5.2   THE DIVISION OF LABOUR BETWEEN MEN AND WOMEN

Some recent data on a selection of industrialised countries are shown in Table 5.1,
which is based on information given in Goldschmidt-Clermont & Pagnossin-
Aligisakis (1995). In the table, the information available on 'productive activities'
is classified into two categories: market-oriented productive activities and non-
market oriented productive activities. The former category refers mainly to gainful
employment. The latter comprises activities such as unpaid household work, re-

Time allocation and gender, Kea Tijdens, Anneke van Doorne-Huiskes & Tineke Willemsen
(eds.), Tilburg University Press, 1997, © Susan van Velzen

pairs and maintenance of one's own house, household management, unpaid work for the community, etc. On average, the amount of time spent on paid, market-oriented productive activities is about the same as the amount of time spent on unpaid, non-market oriented activities. With the exception of the Netherlands, where 65 percent of productive activities is classified as non-market oriented, no clear pattern of specialisation in either one of the two types of activities can be detected.

Table 5.1   *Division of labour between market-oriented (SNA) and non-market oriented activities (non-SNA) for different countries (figures for women and men separately).*

Country	Year (Pop.)	Total work time		Women		Men	
		SNA	Non-SNA	SNA	Non-SNA	SNA	Non-SNA
Australia	1992 (15+)	44	56	28	72	61	39
Austria	1992 (10+)	49	51	31	69	71	29
Canada	1992 (15+)	52	48	39	61	65	35
Finland	1987/88 (15+)	51	49	39	61	64	36
France	1985/86 (15+)	45	55	30	70	62	38
Germany	1991/92 (16+)	44	56	30	70	61	39
Israel	1991/92 (14+)	51	49	29	71	74	26
Italy	1988/89 (15+)	45	55	22	78	77	23
Netherlands	1987 (12+)	35	65	19	81	52	48
United Kingdom	1985 (15+)	51	49	37	63	68	32
USA	1985 (15+)	50	50	37	63	63	37
Average		49	51	34	66	66	34

Source: Goldschmidt-Clermont & Pagnossin-Aligisakis, 1995, Table D, p.33.

However, when the figures are broken down by gender, a clear pattern of specialisation emerges. Although there are some differences between countries, the general impression from the data is that women spend most of their productive time on non-market oriented activities, whereas men spend most of their productive time on market-oriented activities. On average, women spend only one-third of their time on market-oriented activities, against two-thirds of men's time. Of course, as the figures above refer to aggregates, they only provide us with indirect evidence as to the division of labour within the household. However, the assumption that the gendered division of labour at national level is a reflection of gendered divisions of labour within the household is supported by many cross-national studies (see, e.g., Gershuny & Robinson 1988, 1991; Juster & Stafford 1991; United Nations 1995. An early study is Szalai, 1972) as well as many single-country studies. These studies also show that the pattern of specialisation is especially marked in couples with relatively young children.

5.3   NEW HOME ECONOMICS AND THE INTRAHOUSEHOLD DIVISION OF LABOUR

An influential economic approach which attempts to generate rationales for the actual division of labour within the household was developed by 'New Home Economist' Gary Becker. Becker was certainly not the first within the neo-classical tradition to focus on the division of labour within the family, nor is he the only contributor to the development of the field of New Home Economics. In 1962, Jacob Mincer had already done ground-breaking work with his publication 'Labor force participation of married women: a study of labor supply'. Other important contributions to the New Home Economics are Gronau (1976, 1977, 1986), Pollak & Wachter (1975), Kooreman & Kapteyn (1987) and Cigno (1991). However, Becker more than others has devoted considerable attention to the theoretical development of the New Home Economics approach to the division of labour within the family, which is why his work is taken as a starting point for that what follows.

In his 'A Treatise on the Family' (1991 [1981]), Becker formulates a normative theory of the intrahousehold division of labour within the framework of a house-hold production model (see also Becker 1965; Stigler & Becker 1977). In this model, households are assumed to derive utility not directly from market goods and leisure, as the traditional microeconomic approach to labour supply has it, but from 'commodities', such as children, health and prestige. Households cannot buy these commodities on the market, but have to produce them 'in house' using time, market goods and some environmental parameters as inputs in the production process.

The household's decision-making problem in this household production framework is - given time, income and production technology constraints - how time and goods can be allocated to maximise utility. Becker shows that, given some assumptions, this problem for two one-person households is solved most efficiently by co-ordinating efforts and forming a two-person household. If one person then specialises more in market work, while the other specialises more in household work, the total production of the household may increase. This theorem is straight-forward if two people have different comparative advantages for household and market work, because in this case each person can concentrate his or her time and effort doing the things he or she does best. However, it is also true for two 'intrin-sically identical' individuals (iii) if the productivity of household and market time is affected differently by human capital and the returns on human capital invest-ments are positively related to the amount of time spent in the sector in which the human capital is put to best use. A certain degree of specialisation is also efficient in this case, because it provides incentives for both individuals to each accumulate a different type of human capital. One person can specialise in market work and invest more in 'market-specific' human capital, such as on-the-job-training. The other one can specialise in household work and invest more in 'marital-specific' human capital, such as 'classes in child care, cooking or art history' (Becker 1991: 27). Obviously, the gains from specialisation will probably be reduced if people derive a lot of pleasure from certain activities per se, or if the time of two persons are imperfect substitutes or perhaps even complements. However, the main point is that unless very specific circumstances hold, two people - even two intrinsically identical individuals - can increase their efficiency to the benefit of both through co-operation by moving from Jacks-and-Jills-of-all-trades to more specialised workers.

Incidentally, this implies that an efficient division of labour need not necessarily be a *gendered* division of labour. Within the New Home Economics framework, a division of labour between men and women is only rational if women have a comparative advantage in non-market oriented activities, i.e., if women have a higher value of time spent at non-market oriented activities relative to market earning power as compared to men. It is often argued that women have such an advantage, basically because they traditionally have been made responsible for the care for children and the household (cf. Becker 1991: 62-63; Gronau 1976: S202). This is then used to explain the rationality of a gendered division of labour. The main thrust of the analysis, however, is that "the fundamental source of much of the gain is (...) the advantage of specialised investment and the division of labor" (Becker 1991: 36, also 78).

5.4   THE ASSUMPTION OF A SINGLE 'HOUSEHOLD UTILITY FUNCTION'

An important assumption on which the rationality of an intrahousehold division of labour is based is that household preferences on commodities to be produced can be represented by a single 'household utility function'. It is not assumed that all individuals within a multi-person household are similar in their tastes and preferences. However, implicitly or explicitly, it is assumed that negotiations over what to produce, in what quantities and how to divide it between the different household members have already taken place before the household members co-ordinate their efforts and decide on the optimal use of time and money inputs. Essentially, this agreement on what to produce and how to divide it can come about in one of two ways: it is either established in a contract, following the search process in the 'marriage market' for the best possible match (Becker 1973, 1991; also Cigno, 1991), or it is established by introducing an 'altruistic head of the household' (Becker 1991: chapter 8. Cf. Samuelson 1956).

In the marriage market scenario, individuals only form a household together and engage in specialised investments after they have signed a contract stipulating how the 'gains from co-operation' are to be divided. This contract is assumed to be both legally binding and complete, i.e., it is assumed to have taken into account all future contingencies that arise during a relationship. Given the existence of such a contract, bargaining during the relationship is virtually negligible and specialised investments are made (cf. Becker 1991: 14; Pollak 1994: 149). Without such a contract, people are not willing to undertake specialised investments, at least not to the extent deemed efficient in the complete and enforceable contract-case. This may seem a bit strange at first, as prospective partners are supposed to have found each other in the marriage market. By definition, this is a market in which connections are made between people who are each other's best match. As there is obviously no better match than the best match, it seems superfluous to have these people sign a contract. The fact that such a contract is necessary for people to engage in specialised investments can only mean that there are actually better matches than the one being contracted for, including the 'match' of being single. Each partner is thus faced with the risk of being deserted. Presumably, this is because the costs involved in scrolling down the marriage market are relatively high, and no one is able to check out all options (cf. Becker, Landes & Michael 1977). This is what Frank (1988: 192-193) calls the 'commitment problem in the relationship market'. Only when the uncertainty which arises out of a not-completed search is abolished by having people engage in enforceable contracts, are people willing to undertake specialised investments.

In the altruistic head of household scenario, bargaining over what to produce and how to divide it does not take place because it is in everybody's interest to maximise the utility function of the altruistic head of the household. Household preferences blend into the preferences of the altruistic head of the household given two assumptions:

1. there is at least one altruist within the household, i.e., someone whose well-being depends positively on the well-being of the other household members;
2. there is one (and only one) altruist in the household who always has the last word, i.e., controls the last action in a temporal sequence (Hirshleifer 1977: 501-502; see also Pollak 1985, especially the discussion on 598-600; Manser & Brown 1980: 37-41).

Given these two assumptions, if disagreements ever arise, these disagreements stop as soon as an altruistic member of the household has gained the power always to have the last word. From that moment on, every member is geared towards maximising the altruist's utility and bargaining over what to produce and how to divide it ceases.

The conclusions on the efficiency of a certain division of labour are to a great extent driven by these very specific assumptions on the possibility to model a household as if it were maximising a single household utility function. The following quote from 'A Treatise on the Family' serves to illustrate both the breadth and the limits of this approach. The quote is taken from Becker's response to critics who objected to his alleged focus on intrinsic differences in comparative advantages - and the lack of attention to the importance of power differences between men and women - as an explanation of the division of labour. After having argued that a division of labour based on intrinsic differences in comparative advantages does not imply there is no exploitation within the household, he goes on to say that:

> "(...) (E)xploited women may have an 'advantage' at unpleasant activities only because (...) exploited persons are not allowed to participate in activities that undermine their exploitation. No definite judgement needs to be made for the analysis (...), because it does not depend on the *source* of the comparative advantage of women at household activities, be it discrimination or other factors. It requires only that investments in specific human capital reinforce the effects of comparative advantage" (Becker 1991: 62-63; emphasis in original).

'No definite judgement needs to be made' because the greater part of the analysis is concerned only with the efficiency of a division of labour *given* the existence of an a priori 'agreement' between household members on how to divide the gains from co-operation (but see the Treatise, chapter 11). The conclusion which logically then follows is that a certain specialisation of labour and investments within the family is always efficient, as it will maximise the total gains from co-operation. However, if no a priori agreement on the division of the gains from co-operation can be assumed, this conclusion no longer follows. Then, the division of labour is likely to be determined by more considerations than maximising the gains from co-operation only.

5.5   MARKET-SPECIFIC AND MARITAL-SPECIFIC HUMAN CAPITAL

The problem of specialised investments in a context in which no single household utility function can be assumed is that specialisation is only efficient if people actually co-operate. Obviously, whether or not it is efficient to be a Jack-or-Jill-of-all-trades or a specialised worker depends very much on whether or not other specialised workers with complementary skills are available. The dangers of specialisation are nicely phrased in a more general publication on the division of labour written by Becker & Murphy (1992: 1146):

> "Although workers in modern economies have considerable knowledge of principles and have access to complicated technologies, a typical worker also commands a very much smaller share of the total knowledge used by the economy than do workers in simpler and more backward economies. (...) Highly specialised workers are surely experts in what they do, and yet know very little about the many other skills found in a complex economy. Modern expertise comes partly at the expense of narrowness, and of ignorance of what other people do".

The extent of the gains from specialisation depends to a large degree on the success of co-ordinating specialised individuals. The 'narrowness' and 'ignorance' which follows from specialisation implies that specialisation is only fruitful if the costs of combining specialised workers into a productive unit are relatively modest (Becker & Murphy 1992: 1137). If it is difficult to co-ordinate people's actions and if, for example, contracts cannot be enforced, then specialisation is not a sensible strategy. Arguably, within the context of the economics of the household, these dangers of specialisation are especially important because the 'narrowness' and 'ignorance' which follow from specialised investments are more problematic for some than for others.

However beneficial within the co-operative household, if co-operation stops, an investment in marital-specific human capital is not as useful and valuable as an investment in market-specific human capital. The difference mentioned most often between the two types of human capital refers to the difference in portability between relationships. Market-specific human capital can be defined as increasing productivity more in the market than in the home and is assumed to be portable between households. Marital-specific human capital can be defined as increasing productivity more in the household than in the market and is assumed to be less useful once the particular co-operation stops. If the relationship ends, any skills pertaining specifically to having a relationship in general fall in value until the person who has them enters a new relationship; any which pertain specifically to that relationship vanish anyway. This clearly puts those with mainly marital-specific human capital investments at a disadvantage if a specific co-operation stops (see, e.g., Becker 1974; Becker, Landes & Michael 1977: 1152; Cigno 1991: 71).

Apart from the differences in portability between relationships, there are two other differences between the specialised types of investment that are relevant here. First, it may be argued that investments in marital-specific human capital never result in as high a productivity gain as investments in market-specific human capital. Even if marital-specific skills were portable between households and perhaps marketable, they would not be worth as much as market-specific human capital investments. As Ott (1992: 70-71) points out, this is likely to be the case because, as the production of more and more things were taken from the home and into the market, only a selective cluster of goods remained. The presumably more heterogeneous character of those goods made them less suitable for market production. A second notable difference between the two types of human capital is that marital-specific human capital is less 'excludable' than market-specific human capital, as the commodities produced with this type of human capital in general have some public goods characteristics.

The asymmetry in portability and productivity of the two types of human capital as well as the differences in excludability result in specialisation within the household causing or increasing differences in bargaining power between two co-operating individuals. This power difference arises from the fact that the individual who specialises in market-oriented activities is less dependent than his or her partner on the continuation of the co-operation and has greater potential for exiting the relationship unharmed. This gives that person the possibility to threaten termination of the co-operation in order to extract a more favourable division of the gains from co-operation than previously agreed upon. Such threats are not credible if individuals have been able to reach an a priori consensus over the division of the gains from co-operation. In that case, the co-operation between specialised individuals with complementary tasks is guaranteed, and the asymmetry in portability between relationships is not problematic. However, the asymmetry does become important, and the threat to terminate the co-operation more realistic, if the altruistic head of the household does not always have the last word, if whatever agreement is reached before the co-operation started is not enforceable, or does not cover all eventualities that may arise within the relationship. In such instances, the possibility of bargaining during the co-operation can no longer be ignored, and decisions on the division of labour within the household gain a strategic aspect in addition to an efficiency aspect; rational individuals have to take into account that "relations of influence, dependence, and domination arise right out of 'mutually beneficial' trade" (Hirschman 1980 [1943]: vii; cf. Okin 1989: 137-138). Whereas both do want to make use of the advantages of a division of labour, neither party is likely to want to end up drawing the short straw, i.e., end up with a large stock of marital-specific human capital and a small stock of market-specific human capital.

Within frameworks based on the existence of a single household utility function, this strategic aspect cannot be incorporated in any systematic manner because the possibility of conflicts is assumed away. Thus, in order to incorporate strategic behaviour into the analysis, it is necessary to extend the analysis. Within neo-classical economics, this has been done by including a 'strategic aspect' in several different but related co-operative bargaining models. These models differ from those formulated within the New Home Economics tradition in that they do not assume a joint household utility function. Instead, they model the household as consisting of individuals with possibly conflicting preferences, and assume that individuals resolve these differences in the manner prescribed by some explicit bargaining rule. More importantly, they explicitly model the effects of differences in bargaining power as a result of the asymmetric effects of accumulated specialised human capital. Thus, it is possible to analyse the division of labour not as an outcome determined by comparative advantages only, but also as determined by distributional considerations. In section 6, two of these models are discussed. First, however, the general idea behind the co-operative bargaining approach to the household decision-making process is presented (Ott 1992; cf. Hargreaves Heap & Varoufakis 1995: 122-127; Gravelle & Rees 1992: 380-388; Harsanyi 1977 for a general discussion on bargaining models).

5.6   THE NASH-BARGAINING APPROACH TO HOUSEHOLD DECISION-MAKING

The main criticism that gave rise to the first formulations of co-operative bargaining models applied to the household decision-making process is that the New Home Economics approach consists of two *related* but in essence *separate* frameworks. One framework allows for an analysis of whether or not it is rational for individuals to co-operate and form a household together. The other framework allows for an analysis of the most efficient division of labour for these individuals if they have been able to agree on the division of gains from co-operation. The two frameworks are related but separate because the 'bargaining problem' of how to divide gains from co-operation is left unaddressed.

A more fundamental criticism is that it is also methodologically unsound to use such a thing as a single 'household utility function' if the whole foundation of micro-economic analysis rests on the assumption of the rational individual decision-taker as the basic unit of analysis. As Chiappori (1992) puts it '(m)odelling a group (even reduced to two participants) as if it were a single individual (...) should be seen as a (...) holistic deviation' (quoted in Woolley 1993: 493).

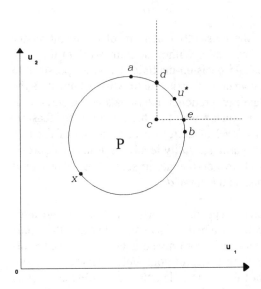

Figure 5.1

Figure 5.1 may be used to illustrate the shortcomings of the 'split-approach' to the household decision-making process. The figure shows a so-called 'payoff space'

69

P, the set of all technically feasible combinations of individual utility levels when two individuals, person 1 and person 2, co-ordinate their actions. For convenience, the payoff space is drawn as a circle, but this need not be the case. The utility levels of both 1 and 2 are assumed to depend positively on the amount of commodities consumed. The amount each can consume depends on the total amount they produce when they co-operate. This total amount may be more or less, depending on how they choose to allocate their time, money and effort. Thus, for example, point *x* denotes the minimum utility level person 1 and person 2 can possibly attain given the resources and technologies available to them. This outcome corresponds with a situation in which all available time, money and effort are put to their most inefficient use. Another possible allocation is point *a*, which represents a choice for a more efficient division of labour, resulting in a higher total output and higher utility levels for both 1 and 2.

The question whether or not these two individuals are better off co-operating is easily answered once point *c*, 'the fall-back point', is taken to represent the maximum utility levels feasible if the two persons do not co-ordinate their efforts. In our example, such non-co-operative behaviour is clearly not optimal, as there are 'gains from co-operation'; point *c* lies inside the payoff space, and not above or to the right of it. As can be seen from the figure, there are many technically feasible production possibilities such that both individuals are better off co-operating than not co-operating (i.e. all the points covered by the triangle *cde*). The 'postulate of individual rationality' implies that rational individuals in this case always choose to co-operate.

A subsequent question, i.e., what is the most efficient form of co-operation for these two individuals, is not answered as easily. Within the framework of the New Home Economics approach to household decision-making, it is only possible to indicate a range of possible solution concepts. This is due to what is known as the 'joint rationality or efficiency postulate': two rational individuals will always allocate their time and money resources in such a way that there is no other feasible allocation which would yield a higher level of utility for at least one of the two partners (without decreasing the other partner's utility level). In terms of figure 1, this implies that rational individuals always co-operate in such a way that would result in one of the utility combinations on the curve *de*.

The *exact* form their co-operation takes depends on whatever it is the two individuals stipulate in the contract they are assumed to have signed before they start to co-operate (in the marriage market scenario), or on who is declared to be the altruistic head of the household (in the altruist head of household scenario). Without further information on this, all sorts of divisions of labour are feasible as long as they result in one of the many utility combinations on the curve *de*. Depending on the bargaining power of the two individuals, the most efficient division of labour is a division that ends up satisfying the wants of person 2 most (point *d*), satisfying the wants of person 1 most (point *e*), or satisfying the wants of both to some extent.

Nash-bargaining as a solution concept

At the beginning of the 1980s, both Manser & Brown (1980) and McElroy & Horney (1981) presented an application of the 'Nash-bargaining problem' which solved the bargaining problem identified above, and allowed the outcome of the decision-making process to be pinpointed to a single outcome.

In the Nash-bargaining approach, the outcome of the household decision-making process is modelled as the outcome of a 'game' played by two 'players' "whose interests are neither completely opposed nor completely coincident" (Nash 1953: 128). These two players are assumed to be 'co-operative', i.e., they "are supposed to be able to discuss the situation and agree on a rational joint plan of action, an agreement that should be assumed to be enforceable" (Ibid). In addition, it is assumed that their preferences can be represented in terms of cardinal utility functions, i.e., functions which are unique up to order-preserving linear transformations. The rules of the game stipulate that both players have to state how they wish to divide the gains to co-operation simultaneously and independently of each other. If both the 'payoff demands' lie in the 'payoff space' of the game (set P in figure 1), then the two players' demands are mutually compatible; a division of labour is feasible which allows the household to produce the desired combination of payoffs. In this case, after having signed an enforceable contract in which it is agreed that each player will receive the payoff that he or she demanded, the co-operation can begin. In contrast, if the demands lie outside the payoff space, then the players' demands are incompatible. There is no feasible division of labour which can actually produce the desired combination of payoff demands. In this case, the players will not co-operate. Then, the 'gains from co-operation' will not be realised.

How is it possible to predict the outcome of such a bargaining game? John Nash was the first to observe that with the help of 'certain idealisations', i.e., "assuming that the two individuals are highly rational, that each can accurately compare his desires for various things, (...) and that each has full knowledge of the tastes and preferences of the other" (Nash 1950: 155), the game has a definite solution. He came up with a seemingly simple idea, captured in the 'symmetry postulate' (Nash 1950, 1953; see also Harsanyi, 1977: chapters 8 & 9). Loosely formulated, this postulate says that if two individuals are exactly the same, then the only rational thing which can be expected to emerge from a bargaining game between the two is that they agree on a 50/50 division of the output. After all, in such a symmetrical situation there is no reason to expect that one player will be able to get a better deal than the other.

The symmetry postulate combined with some other assumptions (four in total: joint rationality, symmetry, linear invariance and independence of irrelevant alternatives) make it possible to predict the outcome, also where the two players are not

71

intrinsically identical individuals. The outcome of the bargaining problem depends on the 'bargaining power' of the two individuals. This is operationalised as their utility if no co-operation takes place, the position to fall-back on if they do not manage to reach an agreement (point c in figure 5.1). Point u^* then represents the outcome of the game, i.e., the payoff demands formulated by the players and agreed upon in a contract. It is the point where the curve de is cut by the 45^0 line from point c, which splits the area dce into two symmetrical parts. Mathematically, this outcome is found by maximising the 'Nash product', $(U_1-c_1)(U_2-c_2)$, given the constraints imposed on the production possibilities of the household. This solution incorporates the idea that a rational player with a relatively high fall-back position will not agree to co-operate unless he or she gets a relatively large share of the total output.

The advantage of the bargaining approach as compared to the New Home Economics approach to household decision-making is that the 'bargaining problem' of how to divide the gains from co-operation - and consequently the problem of how best to divide time, money and effort - is incorporated into the same framework as the problem of whether or not to co-operate. A consequence of being able to integrate all these issues is that changes in the preferences of the household can be treated endogenously. A change in the external alternatives of two individuals results in a different weighting of the (stable) preferences in the Nash-product and thus in a systematic change in the preferences of the household. Whereas approaches stipulating a single household utility function can only explain changes in household preferences as determined by changes in prices or changes in household income, within the bargaining approach changes in the fall-back positions of people also matter (see for applications, e.g., McElroy & Horney 1981; Manser & Brown 1980; McElroy 1990; Chiappori 1988, 1992; Kooreman & Kapteyn, 1990 Lundberg & Pollak, 1993; Pollak, 1994).

5.7   STRATEGIC BEHAVIOUR AND THE DIVISION OF LABOUR

The superiority of the Nash-bargaining approach to household decision-making above those based on a single household utility function is due to the fact that the former encompasses the latter and allows for a tight fit between individual preferences and household preferences. However, as long as the co-operative bargaining approach to the division of labour is static, and contracts are always enforceable and complete, the conclusions on the division of labour will be the same as those arrived at within the New Home Economics framework. Decisions on the division of labour will then still be based on considerations of maximising the total gains from co-operation only, and would not include distribution considerations. For applications on the division of labour within the family, the bargaining framework seems especially useful once a dynamic approach is taken. Recently, several dynamic applications of the Nash-bargaining approach have been formulated. These

72

models explicitly model the strategic aspect of specialised investments by some-how assuming limits to contracting.

One such model is a dynamic version of the Nash-bargaining approach to house-hold decision-making, formulated by Notburga Ott (1992, 1995). Ott's model can be interpreted as a combination of the household production models discussed in section 2 and the Nash-bargaining approach to household decision-making dis-cussed in section 5. Individuals are assumed to derive utility from commodities which are produced by the household by means of the time, money and effort available. As before, it is assumed that there are gains from co-operation and that the realisation of these gains requires binding contracts. Similar to the Nash-bargaining approach described above, it is assumed that people decide on the divi-sion of gains from co-operation on the basis of their bargaining positions before they actually start to co-operate (in Ott's model - the utility levels when single). However, the gains from co-operation are less than in the approaches discussed so far, because people do not make full use of the advantages of specialised invest-ments.

The strategic aspects of time allocations and investments enter Ott's model be-cause she assumes that increasing asymmetries in bargaining power which result from specialised investments mean some contracts cannot be enforced and are therefore not engaged in by rational individuals in the first place. Some forms of co-operation imply such large losses of bargaining power for one of the two part-ners - i.e., for women, fertility decisions in combination with interruptions of mar-ket work - that they *cannot be contracted upon*. Although such divisions of labour are 'technically feasible', they are not 'rationally feasible' (cf. Ott 1992: 102). In terms of the gains from co-operation, this 'underutilisation' of the household's capital means that the household produces less than is technically feasible; the curve *de* in figure 1 shifts downwards.

A second model which incorporates the strategic aspect of decisions on time allo-cation is formulated by Kai Konrad & Kjell Erik Lommerud in a recent discussion paper (1996. Also see 1995). The model they propose can be placed in the tradition of public economics studies that look at individual incentives to provide public goods (see e.g. Warr, 1982; Bergstrom, Blume & Varian 1986). Individuals are as-sumed to derive utility from both private goods as well as from what is defined as 'the family public good': i.e., well-raised children or a clean and nicely decorated home. The decision-making process in the household is modelled as a two-stage game. In the first stage, both partners have to make an 'education investment' de-cision, i.e., they have to determine how much to invest in their labour market pro-ductivity. This first stage is modelled non-co-operatively; it is assumed that "these investments have a long-lasting effect on spouses' labour market productivity, and are likely to be made non-co-operatively, that is, without having reached full agreement with the spouse" (Konrad & Lommerud 1996. Cf. Lundberg & Pollak 1993). In the second stage, both partners have to decide about their contributions to the public good, i.e., on their time allocations. This stage is modelled as a co-operative game. Because it is assumed that the contracts engaged in at this stage are fully enforceable, the household decision-making process in stage 2 is an efficient one. Still, as in Ott's model, the household does not produce as efficiently as technically possible in this second stage because the education investment decisions made in stage 1 influence the fall-back positions in stage 2.

The crucial assumption made in Konrad & Lommerud's model is that even where two persons do not co-operate, they are still connected to each other because of their mutual concern for the family public good. This assumption means investments in specialised human capital gain a strategic aspect: assuming individuals are otherwise identical, whoever produces more of the public good ends up in a weaker bargaining position than the one who produces more of the private good. This is so, because in a non-co-operative state the returns from investments in market-specific human capital accrue to the individual who has invested in it and to no one else. On the other hand, returns from investments in marital-specific human capital (public goods-specific human capital) benefit the total household because, by definition, the public good produced is non-excludable. For the educational investment decisions made in the first stage, this means that both persons overinvest just to prevent ending up as the one with a comparative advantage in the production in the public good. "The situation is one with an arms race externality: when both persons overinvest in this way, the difference between fall-back utilities remains constant (at zero) -- so in the end overinvestment only reduces welfare without altering the intrafamily distribution" (Konrad & Lommerud 1996: 15). The decision-making process in the second, co-operative stage is still 'efficient', but because of the different effects of specialised human capital investments on individuals' bargaining positions, the household does not gain as much from the co-operation as technically speaking it could have done.

Basically, then, both models focus on the causal relationship between asymmetries in specialised investments and the inability to enforce contracts. Ott assumes that some divisions of labour which imply large asymmetries in specialised investments cannot be contracted for because the resulting effects on bargaining power would allow one of the two partners to break the contract. Konrad & Lommerud assume something similar when they state that, because of the long-lasting effect on spouses' labour market productivity, decisions on investments in education are likely to be taken non-co-operatively. (It should be noted that both these assumptions presumably only make sense if there is room for some uncertainty. This makes it somewhat problematic to assume that individuals are certain of a co-operative outcome at some point. This issue is not addressed here, but it is discussed in Ott (1992, chapter 9). Also refer to Lommerud (1989)). Given these limits to contracting, rational individuals are assumed not to make use of the advantages of specialisation to the extent technically possible. The main reason is that in both models investments in market-specific human capital have different effects on bargaining power than investments in marital-specific human capital. Admittedly,

74

the two models focus on two quite different mechanisms. Ott's model models the fall-back position as a break-up of the household and especially focuses on the differences in portability between households. Konrad & Lommerud's model models the fall-back position as a non-co-operative, multi-person household and points to the differences in excludability of the goods produced with either one of the two types of human capital. Notwithstanding these differences, I have argued that both models can be used to send the same message: the asymmetric effects of specialised human capital make complete and enforceable contracts impossible. Therefore, the gains from specialisation within the family will be less than those technically feasible.

5.8 CONCLUSION

In conclusion, it is perhaps worthwhile to restate that the models discussed in this chapter model the behaviour of individuals within the context of the household decision-making process assuming that individuals behave according to a considerable number of rationality postulates. Depending on the specification of the situation, they prescribe what should happen in families consisting of instrumentally rational individuals. But, "all the same, the main purpose of (game) theory is very definitely to help the positive empirical social sciences to predict and explain real-life human behaviour in various situations" (Harsanyi 1977: 16). The question which remains therefore is how the above may be relevant to our understanding of the actual division of labour between men and women.

The basic lesson to be drawn from the discussion in this chapter is a general one, i.e., that "there are truly non-co-operative game situations, where a prudent decision-maker cannot put much confidence in his opponent's willingness to keep agreements" (Harsanyi 1977: 278). The 'truly non-co-operative situation' pointed out in the above is the situation which may arise if investments in specialised human capital result in such asymmetric bargaining situations that theoretically mutually beneficial relations give birth to 'relations of influence, dependence and domination'.

In real-life situations, it seems fair to say that individuals may behave more or less rationally in dealing with this mechanism. Those who are more rational will try to prevent asymmetric dependency by means of certain strategies. These strategies in turn will result in welfare losses related to an underinvestment in marital-specific human capital. Those that are less rational will not be fully aware of the disadvantages of specialisation, perhaps because of the importance of tradition, social norms or because of the complexity of the situation. These persons are likely to end up in a position of asymmetric dependency on their partner. Whenever conflicts of interest within households occur, these people will try to avoid escalation of the situation, simply because they have more to lose in case of a break-up. This implies that the more dependent partners are likely to subordinate their own interests to the interests of the more powerful partner. This may result in substantial inequalities within relationships. Either way, whether real-life people are thought to be more or less rational in their behaviour, policy makers who find that the mechanisms described in this chapter make some sense of reality have a clear mission: to focus on policy measures which help individuals to overcome the problems of the asymmetric effects of specialised investments and allow them to engage in mutually beneficial arrangements.

REFERENCES

Becker, G.S. 1965: A theory of the allocation of time. *Economic Journal, 75*, 493-517.

Becker, G.S. 1973: A theory of marriage: part I. *Journal of Political Economy, 81*, 813-846.

Becker, G.S. 1974: A theory of marriage: part II. *Journal of Political Economy, 82*, S11-S26.

Becker, G.S. 1991: *A treatise on the family, enlarged edition* (1st edition 1981). Cambridge/London: Harvard University Press.

Becker, G.S. & Murphy, K.M. 1992: The division of labor, coordination costs and knowledge. *The Quarterly Journal of Economics, 107*, No.4, 1137-1160.

Becker, G.S., Landes, E.M. & Michael, R.T. 1977: An economic analysis of marital instability. *Journal of Political Economy, 85*, 1141-1187.

Bergstrom, T., Blume, L. & Varian, H. 1986: On the private provision of public goods. *Journal of Public Economics, 29*, 25-49.

Cigno, A. 1991: *Economics of the family*. Oxford: Clarendon Press.

Chiappori, P.A. 1988: Rational household labor supply. *Econometrica, 56*, 63-89.

Chiappori, P.A. 1992: Collective labor supply and welfare. *Journal of Political Economy, 100*, 437-467.

Frank, R.H. 1988: *Passions within reason. The strategic role of emotions*. New York/London: W.W. Norton & Company.

Gershuny, J. & Robinson, J.P. 1988: Historical changes in the household division of labor. *Demography, 25*, No.4, 537-552.

Gershuny, J. & Robinson, J.P. 1991: The household division of labour: multinational comparisons of change. In European Foundation for the Improvement of Living and Working Conditions, *The changing use of time: report from an international workshop* (pp.153-184). Luxembourg: Office for Official Publications of the European Communities.

Goldschmidt-Clermont, L. & Pagnossin-Aligisakis, E. 1995: Measures of unrecorded economic activities in fourteen countries. *Occasional Papers Human Development Report Office*, No.20. New York: Human Development Report Office.

Gravelle, H. & Rees, R. 1992: *Microeconomics. Second edition* (First edition 1981). London/New York: Longman.

Gronau, R. 1976: The allocation of time of Israeli women. *Journal of Political Economy, 84*, No.4, Pt.2, S201-S220.

Gronau, R. 1977: Leisure, home production, and work; the theory of the allocation of time revisited. *Journal of Political Economy*, *85*, No.6, 1099-1123.

Gronau, R. 1986: Home production, a survey. In O. Ashenfelter & R. Layard (eds.) *Handbook of labor economics*, Volume 1 (pp.273-304). Elsevier Science Publishers.

Hargreaves Heap, S.P. & Varoufakis, Y. 1995: *Game theory. A critical introduction*. London/New York: Routledge.

Harsanyi, J.C. 1977: *Rational behaviour and bargaining equilibrium in games and social situations*. Cambridge [etc.]: Cambridge University Press.

Hirshleifer, J. 1977: Shakespeare vs. Becker on altruism: the importance of having the last word. *Journal of Economic Literature*, *15*, No.2, 500-502.

Hirschman, A.O. 1945, expanded edition 1980: *National power and the structure of foreign trade*. Berkeley [etc.]: University of California Press.

Juster, F.T. & Stafford, F. 1991: The allocation of time. Empirical findings, behavioral models, and problems of measurement. *Journal of Economic Literature*, *24*, No.2, 471-522.

Konrad, K.A. & Lommerud, K.E. 1995: Family policy with non-cooperative families, *Scandinavian Journal of Economics*, *97*, No.4, 581-601.

Konrad, K.A. & Lommerud, K.E. 1996: The bargaining family revisited. *Discussion Paper* No.1312. London: Centre for Economic Policy Research.

Kooreman, P. & Kapteyn A. 1987: A desegregated analysis of the allocation of time within the household. *Journal of Political Economy*, *95*, 223-249.

Kooreman, P. & Kapteyn, A. 1990: On the empirical implementation of some game theoretic models of household labor supply. *Journal of Human Resources*, *25*, 584-598.

Lommerud, K.E. 1989: Marital division of labor with risk of divorce: the role of 'voice' enforcement of contracts. *Journal of Labor Economics*, *7*, No.1, 113-127.

Lundberg, S. & Pollak, R.A. 1993: Separate spheres bargaining and the marriage market. *Journal of Political Economy*, *101*, No.6, 988-1010.

Manser, M. & Brown, M. 1980: Marriage and household decision-making: a bargaining analysis. *International Economic Review*, *21*, No.1, 31-44.

McElroy, M.B. 1990: The empirical content of Nash-bargained household behavior. *Journal of Human Resources*, *25*, No.4, 559-583.

McElroy, M.B. & Horney, M.J. 1981: Nash-bargained household decisions: towards a generalisation of the theory of demand. *International Economic Review*, *22*, No.2, 333-349.

Mincer, J. 1962: Labor force participation of married women: a study of labor supply. Abridged version reprinted in: A.H. Amsden (ed.) (1980). *The economics of women and work* (pp.41-51). Harmondsworth/New York: Pinguin Books.

Nash, J. 1950: The bargaining problem. *Econometrica*, *18*, 155-162.

Nash, J. 1953: Two person cooperative games. *Econometrica*, *21*, 128-140.

Okin, S. Moller 1989: *Justice, gender and the family*. S.l.: BasicBooks.

Ott, N. 1992: *Intrafamily bargaining and household decisions*. Berlin [etc.]: Springer-Verlag.

Ott, N. 1995: Fertility and division of work in the family. A game theoretic model of household decisions. In E. Kuiper & J. Sap (eds.) *Out of the margin. Feminist perspectives on economics* (pp.80-99). London/New York: Routledge.

Pollak, R.A. 1985: A transaction cost approach to families and households. *Journal of Economic Literature, 23,* 581-608.

Pollak, R.A. 1994: For better of worse: the roles of power in models of distribution within marriage. *American Economic Review Papers and Proceedings, 84,* No.2, 148-158.

Pollak, R.A. & Wachter, M.L. 1975: The relevance of the household production function and its implications for the allocation of time. *Journal of Political Economy, 83,* No.2, 255-277.

Samuelson, P.A. 1956: Social indifference curves. *The Quarterly Journal of Economics, 70,* No.1, 1-22.

Stigler, G.J. & Becker, G.S. 1977: De gustibus non est disputandum. *American Economic Review, 67,* No.2, 76-90.

Szalai, A. (ed.) 1972: *The use of time. Daily activities of urban and suburban populations in twelve countries.* The Hague/Paris: Mouton.

United Nations 1995: *Women and men in Europe and North America 1995.* Geneva: United Nations.

Warr, P. 1982: Pareto optimal redistribution and private charity. *Journal of Public Economics, 19,* 131-138.

Woolley, F.R. 1993: The feminist challenge to neoclassical economics. *Cambridge Journal of Economics, 17,* 485-500.

ACKNOWLEDGEMENTS

I would like to thank Elisabeth Harrison-Neu and Notburga Ott for their comments on an earlier version of this paper, presented at the conference 'Time allocation and gender. The relationship between paid labour and household labour', Amsterdam, November 30-December 1 1995.

BIOGRAPHICAL NOTE

Susan van Velzen studied political science and has worked as a PhD-student at the Department of Economics, Faculty of Economics and Econometrics of the University of Amsterdam since 1994. She is affiliated with the Tinbergen Institute as well as with the Amsterdam Graduate Centre for Comparative and Multicultural Gender Studies, the Belle van Zuylen Institute.

6   Parental time allocation and day care

Henriëtte Maassen van den Brink
Wim Groot

6.1   INTRODUCTION

Time allocation patterns of households are changing rapidly. These trends are most pronounced and most visible in the rapid increase in female labour force participation rates. What the overall changes do not reveal among all men and women is that the time allocation patterns of younger cohorts are changing much more rapidly than those of older cohorts. The remarkable increase in labour force participation of women during the last ten to fifteen years is, for example, to a large extent dominated by the increase in labour supply of women with young children. The long-term implications of changing time patterns among younger cohorts are, of course, also much more important. This makes it all the more relevant to take a closer look at the time allocation of men and women with young children.

This chapter is about the time allocation of households with children under the age of four. We address the following questions: How do these men and women spend their time? How do women in paid employment differ from jobless women in the way they spend their time? What, if any, are the differences in time allocation of the individuals with a high level of education compared to those with low levels of education? More in particular, this chapter raises the question of how the use of childcare services affects the amount of time couples devote to household work and paid labour.

We are also interested in the effects of individual characteristics - such as level of education, working experience, and number of children - on the time allocation of both partners and on the use of childcare arrangements. In this respect, a number of questions can be raised, such as: Does the price of childcare services, the level of wage rate, and total family income affect the use of these services and the participation in the labour market of women and men? And, is there a relationship between the number of hours the male partner spends on care of his children and the use and costs of childcare facilities? In addition to establishing these relationships, we would like to obtain an idea of the extent of these effects.

Time allocation and gender, Kea Tijdens, Anneke van Doorne-Huiskes & Tineke Willemsen (eds.), Tilburg University Press, 1997, © Henriëtte Maassen van den Brink & Wim Groot

The outline of this chapter is as follows. In Section 2 we give an overview of the literature with regard to time allocation and division of labour in families. Section 3 describes the data. In section 4 a descriptive analysis is presented of the time allocation of parents with young children and the use of childcare centres. Section 5 contains the estimated results of the influence of costs of childcare, wages and income on the use of day care and participation in the labour market. Section 6 concludes the chapter.

6.2 PARENTAL TIME ALLOCATION: A SURVEY OF THE LITERATURE

Research by the *Centraal Bureau voor de Statistiek* (Statistics Netherlands; CBS) on time use patterns shows that women and men devote a similar amount of time to their personal care, eating and sleeping (CBS, 1994). Men and woman also have an approximately equal total amount of leisure time at their disposal. Women, however, devote more of their time to household work and looking after the children, while men spend more time in the labour market. There are also important differences between households. For instance, couples consisting of partners who are both working in the labour market have less leisure time than couples in which a single partner, or neither partner, is employed. In the former case, both women and men are subject to a greater work load than in the latter. Meijer (1996) concludes that the women in such couples carry the greater load. She observes that, on average, women with a child under five spend more time on care for the child, working, and doing household work, compared to both their own partner and compared to other women. Unemployed women whose youngest child is over five, women in paid employment without children, and male partners have the lowest work load. The greatest difference in average workload between women and men is observed when the children are under five and the woman is in the labour market for more than 24 hours a week.

If both partners participate in the labour market it is mainly at the expense of the following activities: preparing meals, cleaning the home, doing the laundry, looking after clothes, and shopping. The amount of time these couples spend looking after the children also decreases slightly. This decrease is mainly attributable to:

1. the decrease in the number of women who take care of these tasks.
2. the decrease in time that women devote to these activities.

Similar results are found by Van der Lippe (1992) who shows that the time devoted to household work and care for children decreases greatly when women spend more time in paid employment.
Men whose partner is in paid employment generally devote slightly more time to household work and care for the children than men whose partner is not in paid employment. The increase in time devoted to these activities is small compared to the decrease in time that women spend on these activities once they enter paid employment (CBS, 1994). The result is that the overall share of men in these activi-

ties increases only slightly when their partner enters gainful employment. Only among couples with young children is the decrease of the women's participation more or less compensated by their partner's participation in household work and care for children. However, this is mainly attributable to the fact that women with young children devote less time to household work and to care for the children when they enter paid employment. Again, the same conclusion was drawn by Van der Lippe (1992). She finds that the share of men in these tasks is about equal regardless of the amount of time (if any) their wives spend working outside the home.

Furthermore, Van der Lippe (1992) finds that household work is most evenly distributed in households without children. The arrival of children generally gives rise to specialisation. Women apply themselves to the housework and care for children, men to paid employment outside the home. The presence of children means an increase in household work and childcare of about 17 hours per week for the woman, while the share of the husband in these tasks remains about the same.

Results of research by Maassen van den Brink & Groot (1994a) and Maassen van den Brink (1994) also confirm a number of stereotypes concerning women and men. In the first place, men are found to contribute little to the household work. Their contribution remains small even when children enter the household. And, if women enter the labour market, men do not relieve their partners of household work. Men do little to adapt to changes in the family composition. It is mainly the woman who adapts to such changes. The number of children and their age influence the way women, in particular, spend their time. Men's time allocation is much less affected by the family situation. Women with young children spend less time in paid employment and devote more of their time to the children and the household. Men in the same situation spend more time in paid employment than their partners. Children exert little influence on the way men spend the rest of their time.

Secondly, Maassen van den Brink & Groot (1994a) confirm the dominant influence of the traditional division of labour among women and men. Men are oriented towards gainful employment outside the home, women towards unpaid labour in the home. As a result, the value of the woman's unpaid labour exceeds that of her paid labour by far and her contribution to the total value of domestic work is greater than that of men. The average value of paid and unpaid labour of women and men is about equal. However, the value of men's labour largely stems from paid employment, that of women largely from unpaid housework. With respect to paid employment, women contribute a mere 20% to the total value of paid and unpaid labour. So, although the total productive contribution of men and women is approximately equal, women enjoy much less economic independence. The lack of independence is caused by the type of products that women specialise in, namely household and domestic services, which are not marketable (i.e. priced and sold on the market).

Although the division of household work and care for children among men and women is patently unequal, this inequality is not usually considered unfair. Aarts & Hermkens (1994) show that between 85% and 95% of households view this unequal division of domestic work as fair. Nonetheless, 75% of the population does believe that household work should be divided equally and an even greater percentage states that care for the children is equal to the responsibility of both women and men (e.g. Chapter 4 in this book, Van der Vinne)

Even though the majority of the population does not consider the actual division of labour to be unfair, the unequal division does give rise to conflicts (very) frequently in 16% of households (Maassen van den Brink & Noom, 1994; Maassen van den Brink, 1994; Maassen van den Brink & Groot, 1994b). The consequences of these conflicts for the participation in the labour force were investigated by Maassen van den Brink & Groot (1994b). The conclusion is that the more this division of labour gives rise to conflicts, the more hours men tend to spend in paid employment outside the home and the less time women spend on this activity.

6.3 THE DATA OF THE 'TIME ALLOCATION AND DIVISION OF LABOUR' SURVEY, 1995

The data for the analysis are taken from the 'Time Allocation and Division of Labour Survey 1995'(The survey was carried out in co-operation with DESAN market research, Amsterdam.) This survey gathered information on time allocation, childcare use, wages, and individual characteristics. The 1995 survey was partly a replication of the survey 'Women on Work' in 1991 (Maassen van den Brink, 1994). The target population of the 1995 survey consisted of women between 18 and 65 with children and/or a partner. Men, women outside the stated age range, and single women without children are excluded. Over-sampling took place among women with children under four. A telephone survey among this target population, resulted in 4,974 successful interviews. The over-sampling ensured that 1,299 of these interviews were with women with children under four (26%). Of the remaining 3,675 interviews, 671 were again with women with children under four.

Of the 4,974 respondents in the telephone survey, 2,170 women were invited to participate in a written follow-up survey. Of those invited, 89.9% agreed to participate. These 1,950 women were sent two questionnaires: one for the woman and one for her partner. An addressed envelope was provided for return of the completed questionnaires. To encourage the return of the questionnaires, a prize of NLG 2,000 was announced. This sum would be raffled among those who returned the questionnaires. After a period of three weeks, the participants were sent a reminder to return the completed questionnaires. If these were not returned after a further two weeks, a second reminder was sent. After a further two weeks, those who had still failed to return the questionnaires were contacted by telephone and informed that they could still win the prize of NLG 2,000 if they returned the questionnaires. On 1 October 1995 the prize was raffled.

All in all, 1,109 women returned the completed questionnaires in the written survey. This is almost 57% of the 1,950 original participants. Of these 1,109 women, 261 had children under four. Table 6.1 gives an overview of the response to the telephone and written survey.

Table 6.1 Overview of response to written survey

	Number	Percentage
Invited to participate	2170	100.0%
Willing to participate	1950	89.9%
Net response/actually participated	1109	56.9%

Table 6.2 shows the analysis of responses to the childcare questions and some of the personal characteristic questions.

Table 6.2 Analysis of responses in written and telephone survey: women with children under four

	market work		non market work	
	Telephone survey	Written survey	Telephone survey	Written survey
uses day care facilities	0.25	0.27	0.04	0.06
uses subsidised day care	0.16	0.17	0.02	0.03
uses private day care	0.08	0.07	0.02	0.04
company day care	0.04	0.05	0.00	0.00
company day care in private day care centre	0.29	0.18	0.00	0.00
company day care in subsidised day care centre	0.58	0.40	0.00	0.00
host parents	0.04	0.05	0.00	0.00
nursery school	0.32	0.28	0.38	0.38
other day care	0.01	0.01	0.01	0.02
paid private childminder	0.37	0.42	0.13	0.08
unpaid private childminder	0.51	0.45	0.66	0.64
hours paid labour	19.18	19.13	0.00	0.87
net income of female partner	1426	1441	409	621
net income of male partner/husband	2814	2779	2737	2985
age female partner	32.16	32.19	31.12	31.90
years of education female partner	13.45	13.66	11.77	12.21
number of cases	1004	149	964	112

The choice to use a publicly funded or private day care centre was made by the respondents themselves. In the telephone survey the interviewer referred to the definitions of the different forms of childcare use. In the written survey the respondents indicated which type of childcare they use. This method corresponds to those SGBO surveys (1995) in which local governments themselves indicated if a child-care centre is publicly funded or not.

In this chapter we use information of time allocation patterns of both partners from the written survey. Eight categories of time allocation are distinguished: paid employment outside the home (including time spent in commuting), unpaid activities outside the home (e.g., volunteer work, further education), unpaid work in the home (cleaning, preparing meals, doing the washing up), unpaid activities relevant to the household (shopping, repairs), care for the children, care for one's partner, personal care (sleeping, eating, washing), and leisure time activities (hobbies, sport, going out). In Section 4 we also use information taken from the telephone survey such as level of education, experience, number of children, wages, and family income.

6.4   PARENTAL TIME ALLOCATION: AN EMPIRICAL STUDY

On the basis of the literature survey in Section 2, a number of conclusions can be drawn. Firstly, it can be concluded that it is still the woman in the household who does most of the household work and who looks after the children. Whether or not husband and wife are in paid employment has little effect on this. Secondly, women increasingly have to combine child rearing, household work and paid employment. In some cases, the ongoing workload that women experience is allevi-ated by making use of paid services of others, e.g. child day care services or do-mestic help. Thirdly, the combination of paid employment, household work, and care for children represents a considerable workload. This load is a source of con-flict within the home. Fourthly, the number of men who are willing to make an equal contribution to the household work and childcare is very limited. Finally, in their time allocation decisions men tend to take into account neither the work load of their partner, nor the household situation. When women enter paid employment, men do little to accommodate this reallocation of their partner's time by increasing their share of household work or care for the children.

In the remainder of this section, we investigate the effects of child day care on the other categories of time allocation. In Table 6.3 the average number of hours de-voted to the eight activities distinguished are tabulated by participation in the la-bour market and by level of education.

Women in paid employment devote an average of almost 22 hours per week to their job. They spend on average 24 hours per week doing household work. On av-erage, care for the children takes up 30 hours and care for their partners an addi-tional 11 hours. These women have an average 16 hours a week for leisure. Women who are not in paid employment spend about 32 hours doing household work, 36 hours looking after the children and over 15 hours looking after their partners. They have about 21 hours a week of leisure time.

A comparison between participating and non-participating women in the labour market reveals that employed women with children devote less time to the following activities (difference in average number of hours is given in parentheses): care for the children (10 hours less), household work (8 hours less), leisure time activities (6 hours less), and looking after the partner (4 hours less).

More highly educated employed women spend significantly more time in paid and unpaid activities outside the home than less well educated employed women. It is the amount of time devoted to care for the partner especially that decreases: more highly educated women in paid employment devote significantly less time to this activity than their less well educated counterparts.

Among women who are not gainfully employed, the only significant difference between the higher and lower education is in the time devoted to personal care: the former devote significantly more time to this activity (61.9 vs. 50.6 hours a week).

Table 6.3 Time allocation of women with young children. Average hours a week devoted to eight categories of activities by education and participation in the labour market

	market work			non market work		
Q: How much time per week do you devote to the following activities?						
	All women	Higher education	Lower education	All women	Higher education	Lower education
market work	21.8	25.8	19.5	0	0	0
unpaid activities outside the home	2.8	4.5	1.8	2.0	12	2.4
unpaid work in the household	17.9	16.2	18.9	26.4	24.3	27.1
unpaid activities relevant to the household	6.3	6.4	6.2	9.2	8.3	9.4
looking after children	29.5	30.1	28.9	36.2	39.0	35.4
looking after partner/husband	11.3	9.9	12.1	15.3	14.8	15.4
personal care	55.5	57.4	54.4	53.2	61.9	50.6
Leisure time activities	16.5	16.0	16.8	20.7	22.1	20.5

Table 6.4 contains the allocation of time to the eight activities of women who do and women who do not make use of day care centres for their children. Again, we find that women who use day care spend more time in paid employment than women who do not use such services. The use of day care centres especially enables women to undertake activities outside the home. Women who make use of these services engage more in paid and unpaid activities outside the home.

Besides the activities already mentioned, the use of day care centres does not result in any appreciable differences in the allocation of time among the other categories.

It is striking that there are no real differences in the time devoted to looking after the children. Women who make use of day care centres, spend an average 31.5 hours a week looking after the children. Women who do not make use of such services devote 32.5 hours a week to this activity, a difference of only one hour. Apparently, the use of child day care has little or no effect on the amount of time women spend on care of their children. Children in day care do not appear to enjoy less care or attention from their mothers than children who stay at home.

Table 6.4 Time allocation in average number of hours per week by use of day care of women with young children

Q: How much time per week do you devote to the following activities?			
	All women	Women who use childcare centres	Women who do not use childcare centres
market work	12.8	18.4	11.0
unpaid activities outside the house	2.5	5.1	1.7
unpaid work in the household	21.4	20.2	21.8
unpaid activities relevant tot the house-hold	7.5	7.4	7.5
looking after the children	32.3	31.5	32.6
looking after the partner/husband	12.9	11.6	13.4
personal care	54.6	55.9	54.1
leisure time activities	18.2	18.2	19.0

As was already observed in the literature survey, the woman's participation in the labour market has little effect on the time allocation of the partner. Whether the use of child day care has any influence on men's time allocation has not yet been addressed in the literature. The allocation of time by men with young children has also yet to be addressed. In the present section we look at the question of time allocation of men with young children. Table 6.5 contains the amount of time that these men devote to the activities in the eight categories. The sample consists of the partners of the women in the sample that provided the information in Tables 6.1 and 6.2.

On average, men spend 47.3 hours a week on market work (including overtime and commuting time). Almost 14 hours are devoted to household work and a similar amount of time to care for the children. Care for the partner and personal care take up 11 hours and 54 hours a week, respectively. Leisure time amounts to a little over 20 hours a week.

Table 6.5 Time allocation of men with young children in average number of hours per week by employment status of the partner and use of day care

Q: How much time per week do you devote to the following activities?

	All men	Men whose partner has		Family uses day care facilities	Family does not use day care facilities
		market work	non market work		
Market work	47.3	45.6	49.3	44.7	47.4
Unpaid activities outside the home	2.6	2.8	2.4	1.9	2.7
Unpaid work in the household	7.4	7.9	6.7	15.8	7.0
unpaid work relevant to the household	6.5	6.5	6.6	7.6	6.5
looking after the children	13.9	14.7	13.0	15.2	13.8
looking after the partner	11.4	11.1	11.8	13.1	11.4
personal care	54.1	54.5	53.5	52.7	54.2
leisure time activities	20.1	20.2	19.9	16.1	20.3

A comparison of men whose partners are participating in the labour market with men whose partners are not shows that there are very few differences in time allocation. The only significant difference concerns market work. Men whose wives who do not participate in the labour market spend slightly more time in market work than the men with a working partner (49.3 vs. 45.6 hours a week). As shown in Table 6.4, there are other differences as well, for instance in the amount of time devoted to care for the children and to household activities, but these are not significant.

If families that use childcare services are compared to families that do not, we find that men in the former devote more time to unpaid work in the household, to care for the children, and to care for their partner. It is possible that these differences are attributable to the fact that men in families that use child day-care are better educated and have a higher income. The higher levels of education may be associated with less traditional attitudes concerning division of labour within the household.

A comparison of Table 6.3 and Table 6.4 reveals that fathers of young children on average spend four times as much time in market work than women with young children (about 47.3 vs. 12.8 hours a week). Compared to men, on the other hand, women devote almost three times as much time to household activities (21.4 vs. 7.4 hours a week). They spend 2.5 times more time than men on looking after the children (32.3 vs. 13.9 hours a week). On average, they devote about an equal amount of time to care for each other and to their personal care. They have an equal amount of leisure time.

Even when women are participating in the labour market, the division of unpaid work remains unequal. Working women still devote almost 18 hours to household work; men devote less than eight hours to these activities. These women spend almost 30 hours a week on care of the children; their partners only 15 hours a week.

6.5 INFLUENCE OF COSTS OF CHILDCARE, WAGES AND INCOME ON THE USE OF DAY CARE AND PARTICIPATION IN THE LABOUR MARKET

In this section, we investigate the effects of individual characteristics, such as level of education, experience, and the number of children, on labour supply of both partners, on time spent by the male partner on care for the children, and on the use of child day care. Subsequently we investigate the effects of these variables on characteristics relating to the financial situation of the family, such as wages of both partners, total family income, and the costs of child day care.

In contrast to the previous results, the present results are based on the telephone survey among 4,984 women, of whom 1,970 were women with children under the age of four (see Section 3 A for a detailed description of the data).

Table 6.6 contains an overview of the influence of various characteristics of women on their participation in the labour market, the amount of time the male partner spends on care for the children, and hours of time use of subsidised and private childcare centres. We are mainly interested in the effects of the level of education and the number and the age of the children on these variables.

Women with a higher level of education participate in the labour market more frequently: the participation rate of women with a higher vocational education, or university degree is greater than that of women with an intermediate or lower level of education. Women with a higher level of education also make more use of childcare services. Especially women with a VWO, a HBO, or university degree make significantly more use of these services. In addition, higher educated women more often use paid private child minders.

The partners of women with a university degree devote more time to care for the children than the partners of less well educated women. This corroborates the finding in Section 3 that the division of childcare responsibilities is more equitable among men whose partners have a university degree.

The presence of children still has a great effect on women's participation in the labour market. The more children a woman has, the less she participates in the labour market. Women with children aged between 4 and 12, in addition to young children aged between 0 and 3, participate significantly less frequently. The male partners' contribution is smaller if there are (several) older children present in the household. The division of labour appears to be such in these circumstances that the male partner specialises in market work to support the children and the female partner specialises in the care of the children. When there are several children, less use is made of child day care facilities. This is probably due to the fact that women in this situation participate less frequently in the labour market.

Table 6.6 The influence of individual characteristics on labour supply, time spent caring for the partner, and use of childcare services (t-values in parentheses)

dependent variable:	labour supply of women	number of hours spent on childcare by men	hours of day care
intercept	-32.818**	8.770	-52.723**
	(4.352)	(1.916)	(3.426)
experience	3.495**	0.521	1.468
	(4.933)	(1.240)	(1.076)
experience^2/100	-0.068**	-0.009	-0.003
	(3.796)	(0.835)	(0.086)
Highest level of education of woman			
university	25.044**	7.869**	41.504**
	(5.583)	(2.864)	(4.378)
higher vocational education	18.596**	3.976	24.577**
	(4.489)	(1.606)	(2.736)
VWO or HBS	8.933	4.251	19.979*
	(1.884)	(1.464)	(2.028)
HAVO or MMS	6.896	-0.800	11.017
	(1.654)	(0.320)	(1.223)
MAVO, MULO or ULO	2.170	1.012	0.411
	(0.541)	(0.423)	(0.047)
Intermediate vocational education (MBO)	8.498*	1.301	12.930
	(2.082)	(0.535)	(1.456)
Lower vocational education (LBO)	-7.511	1.393	-5.467
	(1.834)	(0.579)	(0.609)
number of children in age groups:			
0 to 3 years	-6.643**	-0.734	-6.606*
	(5.200)	(0.953)	(2.468)
4 to 5 years	-9.287**	-1.461*	-9.554**
	(8.318)	(2.213)	(3.961)
6 to 12 years	-7.675**	-1.300**	-13.580**
	(8.646)	(2.597)	(5.816)
over 12 years	-5.561*	-0.649	-5.354
	(2.283)	(0.509)	(1.059)
σ	17.620**		26.677**
	(34.191)		(17.043)
Loglikelihood	-3648.65	-6080.67	-1365.52

p<0.05; ** p<0.01

It can be expected that there is a negative relationship between the cost of child-care services and the use of such services: the more expensive these services are, the less use is made of them. Furthermore, the price of child day care is expected to have a negative effect on women's labour market participation. The more expensive these services are, the more women will take the task of caring for the children upon themselves and the less time they will be able to spend in the labour market.

The level of the wage rate is expected to have a positive effect on the labour supply of women and on the use of childcare services. The higher the wage rates, the more attractive it is to enter the labour market and the more expensive it is, in effect, to care for the children yourself. The cost of childcare services notwithstanding high wages make it financially more rewarding to engage in employment than to spend time caring for the children.

The total household income is again expected to have a positive effect on the use of childcare facilities: the higher the income, the easier it is to meet the expenses of childcare services. On the other hand, there is less necessity for women to enter the labour market if household income is high. The contribution of women in such households to the labour supply is therefore expected to be smaller.

Two questions can now be raised. In the first place, we would like to know whether these expectations are corroborated by the data. Do the price of childcare services, the level of wage rate, and total family income affect the use of these services and the participation in the labour market of women? In addition to establishing these relationships, we would like to obtain some idea of the size of these effects.

A difficulty in estimating the effect of wages, total income, and cost on the use of child day care services is that the number of women who make use of childcare services and participate in the labour market is limited. The failure to take into account the fact that we only observe the cost of child day care for those who actually make use of child day care, can seriously distort the results. A second difficulty is that preferences for specific types of child day care may vary considerably. Some parents prefer to use formal day care services, while other have informal arrangements or prefer to look after the children themselves. These differences exert an influence on the price that women are prepared to pay for childcare services. For instance, women who prefer formal childcare services are willing to spend more money on childcare than women who prefer to look after the children themselves. This means that the cost that one is willing to incur for child day care reflects in part preferences for a given type of child day care. These interdependencies complicate the analysis of the effects of the cost of childcare services on the use of these services and participation in the labour market.

To solve these problems, we first establish how much, in theory, the partners in a household would have to pay for childcare, and how much the female partner would be expected to earn if she were in the labour market. The relevant results are reported in Table 6.7.

90

Table 6.7 Determinants of wage rates and prices (t-values in parentheses)

dependent variable:	log net wage rate female partner	log price of day care centre
intercept	-4.781	-3.924
	(4.755)	(4.586)
income/1000		0.216
		(1.042)
years of work experience	0.500*	
	(5.303)	
years of work experience2	-0.010**	
	(4.262)	
hours of paid employment		0.090**
		(9.795)
level of education		
university	3.023**	1.747*
	(5.044)	(2.137)
higher vocational education	2.530**	0.931
	(4.576)	(1.192)
higher general education	1.111	1.331
	(1.755)	(1.540)
intermediate general education	0.980	0.757
	(1.762)	(0.948)
lower general education	0.479	0.205
	(0.895)	(0.259)
intermediate vocational education	1.257*	0.642
	(2.309)	(0.827)
lower vocational education	-0.838	0.038
	(1.536)	(0.048)
number of children in the age range		
0 to 3 years	-0.779**	-0.058
	(4.608)	(0.273)
4 to 5 years	-0.965**	-0.113
	(6.574)	(0.591)
6 to 12 years	-0.814**	-0.486**
	(7.041)	(2.805)
over 12 years	-0.867**	-0.018
	(2.647)	(0.044)
σ	2.360**	2.041**
	(33.187)	(16.815)
Loglikelihood	-2201.06	-745.60

* p<0.05; ** p<0.01

Subsequently, the expected cost of childcare and the expected wage rate are included in the analyses of women's labour supply and the use of childcare services. In addition, preferences for types of childcare services and performing market work are taken into account by including the expected use of childcare services in the analysis of women's labour market participation and by including the expected labour force participation of both partners in the analysis of the use of childcare services. We assume that the heterogeneity in preferences for types of childcare service and participation in the labour market are adequately captured by these

91

variables. The inclusion of these variables is meant to correct the effects of cost and wages on differences in preferences.

In so doing, we also take into account the reciprocal causal relationship between participation in the labour market and use of childcare services. On the one hand, we expect that the use of these services will encourage participation. On the other hand, it is possible that women who spend more time in the labour market make more use of childcare services. In the present research, we take into consideration the direct reciprocal relationship between participation in the labour market and the use of childcare services.[1]

The results of the analysis of the effects of wage rates, prices and income on participation in the labour market and the use of childcare facilities are reported in Table 6.8. The majority of the hypotheses mentioned above are corroborated by the data. If women earn more, their likelihood of labour market participation is greater. The effect of women and men's earnings on participation of both partners is similar. As women are able to earn more, the participation of both men and women increases. As men are able to earn more, however, the participation of both partners in the labour market decreases. These findings suggest that the participation in the labour market of men and women is complementary: the more time the female partner spends in the labour market, the more time the male partner does, and vice versa. Neither the wage rate nor the cost of childcare have a significant effect on the use of child day care facilities. The number of hours that women spend in market work, however, is important: the more time women spend in this activity, the more use is made of child day care facilities. Conversely, the results indicate that women's participation in the labour market is greater as more use is made of child day care facilities. The finding that wage rate and prices of childcare do not affect the use of childcare centres is contrary to the hypotheses mentioned above, but does concur with earlier findings. In an analysis of data pre-dating 1991, Groot and Maassen van den Brink (1994b) also found that these variables were not related. However, a positive reciprocal relationship between participation and the use of childcare facilities was also observed in these previous studies.

The results in Table 6.8 further indicate that the cost of childcare facilities has a positive effect on the number of hours that the male partner spends in caring for the children. This implies that male partners spend more time caring for the children when the costs of childcare are higher. It is possible that this relationship is due to the fact that more highly educated men spend more time caring for the children and that better educated partners with a high income pay more for childcare.

---

[1] For further details see the report 'De relatie tussen arbeidsdeelname en het gebruik van kinderopvang voorzieningen' ('The relation between participation in the labour market and the use of child care facilities', Groot, W. & H. Maassen van den Brink (1994), Report for the Ministry of Health, Welfare and Sport, The Hague).

Table 6.8 The influence of wages, prices and income on labour supply and use of childcare (t-values in parentheses)

Dependent variable:	labour supply woman	labour supply husband / partner	hours taken care of child(ren) by husband/partner	hours use of day care centre
intercept	20.627** (6.272)	68.305** (29.989)	20.370** (6.745)	-24.497* (2.027)
wage rate woman	10.042** (12.159)	10.892* (2.022)	-5.225 (0.732)	-11.883 (0.998)
wage rate husband/partner	-1.571* (2.180)	-12.378** (16.148)	-1.655 (1.629)	1.320 (0.391)
costs of day care centre	-0.346 (0.209)	-3.737 (1.786)	12.821** (4.622)	2.946 (0.458)
Income /1000	-0.158** (3.722)	-0.135* (2.426)	0.137 (1.848)	-0.564** (3.104)
predicted labour supply of woman		-1.089 (1.462)	0.475 (0.481)	3.228* (2.057)
hours market work husband/partner	-0.018 (0.812)			-0.172 (1.599)
predicted hours taking care for children by husband / partner	-0.602** (3.691)			
predicted hours use of day care centre	0.566* (2.367)	0.926 (1.928)	-0.522 (0.820)	
σ	6.355** (35.198)			24.265** (17.215)
Loglikelihood	-5573.85			-1320.13

*p<0.05; ** p<0.01

6.6   CONCLUSION

Previous studies (Groot & Maassen van den Brink, 1994, 1996) have shown that women with high levels of education differ from those with low levels in their use of childcare services. In view of this, we have focused on differences between groups of women concerning their problems in the use of childcare. We have investigated the effects of level of education, number of children, and time spent by the male partner on characteristics relating to the wage rates, total family income and the costs of use of formal childcare centres. We were also interested in how the use of childcare facilities outside the home influences the amount of time couples devote to household work. Time allocation of men with young children was of special interest. The key question is whether the use of day care centres has any effect on the time allocation of men. On the basis of the analyses reported in this paper, we draw two main conclusions.

1. Care for children is still mainly the task of women, even when childcare services are used. Women do not devote less time to care for the children when childcare services are used.

Only among women with higher levels of education who are in the labour market does the (cohabiting) partner sometimes feature as the main provider of care for the children. Still, this occurs in less than 4% of these cases. The partners of women with higher education generally spend more time looking after the children than the partners/husband of less well educated women.

A comparison of women who participate in the labour market and women who do not, reveals that women with young children who are in the labour market devote less time to the following activities (differences in hours are shown in parentheses): caring for the children (10 hours less), household work (8 hours less), leisure time activities (6 hours less), and looking after their spouse or partner (4 hours less). Women who make use of childcare facilities devote about 31.5 hours a week to caring for the children. Women who do not make use of such facilities spend 32.5 hours looking after the children, i.e., a difference of a single hour. Children in day care do not receive appreciably less care and attention from their mothers than children who stay at home.

2. Women's employment and the use of childcare services has little or no effect on men's time allocation.
Men whose child is taken care of in a day care centre devote more time to unpaid work in the household than men whose child stays at home and is cared for by the mother. They devote a little more time to unpaid activities in the household, to care for the children and to looking after their partner. This effect of child day care on men's time allocation is related to the fact that parents who use child day care facilities are better educated, and better educated men probably spend more time caring for the children.

There are no noticeable differences in the pattern of time allocation of men and women who are in the labour market and those who are not. Men whose partners are employed spend less time in the market than men whose partners are not in the labour market. Men whose partner is participating in the labour market devote a little more time to household work and to caring for the children.
Men with young children spend four times as much time in market work as women with young children (about 47 vs. 13 hours). However, women devote three times as much time to unpaid work in the household than men (about 21 vs. 7 hours). Women also spend 2.5 times as much time caring for the children than men (about 32 vs. 14 hours). On average, men and women devote an equal amount of time to each other. They devote an equal amount of time to their personal care and they have an equal amount of leisure time.

If women are participating in the labour market, the division of unpaid labour remains highly unequal. Comparing women and men in market work, we find that women devote almost 18 hours a week to the household and 30 hours a week to the children, men devote 8 and 15 hours a week, respectively, to these activities.

94

REFERENCES

Akerlof, G. 1970: 'The market for lemons: qualitative uncertainty and the market mechanism', Quarterly Journal of Economics 84, p. 488-500

Arts, W. & P. Hermkens 1994: 'De eerlijke verdeling van huishoudelijke taken: percepties en oordelen', *Mens en Maatschappij* 69, p. 147-169

CBS 1993: Kindercentra 1992, 's-Gravenhage, *CBS Publikaties*

CBS 1993: 'Kinderopvang: gebruik en gebruikers', *Sociaal-Culturele Berichten 1993-11,* CBS, Voorburg/Heerlen

CBS 1994b: 'Tijdsbesteding van vrouwen en mannen naar huishoudenstype', *Sociaal-Culturele Berichten* 1994/20, p. 3-32

CBS 1995: Sociaal Economische Maandstatistiek, 's-Gravenhage, *CBS-publikaties*

Groot, W. & H. Maassen van den Brink 1994a: *'De relatie tussen arbeidsdeelname en het gebruik van kinderopvangvoorzieningen',* Rapport in opdracht van de Directie Jeugdbeleid van het Ministerie van Welzijn, Volksgezondheid en Cultuur, Amsterdam/Leiden

Groot, W. & H. Maassen van den Brink 1994b: *'Het rendement van kinderopvang',* Rapport in opdracht van de Directie Jeugdbeleid van het Ministerie van Welzijn, Volksgezondheid en Cultuur, Amsterdam/Leiden

Groot, W. & H. Maassen van den Brink 1996: *'Monitoring kinderopvang: veranderingen in het gebruik van kinderopvang, 1991-1995',* Rapport in opdracht van de Directie Jeugdbeleid van het Ministerie van Welzijn, Volksgezondheid en Cultuur, Leiden/Amsterdam

Groot, W. & H. Maassen van den Brink 1996: *'Knelpunten in de kinderopvang',* Rapport in opdracht van de Directie Jeugdbeleid van het Ministerie van Welzijn, Volksgezondheid en Cultuur, Leiden/Amsterdam, te verschijnen.

Maassen van den Brink, H. 1994: *Female labour supply, childcare and marital conflict,* Amsterdam University Press, Amsterdam

Maassen van den Brink, H. & W. Groot 1994a: *Obstakels: vrouwen tussen arbeidsmarkt en gezin,* Amsterdam University Press

Maassen van den Brink, W. & W. Groot 1994b: 'Labour supply and the welfare costs of marital conflict', *Journal of Economic Psychology* 15, p. 467-486

Lippe, T. van der 1992: 'De verdeling van huishoudelijk en betaald werk in Nederland', *Mens en Maatschappij* 67, p. 128-139

Meijer, L. 1996: *'Moeder met baan besteedt minder tijd aan haar kinderen',* Demos, p. 29-31

ACKNOWLEDGEMENTS

The research was funded by a grant from WVEO/NWO 'Time allocation and Gender, no. 759-717-603. The first author wishes to thank The Netherlands Organisation for Scientific research (NWO) and the Ministry of Health, Welfare and Sport for financial support for collecting the data.

BIOGRAPHICAL NOTE

Henriëtte Maassen van den Brink is Professor of Household Economics at the University of Wageningen and Director of SCHOLAR, the NWO Priority Research Program on Schooling, Labour Market and Economic Growth at the Faculty of Economics and Econometrics of the University of Amsterdam. Her areas of research are economics of time allocation, bargaining, power, labour market and education. She has published in national and international journals and has written in co-operation with Wim Groot several books on division of paid and unpaid labour, marital conflict, delayed exits from the labour market after child births and labour market flexibility of older workers.

Wim Groot is Associate Professor of Economics at Leiden University and Director of SCHOLAR, the NWO Priority Program on Schooling, Labour market and Economic Growth at the Department of Economics of the University of Amsterdam. His areas of research are schooling, labour market and time allocation. He has published a great number of articles in international journals on labour market and schooling. He has written several books on time allocation and labour market issues in co-operation with Henriette Maassen van den Brink.

Part II

Allocation of Time to Paid Work

7   Paid careers and the timing and spacing of births in Germany, Great Britain and Sweden

Siv Gustafsson
Cécile Wetzels

7.1   INTRODUCTION

This paper examines panel data from Germany (GSOEP, 1984-1993, Great Britain (BHPS, 1990-1992, from 1980 retrospective) and Sweden (HUS, 1984-1993) to analyse links between career orientation and the timing and spacing of children in a woman's life.

Microeconomic theory of the family leads us to expect that women with a high degree of human capital (education and/or training) will delay the birth of their first child. However, in cases where the spouse is expected to earn a higher lifetime income women are more likely to become mothers earlier. If we turn our analysis to the timing of subsequent births in connection with timing of work after first birth, microeconomic theory is less conclusive on women's behaviour. Women who are highly economically productive could opt for either a quick return to the labour market or to have a second child fairly soon, since both options would tend to minimise loss of human capital investment and returns from such investment. Less productive women would be less in a hurry.

Differing government policy on the family, such as paid parental leave, the length of the job guarantee period, availability and costs of child day-care provision, and family-related tax and fiscal benefits policy, may explain departures from microeconomic predictions in the three countries surveyed.

The outline of the paper is the following. In section 2 we present economic theory on the timing and spacing of children. In section 3 we analyse how the predictions from economic theory are modified by public policies in the three countries surveyed. Subsequently, section 4 deals with the organisation of the data sets for the purposes of this analysis. Section 5 comprises the empirical analysis on the timing of first child and section 6 the empirical analysis of the choice between returning to work or having a second child. Section 7 concludes the analysis.

Time allocation and gender, Kea Tijdens, Anneke van Doorne-Huiskes & Tineke Willemsen (eds.), Tilburg University Press, 1997, © Siv Gustafsson & Cécile Wetzels

7.2 THEORETICAL CONSIDERATIONS ON TIMING AND SPACING OF CHILDREN

The purpose of this section is to analyse what economic theory can contribute to the understanding of timing and spacing of children, given that some women want to pursue a paid career in addition to raising a family. Following Cigno (1991) we can represent the financing of children as a lifetime budget constraint as follows:

$$(1) \quad \sum_{t=M}^{D}(C_t + B_t)r^{M-t} \leq y + \sum_{t=M}^{D} L_t W_t r^{M-t}$$

The lifetime budget constraint says that expenditures on adult consumption C_t and on children B_t over the relevant life span from marriage age M until the point of time D, (where the financial well-being of the children is no longer the parents' concern, here for simplicity's sake taken as the time of death) must be financed out of the lifetime incomes of the couple over the same period, discounted by the market rate of interest r-1. The husband's discounted lifetime earnings plus capital income are collapsed into a constant y in order to concentrate on the labour force behaviour of the wife. The child variable B_t has to be understood as the total expenditure on children in year t. The woman's market wage at time t is w_t and depends on her stock of human capital at that point in time. Time spent in market work of the wife L_t at time point t can be thought of as a zero one variable: either the wife is a participant in the labour market or she is not. In principle, however, the variable could also have any value between zero and one to indicate part-time labour market participation. We can then write the discounted present value of the lifetime cost of having a child at a particular point in time, t, as:

$$(2) \quad P_t = E_t + W_t + \beta \sum_{\tau=t+1}^{D} L_\tau r^{t-\tau}$$

so that there is a component of direct expenditure E_t including clothing, housing, education and other monetary costs for the child in addition to time or opportunity costs. If we assume that the mother leaves the labour market during the time of having a child, the time costs of the child consist of the wage forgone in that period W_t plus the capital loss of human capital investment not undertaken during the child-caring period. In (2) human capital is assumed to increase linearly with the time spent in market work L_t. The w_t will be larger the longer the period of human capital investment prior to the birth and the capital cost will be smaller the fewer periods are left until time D.

In Figure 7.1 we illustrate some possible cases. Figure 1A shows the birth timing problem of a woman with a large potential growth in human capital i.e. a large β. If she has a child at time t_1 and returns to work at the end of that period, her direct earnings loss will be area A and her human capital investment loss will be

Figure 7.1

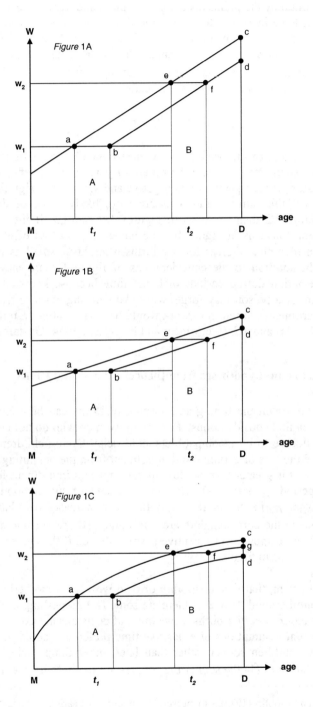

the area delimited by the points abcd. On the other hand, if she waits until time t_2, her wage will have increased to w_2 and the direct wage loss will be area B and her human capital loss will be the area delimited by efcd. A comparison of Figure 1B to Figure 1A shows that if β is small, the human capital loss will be relatively unimportant. Numerous analyses of earnings functions have been carried out according to the Mincer (1974) specification:

$$(3)\ \ln w = \beta_0 + \beta_1 S + \beta_2 \exp + \beta_3 (\exp)^2$$

where the logarithm of the wage (ln w) is determined by years of schooling (S) and years of experience (exp) and the square of years of experience $(\exp)^2$. The results indicate that the square term is negative and statistically significant, which means that real life earnings functions are more likely to be of the character shown in Figure 1C than linear as in Figures 1A and 1B. If the age earnings function is non-linear as in Figure 1C, the human capital loss of an early birth might be considerable; whereas for late births it might be small as indicated by Figure 1C. In addition to the considerations of figure 1 there may be human capital depreciation during periods of home time because knowledge may become obsolete or a person may forget work skills during absence from work. In such cases earnings w_t at return to work would be smaller at point b than at point a in figures 1A, 1B and 1C. (see Mincer and Polacheck 1974, Gustafsson, 1981).

7.2.1   Conclusion: hypotheses from theoretical considerations

Which hypotheses on the timing and spacing of births can be concluded from these human capital considerations? First of all, women who do not consider paid work and childcare to be incompatible should delay having children as long as possible since the loss of earnings and investment from the beginning of time period t_1 to time D is greater than the loss of earnings and investment from the beginning of period t_2 to time D. The postponement of motherhood should be longer the larger β, i.e. the more steeply the wage increases with labour market experience, since the corresponding areas in Figure 1B are considerably smaller than in 1A. The postponement incentive is strengthened if the age earnings function is non-linear as in Figure 1C.

It seems clear, then, that incompatibility of paid work with motherhood tends to favour later motherhood. However there are some factors pushing in the opposite direction in favour of earlier births. If we think of decisions as taken at time point M then the usual assumptions of a positive time preference could make couples prefer to have children sooner rather than later, other things being equal. The larger y in relation to (1) the sooner the couples are likely to have children.[1] Ad-

---

[1] One suggestion by Willis (1973) is to measure 'y' by predicted earnings at age 40 of the husband.

ditionally, the larger the market rate of interest (r) the more unimportant earnings later in life become. This decreases the significance of the capital component in the cost of a child and makes timing less dependent on the human capital of the woman, so that there are fewer incentives to postpone childbearing.

Let us now consider the situation of a woman who already has one child and desires a second, but wants to optimise the timing of the second child with respect to the total costs of the child (P_t) of formula (2). Should she immediately proceed to have a second child, making one longer labour force interruption, or should she first return to the labour market in order to keep up her human capital investment and then make a second labour force interruption for her second child? The trade-off between one period out of work in which clustered childbearing takes place against separate periods out of work for each birth will depend on whether the combined total length of the periods out of work can be the same, or whether there is greater risk of human capital depreciation when staying out for a single long period than when staying out of the labour market for two short periods. If the earnings function is linear as in Figure 1A, the choice between one longer labour market interruption for two births and two shorter absences for each birth gives equivalent results on missed earnings and forgone human capital investment at a zero rate of interest. Further, just as is the case for the timing of a first birth, time preference and a positive rate of interest will speak in favour of clustering, i.e. one labour market interruption with a short interval between successive births. The non-linear nature of the earnings function as in Figure 1C, on the other hand, makes postponement of the second birth and labour force interruption more attractive. If there are major differences in the gradients of the age earnings functions such that less economically productive women with a shallow gradient (β) have little to lose from poor timing of birth and labour market participation while other more productive women have a steep slope (high value on β), we may expect differences in behaviour between these two groups. On the basis of these considerations we will form the hypothesis that more productive women with a high β will either return to work within a year or two or have a second child during this time period, whereas less productive women will do neither.

7.3 EFFECTS OF FAMILY POLICIES ON TIMING AND SPACING OF CHILDREN IN GERMANY, GREAT BRITAIN AND SWEDEN

Government policy on the family in Germany, the United Kingdom and Sweden differs as regards to the degree of public funding and ideology. Our data refers to Great Britain excluding Northern Ireland whereas family policy includes Northern Ireland and thus applies to the United Kingdom as a whole. Public funding for family policy is strong in Germany and Sweden, in contrast to the UK where the cost of children is viewed primarily as the private business of parents. Individual parents can enjoy better provisions than the national average if they work for an employer who, as a result of negotiations, has conceded better provisions during childbearing and parental leaves and/or provide daycare for children of employees. Although there is stronger government involvement in family policies both in Germany and Sweden, the ideology differs in that Germany promotes one earner/one carer families, which implies financial benefits for the breadwinner and little help to combine work and family. Swedish policies, on the other hand, promote equal role sharing within the family. (See Gustafsson, Wetzels, Vlasblom and Dex, 1996 for more details). A summary of family policies is given in Table 7.1.

7.3.1 Parental leave

Maternity leave and benefits will reduce wage loss to the mother (w_t in relation (2)) but the loss of human capital investment will be greater the longer the period of leave. The longest job guarantee period is to be found in Germany, where jobs are held for 24 months after childbirth - four times the British equivalent. Sweden combines a rather long job protection period of 18 months with relatively high levels of pay compensation. Until January 1996, new mothers were entitled to maternity benefits equalling 90 percent of earnings for the first 12 months. The current (1997) regulation is 10 months with 75% for either parent and one month with 90% compensation for the father and one month with 90% compensation for the mother. In addition, three months are compensated at a flat rate for either the father or mother. Parents cannot simultaneously take leave. A Swedish woman therefore has an incentive to have a job first and a child next, since having no earnings before child bearing means that she gets only a small guarantee benefit.

Unlike the Swedish paid parental leave, German parental leave subsidy is not related to previous earnings except for a period of two months following the birth ("the Mutterschutz" period). Currently the mother who cares full-time for her child and refrains from paid labour receives 600 DM per month for 24 months unless her husband has a high income, in which case she may lose the 'Erziehungsgeld' after the seventh month of the job guarantee period. The parental leave subsidy becomes means-tested against family income from the seventh month (Ostner 1993: 102). In addition, Germany has child benefits that increase in line with the number of children (Zimmermann, 1993:210) and tax deductions based on the number of children (Zimmermann, 1993:208). Career-oriented women confronted with German long-leave provisions, but low or no pay compensation may be more eager to return to the labour market even before the job guarantee period has expired because they face both a higher wage loss and a higher human capital loss. However Ondrich, Spiess and Yang (1996) show that German women have been making use of the longer job protection periods as these have gradually been extended.

104

Table7.1   Family Policies in Germany, Great Britain and Sweden

	Germany	Great Britain	Sweden
Maternity and Parental leave			
Job protection	24 mths	6.7 mths	18 mths
Parental benefits	90% of earnings 6 weeks at maximum; DM 600/month, 6 months thereafter means tested	90% of earnings 6 weeks £30, 12 weeks	75% of earnings, 15 mths
Child benefit	DM 200/month, 1st and 2nd chld DM 300/m 3rd+	ú 10/w +/- DM 90/m 1st chld +/- DM 70/m 2nd+	SEK 750/m _ DM 170 all
Child care	kindergarten 64% of age 3-6 9% full day	Private	public daycare 51% 0-2 _ 60% 3-5 full day
Taxation			
Taxation regime	Joint tax for couples since 1948	Couples taxed as individuals since 1991	Couples taxed as individuals since 1971
Basic allowance adults transferable	DM 5616	£ 1720 +/- DM 3800	None
Adults non transferable	No	£ 3445 +/- DM 7700	SEK 10 000 +/- DM 2200
Child allowance	DM 6264	None	None

Source: Gustafsson, Wetzels, Vlasblom and Dex (1996)

Introduced in 1986 at 10 months, they were extended to twelve months in 1988 and to 18 months in 1990 and 24 months in 1992 (Zimmermann 1993). There is reason to believe that career-oriented women are well informed about their potential human capital loss and know that the loss will be smaller towards the end of their careers. In Germany incentives to have a job first and a child next is smaller than in Sweden but the importance of a job protection period should not be underestimated in facilitating the return to work. Albrecht et al (1996) shed an interesting light on the career break effect of parental leave on wages of mothers in Sweden. A number of studies using US data indicate that time out of the labour market has a negative impact on women's wages which exceeds the effect of lost experience i.e. depreciation of human capital. In cross section specifications for Sweden (Albrecht et all 1996), they confirmed expectations that job interruptions adversely affect women's wages, but time used for parental leave during the job protection period did not result in reduced wages. Depreciation of human capital is found to occur during periods of unemployment and periods out of the labour market which exceed the job protection period.

7.3.2 Job guarantee period

Britain's legal job guarantee period (6.7 months in 1996) and period of maternity benefits (18 weeks in 1996) are very small compared to those in Germany and Sweden. The British case approximates the situation which would arise in the absence of public policies and shows similarities with results of US studies. For Britain, Ni Bhrolchain (1983, 1985a) and Martin & Roberts (1984) found that in Britain return time to work after the birth of the latest child was strongly linked to prior interbirth working. Women who returned to work within five years after giving birth to their last child were two to three times as likely as others to have worked between their first and last child.

In Sweden there is a policy referred to in the literature as 'the speed premium'. Effective from 1986, a second child born within 30 months of the first entitles the mother to parental leave benefit based on her earnings before the birth of her first child. This policy developed as mothers whose children were born in quick succession brought cases to the Swedish National Insurance Board claiming that the births were so close that it was impossible to earn similar income between births. The 'speed premium' is widely chosen with 40 percent of Swedish mothers of two or more children having their second child within 30 months (Hoem, 1993). Of course the profitability of a strategy of one career interruption rather than two will depend on a number of factors: the length of the interruptions; income compensation during parental leave; the women's human capital accumulation function; and whether any depreciation effects occur that count for lower wages than a loss of human capital investment in itself. However, this 'speed premium' is a policy instrument if one deems close spacing to be politically desirable, which it might be if the medical concerns of late births are at all important. In Sweden however the speed premium resulted from the effects on income of parents who happened to have a close spacing of childbirths. It has since become a decision parameter for prospective parents.

7.3.3 Childcare

In addition to paid parental leave and job protection the availability and cost of good quality childcare are important in combining paid work and family. In all three countries childcare provision for children under three is less than ideal. Swedish policy is that children in their first year of life should be cared for exclusively by their parents, which is supported by generous paid parental leave. Also there is little childcare available for children younger than 18 months. In 1988 roughly 90 percent of Swedish children under the age of one were exclusively cared for by their parents who were on paid parental leave (SCB 1989). However, for children from about four years onwards there is now in Sweden 'full needs supply' (full behovstäckning) of day-care. Parents' contributions to the costs of public day-care in Sweden are mostly income-linked and averaged less than 10 per cent of total costs for the entire period 1975-1990 (Gustafsson and Stafford, 1992). In 1994 they had increased to 13.4 per cent (Socialstyrelsen 1995).

In Germany there is little all-day childcare although in 1990 some 65 percent of German children aged three to six had a place in local government subsidised good quality kindergartens which are part-day (Zimmermann 1993). Combining children with full-time work in Germany is also more difficult because most schools are organised with morning lessons ending at 1 pm on the assumption that children will be helped with schoolwork at home.

In Great Britain public provision of day care is extremely limited apart from pre-primary education lasting several hours a day. In contrast to Sweden but similar to German kindergartens, working mothers are not given priority. As a result British mothers- like their German counterparts who wish to combine work and family- are forced to rely on ad hoc arrangements and the informal sector. (Sainsbury 1996).

7.3.4   Income tax

Because they are taxed separately, Swedish wives have an economic incentive to increase their working hours relative to their husbands. This contrasts with German wives whose earnings are added to those of their husband before taxation. Consequently a part-time job contributes relatively more to family income in Sweden, because the small incomes of part-time working wives are taxed at lower rates than the larger incomes of full-time working husbands (Gustafsson 1992). Whereas in Germany part-time earnings are taxed on top of husbands earnings, Great Britain occupies a place between the German split-taxation system and the Swedish individual tax system, utilising one transferable basic deduction which is an element of joint taxation, and one non-transferable basic deduction which is an element of separate taxation. The relatively large personal non-transferable deduction in Great Britain represents an incentive to work short hours and earn an income small enough to be within the limits of the personal deduction, to avoid any taxation at all. However such jobs are often ineligible for any type of social security benefit and are often low skilled, dead end jobs.

7.3.4 Conclusion: hypotheses to be posited from family policies

The review of family policies in this section shows that, compared to Germany and Sweden, Great Britain implements few if any policies that modify the market mechanisms governing women's choices. As such the considerations set out in section 2 remain valid. Highly productive women who care both about their paid careers and their families will tend to postpone the birth of their first child but it will make no difference to them whether they space their children around a single career break or they return to work in between children as long as the total career break is of a given duration. Less productive women will be less in a hurry to return to work and also less in a hurry to have a second child. In Sweden we may expect fewer differences between more productive women and less productive women because of policies to combine work and family. In addition the so-called 'speed premium' makes clustering of births a profitable option which should distinguish Swedish women's behaviour from behaviour in the other two countries. In Germany the combination of work and family is not facilitated by social policies, rather the contrary. The incentive for highly productive women to postpone births is therefore strong. Once the first child has been born, a rapid return to paid work is unlikely because of the long job protection period. German women considering spacing their children close together rather than two shorter career interruptions are not influenced by public policies and should therefore be indifferent between the two choices. Because Germany favours full-time maternal care rather than assisting mothers to combine work with family, there could be a demarcation line between the highly productive women who want to combine work and family and others who do not wish or cannot struggle against the 'male breadwinner' organisation of the German society. Individual human capital considerations will be more important in Germany than in Sweden.

7.4 DATA AND COMPARABILITY OF VARIABLE DEFINITIONS ACROSS COUNTRIES

This paper makes use of the German Socio Economic Panel (GSOEP, 1983-1992, annual surveys) the Swedish Household Market and Nonmarket Activities Panel (HUS, 1984-1993, surveys every second year and spell data) and the British Household Panel Survey (BHPS, 1990-1992, retrospective data from 1980). We organised the data sets with date of birth of a child in the household as a starting point. Some births during our observation period are first births, some are second births and some are third births. The surveys contain information on human capital variables, earnings and hours worked of the mother and her spouse. The variable monthly changes in labour market status around childbirth has been defined in the different surveys in the following way.

In addition to human capital and earnings information during the survey year in which the woman gives birth, our 'birth event' approach requires information on changes in the labour market status before and after birth. All three data sets give monthly data on labour market status (See Gustafsson, Wetzels, Vlasblom and Dex (1996)). Each also provides information on whether the woman enters the labour market in a full-time or part-time capacity. Data on changes in labour force status in the HUS spell file include 8 different categories. The category of gainfully employed can be broken down in 5 sub-categories according to hours of work but we only distinguish between full-time (35 hours or more) and part-time (not more than 34 hours). In GSOEP we used survey information on employment experience on a monthly basis which provides different categories on full-time (Voll Erwerbstaetig) and part-time (Teilzeit-geringfuegig) work, which however are not defined in hours worked per week. The dividing line between part-time and full-time might therefore differ from the Swedish one which is something the data does not allow us to investigate.

In HUS, maternity leave can be separated only in the survey year and not in the month-to-month spell data files. In the spell data it is included under 'being on leave', which category also comprises sick leave, vacation, absence from work. In GSOEP maternity leave becomes a separate category of labour force status from the 1988 survey. To arrive at a variable of women on maternity leave before 1988 we used the information on women who chose "other" as their labour force status and matched some other criteria.

Changes in labour force status in the British Household Panel Survey (BHPS) is available from retrospective information (1980-1990). Since the British data are retrospective, women were asked to give the birth dates of all their children, whereas in the Swedish and German panel data only births that occurred during the observation period were included because the monthly labour force status data cover the same period. British respondents had to cover a 10 year period retrospectively and give information on labour force status for each month during each of these 10 years. In her analysis of the quality of retrospective data, Dex (1991) concludes that a broad summary of employment history can be recollected with a reasonable degree of accuracy. She cites a study (Freedman et al (1988)) which indicates in 1985 that 83 percent of respondents confirmed their labour force status for a month of 1980 which could be checked against a data set collected in 1980 from the same respondents. However earnings data are not possible to collect because it is impossible to remember earnings retrospectively. In the annual surveys from 1990 onwards the BHPS collects earnings data but there are no earnings data for earlier years.

The variable 'years of employment experience' for Sweden and Germany was defined in the following ways. In Sweden, respondents whose employment experience since age 16 was requested in a survey predating the year in which the relevant birth was observed have their recorded experience updated by information in the spells. The GSOEP records employment experience from age 15 onwards. In 'biography before respondents enter the panel' we added the time of birth to arrive at experience.

The 'education' variable in the GSOEP is given as two different variables called schooling (Schulabschluss) and vocational training (Berufliche Bildungsab-schluss). Using information on the number of years it generally takes to finish school and vocational training, these two have been added together for the years of schooling variables. In Germany higher education is defined as 'Abitur': 13 years or more. University level means an additional 5 years, making 18 years of schooling in total. In the Swedish data a high school graduate examination ('stu-dentexamen') takes 12 years i.e. nine years of compulsory education and an ad-ditional three years of 'gymnasium'. A university degree takes a further four year, so a Swedish university graduate is coded in the HUS data as having 16 years of education. However we consider a Swedish and a German university graduate to be of similar length. For this paper we used the years of schooling coded in the national data. For within country regressions and standardised higher education to mean studentexamen, abitur or summer school in between country comparisons.

In order to obtain the husband's pre-tax earnings in Sweden as close to the date of birth or to make the earnings data as comparable to German data as possible we used the response to the following question that was asked in all surveys: 'How much do you earn, before taxes at your primary job?'. In 1991 the infor-mation was requested for 1989 and 1990.[2] In some Swedish cases 'income from employment last year were used in connection with hours of work per week in the year under study as an instrument for the missing current earnings. The Swedish earnings data in HUS are reported as earnings per hour, per week, per month or per year. We transformed all earnings information into monthly in-come. The question on hours worked per week is similar in all Swedish surveys and sounds: on average how many hours per week are you currently working at your main job, including paid and unpaid overtime?'. For Germany we used "Arbeitsverdienst brutto letzter Monat" including paid overtime work plus other benefits but excluding vacation benefits. The following survey year the GSOEP includes a question on vacation benefits last year. but there are many missings on this. Because the question is only put to persons in work, there are cases of women on maternity leave who do not answer this question. However, such women will probably also answer the hours worked per week similarly. We have recomputed earnings for both countries into constant prices over 1993[3]. Swedish

---

[2] In 1991 the questions that referred to 1989 and 1990 were posed somewhat differently: Approximately how much did you earn (compensation for gainful employment) before taxes at your primary job in 1989 (1990)? (If your earnings changed during 1989 (1990), estimate your average earnings for the portion of the year during which you were gainfully employed.)

[3] Change in consumer prices=(100+cp92-93)/100= cpindex 92-93 earnings 92*cpindex 93-92= earnings of 1992 at 93 prices;earnings 91*cpindex 92-93*cpindex91-92.e.g. earnings of 1984 at 93 prices are multiplied by 1.83 for Sweden and by 1.23 for Germany.

crowns have been translated into German marks by the purchasing power parity of 1993, which is one DM equals 4.71 SEK in 1993 (OECD Economic Outlook 58, December 1995).

7.5 WHO POSTPONES FIRST BIRTH?

The number of births according to birth order and the number of births observed are given in Table 7.2. In the British data, because they are retrospective, information is available on the birth dates of all children the woman has given birth to as of 1990, so no data is available on only second or third births observed as in the Swedish and German data. In this section we will make use of the information on first births i.e. rows 1,4 and 6 of Table 7.2.

Table 7.2   *Number of Women and Their Births by Birth Order*

	West-Germany	Great-Britain	Sweden
only first child observed	283	355	59
only second child	111	a	51
only third child	52	a	50
first & second child	157	440	60
second & third child	34	a	19
first, second & third child	28	139	8
Number of women	665	934	247

Data: GSOEP(1983-1992), BHPS (1990-1992, retrospective 1980-1990) & HUS (1984-1993)
a = not applicable. Because the British data relies on retrospective information on births: there are no cases of whom we have only information on e.g. 2nd birth.

Table 7.3 shows the mean age of the mother at first birth computed from the micro panel data. There are some common characteristics for all three countries. Firstly, in all three countries more highly educated women tend to have their first child at a later age than their less educated counterparts.

Table 7.3   Age Of Mother At First Birth, all women

	West-Germany	Great-Britain	Sweden
	n	n	n
All first births			
Only 1st birth in data	27.32	25.98	27.89
1st and 2nd birth in data	26.07	24.77	26.77
1st, 2nd & 3rd birth in data	24.26	22.41	-
Higher education			
All first births			
only 1st birth in data	29.3	27.3	29.6
1st and 2nd birth in data	28.4	27.2	30.2
1st, 2nd & 3rd birth in data	25.8	24.6	-
Lower education			
All first births			
only 1st birth in data	26.6	25.4	27.1
1st and 2nd birth in data	25.3	24.1	26.6
1st, 2nd & 3rd birth in data	23.7	21.9	-

Data: GSOEP(1983-1992), BHPS (1990-1992, retrospective 1980-)& HUS (1984-1993); Proportion of highly educated in West-German sample:27.3; in Great Britain 23.2 and in Sweden 28.9. for Sweden only 8 obs. for 1st,2nd&3rd, so it is not reported.

Higher education corresponds to having completed "Abitur" in Germany, having completed "Studentexamen" in Sweden and having completed "A-level" in Great Britain. Second, women who proceed later to have another child have had their first child earlier in life than women who are observed only to have had a first birth. This pattern is true within each educational group and across educational groups for all three countries, except for more highly educated Swedish women. Also the women who were observed to have three children in the data had their first child at a still younger age than those who were observed to have two children. If we had been observing completed fertility spells rather than data censored at the interview date, age at first birth of those women who have only one child during lifetime might have been still higher. Some women will of course go on to have more children after our observation period.

Comparing our three countries we observe some consistent differences. Women in Great Britain become mothers at a younger age than either in Germany or in Sweden. This is true for all subgroups presented in Table 7.2. In Great Britain less educated women have less reason to think about earning a right to a maternity benefit than is the case in Germany and Sweden because the benefits are small anyway. This may lead to earlier motherhood among less educated British women than among their German or Swedish counterparts. However as in the other two countries, more highly educated women in Britain have to consider their labour market prospects and this induces postponement of motherhood as explained in section 2 above. The relatively brief job guarantee period in Britain might make having a child more costly in career terms than would otherwise be the case if it leads to a mother having to give up her job and find a new one before she can return to paid employment. Consequently it might be said that British women are forced to pay more attention to the career costs of having children. On the other hand, British women do not have to build up a right to maternity benefit as Swedish women do, and this works in the opposite direction. Furthermore the British data cover the period from 1980 whereas the German data start in 1983 and the Swedish start in 1984. Demographic trends in all three countries have shown a rise in the age of first-time mothers over time, which works in the direction of younger mothers in Great Britain where the period 1980-1982 is included.

7.5.1   Econometric analysis of age at first birth

Using information from our theoretical considerations and the likely impact of differences in government policies on the family in the three countries surveyed, this paper will now go on to examine the mother's age at first birth in each country. Our theoretical analysis in Section 2 implies that other things being equal, the higher the husband's income, the earlier the birth of the first child. Our theoretical variable for the influence of husband's income is the present value of husband's life-time earnings which we approximate by predicted income at age 40 following Willis (1973). For the Swedish and the German data we have information on husband's income at the birth of the first child and his age at this point in time. We compute predicted income at age 40 of the husband by estimating age earnings functions of the form:

$$(4)\ \ln(y)^b = \beta_0 + \beta_1 S^b + \beta_2 age^b + \beta_3 (age^b)^2 + \varepsilon^b$$

where y is the monthly income of the husband at childbirth, S^b the husband's years of education at time of birth and his age at birth. is ε^b the error term, also measured at birth. Income at age 40 is then computed by moving husband's income to his 40th birthday along the estimated age-earnings curve while assuming that his education remains constant and that the error term is specific to the individual mainly comprising ability and productivity increasing ε^b factors. Predicted income at age 40 is then computed by subtracting the predicted income at age 40 according to the estimation of equation (4) above.

$$(5)\ \text{pred.}\ln(\text{y}40)^b = \beta_0 + \beta_1 S^b + \beta_2 age^b + \beta_2(40 - age^b) + \beta_3(40 - age^b)^2 + \varepsilon^b$$

For Great Britain we have no information on husbands' income at the time of their child(ren)'s birth. Instead we use a variable on the husband's occupational status, according to a 7 categories scale with 7 being the most prestigious occupational group.

Table 7.4 shows regression analyses to explain the mother's age at first birth across the three countries surveyed. These indicate that the effect of the husband's income at age 40 on the timing of motherhood is negative and statistically significant; meaning that the higher the husband's income, the earlier the first birth - as predicted by economic theory. This holds true for Germany as well as for Sweden. We also entered an additional variable on husband's schooling in order to see if his education and career planning had an effect independent of income, which we find to be the case for Germany and Great Britain, but not for Sweden. In Britain first births are timed later the higher the husband's level of education and the higher his positioning on a seven-steps occupational ladder. For all three countries we found that when the husband's income and education are held constant, the more well-educated the woman the longer she postpones motherhood. We also entered a second variable to capture career orientation, namely a dummy variable which is equal to one if the mother is observed ever to have returned to the labour market after her first child otherwise this variable equals zero. This variable is not significant in Great Britain and Germany whereas for Sweden it shows the expected sign implying that career-oriented mothers have their first child later in life. To sum up the results of Table 4, we find the expected impact from a husband's income and mother's level of education. The impact of having more than one child is also as expected (except for Sweden), whereas having ever returned to work after the first child is no indicator of career orientation.

Table 7.4   OLS On Timing Of First Birth In West-Germany, Great Britain And Sweden

dependent var: age of the mother at first birth, (t-values)

	West-Germany	Great-Britain	Sweden
const.	151.459	21.888	44.324
	(6.30)	(19.96)	(13.01)
Income husband at age 40	-16.186	0.483[a]	-8.398
	(-5.48)	(4.35)	(-6.76)
schooling spouse	1.057	0.212	0.202
	(7.65)	(2.30)	(1.28)
education mother at 1st birth=high[b]	3.315	0.923	2.021
	(6.91)	(2.10)	(2.35)
mother returns to work=1[c]	-0.885	0.743	-1.547
	(-1.43)	(1.47)	(-1.98)
second birth=1	-1.039	-1.470	0.234
	(-1.91)	(-2.72)	(0.27)
third birth=1	-2.550	-3.258	1.856
	(-3.03)	(-5.14)	(1.27)
Rsq	0.33	0.17	0.40
N	370	398	99

Data: Germany: GSOEP 1983-1993, West-Germans. Great-Britain: BHPS 1990-1992 and retrospective data 1980-1991. Sweden HUS 1984-1993. N=number of observations. We have less observations than presented in Table 1 because information on the spouse as age and education is missing.

a) *BHPS has no information on earnings: we used information on occupational status of the spouse:1=not in job,2=unskilled,3=partly skilled,4=skilled manual,5=skilled nonmanual,6=managerial&technical,7=professional;*
b) *Education is high: >=12 years of schooling*
c) *return=1 if the mother returns after birth1 and after birth2 or only after 2nd birth.*

7.6   CLUSTERING BIRTHS OR SECOND CAREER BREAK?

In this section we address the question on how women time their re-entry onto the labour market after their first child and between subsequent births. Table 7.5 shows a cross-tabulation of the number of months elapsing since the first child before the mother enters the labour force according to how many births women have had and whether they returned to the labour market between children. As in Table 7.3, the data is first divided into three groups: A. women for whom only first birth were observed; B. women for whom first and second births were observed; and C. women for whom we observe first, second and third births. For women who have more than one child the data is further divided according to whether the women returned to paid employment between births or not. A further distinction is made between labour force participation in part-time work or in full-time work. Not surprisingly we find that the period out of employment is longer when mothers choose not to re-enter the labour market between births than if there is a spell of paid work between births. This is evidenced by comparing columns (3) and (5) with columns (2) and (4) in Table 7.5. However full-time or part-time work is significant in this regard. The time taken before entering into paid work is not influenced by whether the woman takes part-time or full-time employment. This is true for both Germany and Sweden. In both countries a large majority of mothers choose part-time employment rather than full-time 63 percent across categories in Germany and 75 per cent in Sweden. Swedish mothers are assisted in this choice by family policies as parents have a legal right to shorten work hours to six hours a day until their child is eight years old, and then return to full-time in the same job. The employer cannot refuse the mother or father although in the majority of cases it is the mother who cuts her hours of paid work. Employers are also prohibited by law from refusing the mother or father to increase work hours again when their child is eight years old. This daily reduction in working hours is at the cost of the employee: it effectively amounts to two hours unpaid leave a day.

One interesting similarity between the countries surveyed is that women who do return to enter the labour market between births do so after about 12 months in all three countries, although the job guarantee protection periods vary. This might lead one to posit a biologically and emotionally optimum of 12 months full-time baby care coupled with a subsequent return to work on a part-time basis. One difference between Sweden and the other two countries is that a greater proportion of Swedish first time mothers re-enter the labour market between first and second births: 35 percent in Germany and 39 percent in Great Britain compared to 47 percent in Sweden.

Sweden also differs from the other two countries in that the duration of time out of the labour market is no longer for the women for whom we observe only the first child than for women who re-enter between births i.e. 12 to 14 months. In Germany and Britain only first birth mothers wait 17 to 22 months. For women who do not re-enter between births in Sweden and Germany the duration of home time is between 43-49 months i.e. three and a half to five years. In Great Britain, on the other hand, those who do not re-enter between first and second children have a spell of home time of some 58 to 65 months i.e. around five years.

Table 7.5   Number of Months Since First Birth Before Entering Employment

	A: only first birth in data	B: first & second birth in data		C. first, second & third birth in data	
	mother enters after 1st birth	mother enters between 1st & 2nd birth	mother enters only after 2nd birth	mother enters between 1st & 2nd birth	mother enters only after 2nd birth
	(1)	(2)	(3)	(4)	(5)
West-Germany	mean (st.d.) n	mean (st.d.) n	mean (st.d.) n	mean (st.d.) n	mean (st.d.) n
full-time or part-time	21.3 124 (19.2)	12.7 65 (8.3)	47.4 14 (47.4)	11.4 12 (5.7)	43.6 5 (24.7)
full-time	20.3 43 (20.6)	12.1 22 (9.1)	43.0 5 (12.4)	13.3 8 (5.7)	46.0 3 (25.5)
part-time	21.8 81 (18.6)	13.1 43 (8.0)	49.9 9 (17.2)	7.8 4 (7.8)	40.0 2 (14.1)
Great-Britain					
full-time or part-time	17.1 133 (21.3)	12.0 135 (12.6)	58.4 78 (29.1)	7.9 32 (5.9)	65.0 42 (30.9)
Sweden					
full-time or part-time	14.4 36 (10.3)	13.0 39 (6.6)	45.7 7 (18.7)	12.5 2 (6.4)	44.8 4 (20.6)
full-time	12.4 5 (5.4)	14.1 15 (8.5)	59.0 1	-	36.0 1
part-time	14.7 31 (10.9)	12.3 24 (5.1)	43.5 6 (19.4)	12.5 2 (6.4)	47.7 3 (4.2)

Data: Germany: GSOEP 1983-1993, West-Germans. Great-Britain: BHPS 1990-1992 and retrospective data 1980-1991. Sweden HUS 1984-1993. For Britain we are not able to split timing of return to work in full-time and part-time. Full-time means more than 35 hours work per week.

Tables 7.6 and 7.7 show proportional hazard regressions on especially the time spent before entering the labour force after the birth of a first child and that of having a second birth. However these two regressions do not really capture our theoretical model, which says that a highly economically productive mother is indifferent as to whether she has a second child relatively quickly with one career

117

interruption or re-enters the labour market between births and delays the second child. Are women, who are highly productive (have a high β in equation (2)) more in a hurry to pursue one of the two options than women who are less productive? Table 7.6 indicates that in Germany and Great Britain the younger the mother is at the birth of the first child the more eager she is to enter paid employment afterwards. In Table 7.6 we also find that in Germany and Great Britain, women with more human capital accumulated at time of first birth spend more time at home since both education of the mother and years of experience of the mother have a positive effect on the number of months before entering paid employment. This effect is contrary to our expectations that women with more human capital should be more eager to return to paid work. The reason is possibly a selection-effect since only non censured observations are included. Husband's income does not have a significant effect on the timing of labour market re-entry.

In Table 7.7 the only significant factor is that if the mother enters paid work after the first birth it takes her longer to have a second childbirth than if she does not re-enter employment after first birth. This is true for all three countries. In Germany a woman who has a longer employment history prior to motherhood waits shorter before having a second child. If the husband's income is larger, the woman will wait for a longer period before having a second child.

Table 7.6   Proportional Hazards of Months Before Entering the Labour Force After First Birth In Connection With A Subsequent Birth, all first time mothers

	W-Germany	Great-Britain	Sweden
age of the mother at 1st birth	-0.087	-0.059	-0.039
	(-2.47)	(-2.82)	(-0.81)
schooling of the mother at 1st birth	0.098	0.112	-0.009
	(2.52)	(4.19)	(-0.19)
employment experience of the mother at 1st birth	0.072	0.716	0.035
	(2.33)	(3.50)	(0.65)
husband's income before taxes at 1st birth	-0.055		0.114
	(-1.16)		(1.09)
subsequent child	-0.669	0.233	-0.114
	(-4.08)	(2.57)	(-0.46)
LogL	-862.1	-5.280.2	-447.97
N	438	1381	125

Data: Germany: GSOEP 1983-1993, West Germans. Great Britain: BHPS 1990-1992 and retrospective data 1980-1991. Sweden HUS 1984-1993.

Table 7.7   Proportional Hazards of Months Before Having a Second Child
After the First Birth In Connection With Participating In The Labour Force After
The First Birth, all first time mothers

	W-Germany	Great-Britain	Sweden
age of the mother at 1st birth	-0.050 (-1.60)	-0.068 (-2.86)	-0.055 (-0.81)
schooling of the mother at 1st birth	0.010 (0.24)	0.058 (1.80)	0.014 (0.20)
employment experience of the mother at 1st birth	-0.021 (-2.33)	0.042 (1.80)	0.046 (0.63)
husband's income before taxes at 1st birth	0.111 (2.13)		0.194 (1.64)
participating after the 1st birth=yes	-0.802 (-4.55)	-0.646 (-6.84)	-0.291 (-4.42)
LogL	-722.3	-3.304.5	-259.86
N	507	1137	103

Data: Germany: GSOEP 1983-1993, West Germans. Great Britain: BHPS 1990-1992 and ret-
rospective data 1980-1991. Sweden HUS 1984-1993.

The results in this section are mixed and we do not always get the expected sign
on variables fount to have significant effect

7.7   CONCLUSIONS

In this paper we used several waves of micro household panel data to construct
fertility and work histories for women in Germany, Britain and Sweden. We also
constructed explanatory variables such as education, work experience and predicted husband's income in order to compare career and timing and spacing of
births across the three countries. The paper indicates that women become mothers earlier if husbands' incomes are higher and when they have more than one
child eventually-born. First births occur later the higher the mother's and father's
respective levels of education, which is in line with the expectations raised by
economic theory set out in this paper. In a cross tabulation study we find a striking similarity between all three countries in that it takes about a year before a
mother returns to work if she does return at all before having a second child.
However, in our proportional hazard estimate in months before re-entry onto the
labour market we find that women in Germany and Britain with a larger degree
of human capital wait longer to return to work than women with a smaller
amount of human capital. This result indicates that - contrary to our hypothesis -

such women have higher incomes and can afford to stay home longer rather than being more in a hurry to return because of concerns about their career prospects. On the other hand, this result is based on women who are observed to return to work. Women who continuously remain housewives are not included in this particular result.

REFERENCES

Albrecht J, Edin P.A., Sundström M. and Vroman S. 1996: paper prepared for the 1996 ESPE meeting in Uppsala.

Cigno 1991: *Economics of the family*, Clarendon Press, Oxford.

Council of Europe 1993: *Recent demographic developments in Europe and North America 1992*, Council of Europe Press Strasbourg.

Dex S. 1991: *The reliability of recall data*: A Literature Review. Working paper 11 of the ESRC. Research Centre on micro-social change in Britian, University of Essex, Colchester.

Esping-Andersen, G. 1990: *The Three Worlds of Welfare Capitalism*. Princeton: Princeton University Press.

Freedman D. et al 1988: 'The life history calendar: a technique for collecting Retrospective data, *Sociological Methodology*, 37-68.

Gustafsson S.S. and Stafford, F. 1992: Daycare Subsidies and Labour Supply in Sweden, *Journal of Human Resources*, vol 27, no 1, pp 204-230.

Gustafsson S.S. 1981: *Male-Female Lifetime Earnings Differentials and Labour Force History*, in E

Gustafsson, S.S. 1992: Separate taxation and married women's labour supply, a comparison of West-Germany and Sweden, *Journal of Population Economics* 5:61-85.

Gustafsson, S.S, Wetzels C.M.M.P., Vlasblom J. and Dex S. 1996: 'Labour force transitions in connection with childbirth a panel data comparison between Germany, Great Britain and Sweden', *Journal of Population Economics*,9:223-246.

Heckman, J.J., V.J. Hotz and J.R. Walker 1985: New evidence on the timing and spacing of births, *AEA papers and proceeding*, vol 75 no 2, 179-184.

Heckman, J.J., and J.R. Walker 1985: The relationship between wages and income and the timing and spacing of births: evidence from Swedish longitudinal data, *Econometrica*, Vol 58, No 6 (November 1990), 1411-1441.

Hoem B. 1996: *Stockholm Research Reports in Demography*, No 104, Some features of recent demographic trends in Sweden, April 1996.

Hoem, J.M. 1993: 'Public Policy as the Fuel of Fertility: Effects of a Policy Reform on the Pace of Childbearing in Sweden in the 1980s', *Acta Sociologica* vol.36: 19-31.

Joshi, H 1990: The cash opportunity cost of childbearing: an approach to estimation using British data', *Population Studies*, 44.

Klevmarken, A. and P. Olovsson 1993: 'Household market and non-market activities: procedures and codes 1994-1991', Almqvist & Wiksell International, Stockholm.

Martin, J. and Roberts C. 1984: Women and Employment: A lifetime perspective (HMSO, London).

McRae S. 1996: Women's employment during family formation, Policy Studies Institute, London. 1996

Mincer J. 1974: Schooling, experience and earnings, Columbia University Press, New York.

Mincer J. and S. Polacheck 1974: Family Investments in Human Capital: Earnings of women " Journal of Political Economy, 82(2): s76-108.

Nerlove M. and Razin A. 1981:in Essays on the theory and measurement of consumer behaviour, in honour of Sir R.Stone ed. by A. Deaton, Cambridge, Cambridge University Press.

Ni Bhrolchain M 1983: Birth spacing and women's work: some British evidence, LSHTM Centre for Population Studies research paper no. 83-3.

Ni Bhrolchain M 1985a: Birth intervals and women's economic activity: some British evidence, Journal of Biosocial Science 17, 31-4

Ni Bhrolchain M 1986a: Women's paid work and the timing of Births: Longitudinal evidence, European Journal of Population, 2: 43-70.

Ondrich, J., Spiess, K. and Yang, Q. 1996: Barefoot and in a German kitchen: Federal Parental Leave and Benefit Policy and the Return to Work after Childbirth in Germany, Journal of Population Economics, 9: 247-266.

Ostner, I. 1993: Slow Motion: Women, Work and the Family in Germany in Lewis, Jane (ed.) Women and Social Policy in Europe, Edward Elgar Publishing Ltd, Aldershot England.

Ronsen M. & Sundström M 1996: women's return to work after first birth in the Nordic countries--full-time or part-time?, paper presented at ESPE, June 13-15.

Sainsbury, D. 1994: Gendering Welfare States, Sage Publications.

Sainsbury, D. 1996: Gender, Equality and Welfare States, Cambridge University Press, Cambridge.

Socialstyrelsen 1995: Barnomsorgen 1994 (Childcare 1994), Stockholm.

Statistics Sweden, SCB 1989: Befolkningsstatistik, Barnsomsorgundersokningen 1989, s11SM 8901, Stockholm.

Tasiran A 1993: Wage and income effects on the timing and spacing of births in Sweden and the United States, dissertation, Gothenburg.

Taylor, M. (ed.) 1992: British Household Panel Survey User Manual, Volumes A and B, Essex University ESRC Research Centre on Micro-Social change.

Wagner, G.G., J. Schupp and U. Rendtel 1991: 'The Socio-Economic Panel of Germany, Methods of Production and Management of longitudinal Data', DIW discussion Paper 31a, Berlin.

Willis 1973: A new approach to the economic theory of fertility behaviour', Journal of Political Economy, 81.

Zimmermann, K.F. 1993: Responses to Taxes and Benefits, Germany in Atkinson A.B. and Mogensen G.V. (eds.), *Welfare and work Incentives. a North European Perspective*, Clarendon Press, Oxford.

BIOGRAPHICAL NOTE

Siv Gustafsson is a Professor of Economics of the University of Amsterdam and director of the research group 'Comparative Population and Gender Economics'. She is a member of the Board and president elect for 1998 of The European Society for Population Economics (ESPE). She has published on welfare states, day-care subsidies and women's labour supply, simulations on the effects of separate taxation on women's labour supply, wage structures and the male / female wage differential using household unicro panel data from several countries including Sweden, Germany, the Netherlands, Great Britain and United States.

Cécile Wetzels (1968) is finishing her PhD in Economics at the University of Amsterdam/Tinbergen Institute. Her research interest lies in economics of fertility and women's participation in paid work: empirical analyses comparing welfare states.

8 Time allocated to paid work by women in Western and Eastern European countries

Tanja van der Lippe

8.1 INTRODUCTION

The history of labour-force participation by Eastern European women and their Western European counterparts differs greatly. In Western European countries, women's labour force participation had increased enormously over recent decades. If in the early 1960s, 40% of women in the 15 to 64 age group participated in the labour force, by 1988 this percentage has increased to 54 (ILO 1984; OECD 1990). In contrast, Eastern European women's labour force participation was already high in the 1960s, averaging 75% (Robinson, Converse & Szalai 1972; ILO 1984), and in 1993 the participation rate was between 80% and 90% (Treiman & Szelenyi 1993). At the end of the socialist system almost the whole of the potential female working population was engaged in full time, paid work, and this remains the case today. Full-time housekeeping, as it used to exist and still does to some extent in Western European countries, neither is, nor was an alternative for Eastern European women. Furthermore, unemployment as it is known in western societies did not exist in the socialist economies. However, since 1989, unemployment has been growing in Eastern Europe and it is expected that women's unemployment rates will be higher than those of men (Einhorn 1993; Funk & Mueller 1993). In Western Europe, women's labour-force participation in the Scandinavian countries has always been higher than elsewhere in the region, and was as high as in Eastern Europe in 1992. However, part-time work is much more common in the Scandinavian countries than in Eastern Europe.

A number of factors are known to influence the labour-force participation of women - the presence of (young) children restricts opportunities for participation while a higher educational level and good career prospects encourage participation. It is not known, however, whether the influence of these characteristics on women's paid work differs from country to country, and if so to what extent. Undoubtedly, women's paid work not only depends on their individual characteristics but is probably also connected to the institutional characteristics of the country where they live. The comparison between Western and Eastern European countries can be

Time allocation and gender, Kea Tijdens, Anneke van Doorne-Huiskes & Tineke Willemsen (eds.), Tilburg University Press, 1997, © Tanja van der Lippe

of importance in this respect. Up until now, the literature has not focused specifically on this comparison. Does, for example, having small children exert the same influence on the paid work of women in Western and Eastern European countries or are the institutional features of countries the primary explanations for different labour patterns? In this paper I will concentrate exclusively on women's working time, as men's paid work differs little in European countries.

My aim in this paper is to explain women's paid labour patterns in different Eastern and Western European countries using both individual and institutional characteristics. I will concentrate on the time women spend on the labour market. The paper is organised as follows: theoretical arguments are developed in section 2 on why and how women decide on the length of time they perform paid labour. Section 3 describes the data used in this paper, and how the various characteristics are measured. In section 4 the empirical analyses, including individual and country characteristics, are performed. Conclusions will be given in the last section.

8.2 THE ALLOCATION OF TIME TO PAID WORK: THEORETICAL ARGUMENTS

There is a rich literature available on women's labour force participation. Many studies have been undertaken to explain the participation of women in the labour market. Some of these focus primarily on the influence of individual characteristics, i.e. they try to explain women's paid work in one specific country (Van Doorne-Huiskes 1979; Ferber 1982; Geerken & Gove 1983; Blossfeld 1987). Others go into more detail on the impact of institutional features, and usually compare two or three countries (Jenson, Hagen & Reddy 1988; Arber & Gilbert 1992; Lewis 1993; Van Doorne-Huiskes, Van Hoof & Roelofs 1995). This paper utilises the insights of these various studies, both on an individual and on an institutional level.

My basic assumption in the present study is that in their time allocation strategies women pursue certain goals but, due to constraints, can never fully realise all of their goals and therefore have to make choices (Siegers 1992; Van der Lippe & Siegers 1994). These choices are dependent on constraints at household level and are embedded in the institutional context in which women live. Although I refer to individual and institutional characteristics as constraints, one could also view these as resources that facilitate certain behaviours. In other words, constraints and resources are two sides of the same coin. The structure of the explanation can also be seen in figure 8.1.

Figure 8.1 Individual characteristics and institutional context of influence on paid work of women

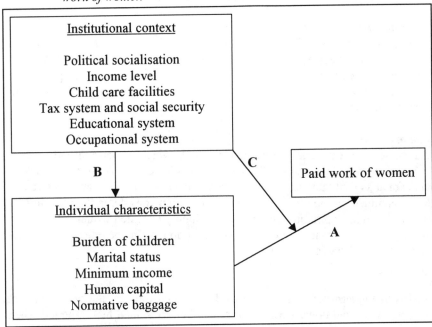

Individual characteristics
I will start with discussing the effect of individual characteristics (which are given with arrow A in figure 1). Studies so far indicate the following characteristics to be relevant in women's decisions to spend time on the labour market.

- The burden of children:
I expect the presence of children to result in a more unequal division of labour between partners (Gronau 1986; Coverman 1985). The presence of children increases the amount of time and money needed to run a household, especially the time spent on household labour (Knulst & Van Beek 1990). I expect the presence of a child causes the father to increase paid work and the mother to increase her unpaid household work at the expense of paid work.

- Marital status:
A single woman has domestic responsibilities for herself only; when she gets married, the amount of household work increases, as there are now two people to care for. Although economies of scale exist - two single households involve more domestic work than a single two-member household - research shows that, ceteris paribus, married women do more domestic work than single women (Van der Lippe & Niphuis-Nell 1994). Being married increases the burden of domestic work for women at the expense of paid work. Furthermore, being married - at least in Western European countries - often means that the economic need for women to

125

work full-time decreases as their husband provides an income too. On this basis, I expect married women to perform less hours of paid labour than single women.

- Minimum income:
If a woman is married and the husband's wage is too low to maintain a family, his wife will have to take a paid job to supplement the family income. Both spouses have to spend more time on paid labour in order to make a living (Hagenaars & Wunderink-Van Veen 1990). If a woman is single, she has to earn money to maintain her own household.

- Human capital:
Human capital constitutes all knowledge and skills which increase an individual's productivity in the labour market (Becker 1975). Women try to use their stock of human capital as profitably as possible. Investments in productive capacities can be made to maximise life time income. Education is often considered the most important form of human capital investment. For the highly educated woman, devoting a lot of time to the labour market can be very rewarding as the benefits - both financial and in terms of status - can be high.

- Norms:
Women with modern norms are more likely to spend time on the labour market than women with traditional norms. Norms can be determined by the period when women grew up and the way in which they were brought up. The norms of younger people are more oriented to an equal division of labour than those of older people (Van der Lippe & Siegers 1994). I expect therefore that younger women will perform more paid labour.

Institutional context
The institutional context influences paid labour of women in two different ways, which can also be seen in figure 8.1. First, the context influences behaviour via women's individual circumstances. If, for example, the national political socialisation forces women into paid work, traditional or modern norms are no longer a factor. In figure 1 this effect is given by arrow B, and I will call this the 'main' effect of the institutional context on behaviour. Second, an interaction effect can be distinguished between the institutional context and individual characteristics of women: the institutional context only influences one specific group of women. For example, childcare tasks at home decrease if outside facilities exist. This means that women with children are able and available to participate on the labour market during the hours that children are cared for by public child care. The influence of the presence of children on women's participation in the labour force will change due to the presence of public child care. So, although state-funded childcare is an institutional effect on paid work, its influence runs via the individual level. This effect is indicated by arrow C in figure 8.1.

126

So, I assume the institutional context always influences behaviour of women via their individual characteristics. Although macro-hypotheses provide insight into the paid working time of women between countries in general, they do not provide insight into the mechanisms with which the institutional context influences women's paid labour. For example, the ideology hypothesis that communism and social-democracy result in more equal positions for women and men on the labour market does not provide insight into the way these ideologies affect women's choices (Chatab, Van Doorne-Huiskes & Ultee 1987). The same applies to the economy hypothesis derived from the theory of industrial societies, which states that the higher the level of economic development, the more equal the positions of men and women in the labour market will be (Chatab, Van Doorne-Huiskes & Ultee 1987). In figure 8.1, macro-hypotheses can be presented with an arrow between the institutional context and women's paid work. Macro-hypotheses alone are inadequate to the understanding of mechanisms by which these general institutional levels influence the paid working time of women; we need to go back to the individual level.

With respect to institutional constraints, I will focus on those national characteristics which are most relevant to the allocation of time to paid work by women, namely: political socialisation, income level, the availability of public child care, the nature of tax systems, social security regulations, the degree of equality between men and women in educational systems, and the degree to which national labour markets are segregated by gender (Van der Lippe 1995). Each of the institutional constraints distinguished will be discussed briefly.

- Political socialisation:
An important difference between Western and Eastern Europe was the communist ideology prevalent in the latter, which obliged both men and women to have a paid job. I expect that this socialisation still influences choices in Eastern Europe today. Political socialisation relates to women's individual norms. I not only expect that younger women perform more paid labour, but also that the younger women who have grown up in a socialist system will perform more paid labour.

- Income level:
If the average family income level in a country is lower, I expect women to participate more in paid labour. As with political socialisation, this is again a main effect of the institutional context on characteristics of women (arrow B). Due to the fact that a minimum income is needed per household, married women perform paid work. Due to the low income level in Eastern European countries over the last decades, I expect that more women were working in the Eastern European countries than in Western European countries. In Eastern Europe, wives' salary wages were a necessary addition to family income (Andorka & Harcsa 1992).

- Childcare facilities, tax systems and social security regulations:
When state funded childcare is available, childcare tasks can be outsourced, thus enabling women with children to participate in the labour market. This is an exam-

ple of an interaction effect. How does this hypothesis apply to different countries? I expect that in the 1960s the extensive childcare services in Eastern Europe meant women worked more in the labour market than women in Western Europe. Due to the egalitarian view of men and women, socialist economies stimulated the creation of facilities to enable both men and women to participate in the labour market, this in contrast to market economies where almost no childcare facilities were available at the beginning of the 1960s. Maternity leave facilities were also quite extensive in the socialist regimes (ILO 1985). Due to the growth in childcare facilities in Western European countries since the 1960s, it can be expected that over time their effects on the division of labour will have brought conditions in Eastern and Western European countries closer. In Scandinavian countries especially the extensive availability of childcare services facilitates opportunities for women with children to work. These kinds of facilities are less extensive in most other Western European countries, and I expect that the effect of childcare services will be proportionately less in those countries. Following the collapse of communist regimes the future of childcare services is uncertain.

With respect to tax systems and social security regulations, differences exist in whether they stimulate or penalise married women with a job. The more accommodating these rules and regulations are to working married women - i.e. the more tax and social security regulations are based on an individual approach, rather than a family approach - the more likely it is for married women to participate intensely in the labour market. This is another example of an interaction effect. Tax and social regimes in the Scandinavian countries make work for married women more financially attractive than those of other Western European countries. I expect this will result in more Scandinavian women participating longer in labour force than counterparts elsewhere.

- Degree of gender inequality in educational and occupational systems:
Where educational and occupational opportunities are equal for men and women, the latter will have access to the means of improving their chances on the labour market and will be more inclined to engage in paid work. If employment is profitable enough, it is highly probable that women will continue working for pay when their family situation changes. In both Eastern and Western European countries the differences in educational level between men and women have decreased in recent decades (ILO 1985). Whether differences exist in the educational level of women between countries is unknown, but the percentage of women in a country with tertiary education can be used as an indicator here. With respect to occupation, many women are still concentrated in a narrow range of female occupations (ILO 1987). Therefore, I do not expect much change in paid labour over time due to the occupational system in Eastern and Western Europe. But again, the extent of differences between countries in women's occupations is unknown. The rate of occupational gender segregation in the various countries can be used as an indicator here.

128

8.3   DATA AND VARIABLES

Data sets
The analyses presented here utilise data from the Multinational Time Budget Archive (Gershuny, Jones and Baert 1991; Multinational Time Budget Archive; Statistics Finland; Statistics Sweden) and the data collected for the 'Social Stratification in Eastern Europe after 1989: General Population Survey' (Treiman & Szelenyi 1993). The Multinational Time Budget Archive is assembled by the European Foundation for the Improvement of Living and Working Conditions. The archive contains 15 European countries: Denmark, Sweden, Finland, France, the Netherlands, the United Kingdom, former West Germany, Belgium, Italy, former Yugoslavia, Hungary, Poland, Bulgaria, former Czechoslovakia and former East Germany. These data range from 1965 to 1991. The 'Social Stratification in Eastern Europe' Survey was conducted in 1993 and 1994 in six countries: Bulgaria, the Czech Republic, Hungary, Poland, Russia and Slovakia. National probability samples of approximately 5,000 members of the adult population were surveyed for each country, using a questionnaire common to all countries. As Czechoslovakia became the Czech Republic and Slovakia in 1990, these two countries remain separate in the analyses.

Together the data cover nearly 30 years, although the exact period as well as type of data differs from country to country. For Italy, for example, only a single study is available, whereas there are no less than three for the United Kingdom and Hungary. A further disadvantage is that the material used from Western Europe is somewhat dated; for Eastern European countries, of course, the most recent survey dates from 1993. The sample is restricted to women aged between 20 to 59 and sample sizes are given in table 8.1.

Variables
The dependent variable, how much time women spend on paid work, is measured as follows. In the Multinational Time Budget Archive the data are collected by means of a diary method, which means that respondents are asked to record a certain period of their time expenditure by means of a diary. The actual working-out of the diary method varies considerably between countries. In some studies, the main activity is noted in fixed interval units (for example, in 15-minute periods) while in others intervals are left free (i.e. the starting and finishing times of activities is indicated). The period of time during which the diary is kept also differs. In some cases, respondents are required to keep diary for just a single day, while in other instances they are asked to do so for a whole week. Shortcomings notwithstanding, the diary method is considered the most reliable way of measuring how people spend their time (Andorka 1987; Juster & Stafford 1991) and gives an acceptable approximation of people's actual situation (Knulst & Van Beek 1990). The method prevents respondents from exaggerating durations of their favourite activities while neglecting time absorbed by day-to-day concerns and trivialities. Thus, the actual subject

Table 8.1   Sample sizes and date of surveys used

Country	Women
United Kingdom	
1961	887
1975	989
1985	1138
Belgium	
1965	979
Netherlands	
1975	564
1980	1323
1985	1335
(Former) West Germany	
1965	1192
France	
1965	2438
1974	2431
Italy	
1980	1058
Denmark	
1964	1317
1987	1212
Sweden	
1991	2999
Finland	
1979	4277
1987	5238
(Former) Yugoslavia	
1965	1259
(Former) East Germany	
1965	925
Bulgaria	
1988	7417
1993	1240
(Former) Czechoslovakia	
1965	894
The Czech Republic	
1993	1602
Slovakia	
1993	1819
Hungary	
1965	1038
1977	2563
1993	1010
Poland	
1965	1640
1993	943
Russia	
1993	1760

Source: Multinational Time Budget Archive, Survey 'Social Stratification in Eastern Europe'

under study is not overstated, which sometimes happens when specialised questionnaires are used. In the 'Social Stratification in Eastern Europe' Survey data on paid work were not collected by means of the diary method but, instead, through the following question: 'How many hours did you work last week? Please tell me the number of hours you actually worked in all your full-time and part-time jobs or business, including family agriculture, but not including household chores.' Although this is a rather rough indicator of working time, there is no other information available. However, since it concerns the amount of paid work which people normally know very well, it does not seem to be a major problem.

The individual characteristics which are expected to influence women's paid working time are presence and age of children, marital status, income level, age and level of education. Unfortunately, for married women the husband's income is unknown. For the presence and age of children, the presence of children in a certain age group is used. Three categories are distinguished: no young children present, children younger than 5, and youngest child between 5 and 14. For marital status, two categories are distinguished, single and married. Widowed or divorced women are included in the single category. Age is a continuous variable and level of education is indicated in three categories: uncompleted secondary or less, completed secondary, and above secondary education. Since we have data for a period of 30 years, a variable is also included which indicates when the survey was carried out. Five time periods are distinguished: 1961-1970, 1971-1977, 1978-1982, 1983-1991, 1992-1993. The means and standard deviations of the variables are given per country in table 8.2. It is clear from table 8.2 that women in Eastern European countries work far more hours per week than women in Western European countries.

Again unfortunately, institutional indicators are not yet available. Although I do have a number of hypotheses on the institutional context which I want to test, information on the institutional context still has to be collected. However, the empirical analyses already shows the importance and impact of the institutional indicators.

Table 8.2   Means and standard deviations of the variables used in the analyses by country

	United kingdom	Belgium	Netherlands	West Germany	France	Italy	Denmark	Sweden	Finland
Paid work in hours per week	18.25 (20.08)	20.37 (28.86)	8.20 (14.66)	16.08 (27.37)	21.10 (28.92)	16.72 (26.67)	19.30 (26.82)	22.30 (29.71)	27.58 (28.50)
Married	.80 (.40)	.81 (.40)	.85 (.35)	.79 (.41)	.76 (.43)	-	.77 (.42)	.76 (.43)	.73 (.45)
Children									
no (young) children	.48 (.50)	.41 (.49)	.35 (.48)	.48 (.50)	.40 (.49)	.53 (.50)	.49 (.50)	.46 (.50)	.50 (.50)
youngest child < 5 years of age	.23 (.42)	.14 (.35)	.29 (.45)	.19 (.39)	.24 (.43)	.20 (.40)	.28 (.49)	.27 (.44)	.24 (.42)
youngest child 5-14 years of age	.29 (.45)	.41 (.49)	.27 (.44)	.32 (.47)	.36 (.48)	.27 (.45)	.23 (.42)	.27 (.45)	.26 (.44)
Age	38.08 (11.69)	41.10 (10.68)	33.55 (13.19)	39.64 (11.35)	38.16 (10.94)	40.00 (11.20)	38.93 (11.15)	38.70 (10.68)	37.91 (11.28)
Education									
uncompleted secondary or less	.46 (.50)	.44 (.50)	.53 (.50)	.47 (.50)	.54 (.50)	.72 (.45)	.65 (.48)	.60 (.49)	.53 (.50)
completed secondary	.33 (.47)	.42 (.49)	.30 (.46)	.32 (.47)	.33 (.47)	.16 (.36)	.25 (.43)	.14 (.35)	.23 (.42)
secondary plus	.03 (.18)	.07 (.26)	.11 (.32)	-	.09 (.28)	.12 (.32)	.08 (.28)	.26 (.44)	.24 (.43)
Period (time of survey)									
1961-1970	.32 (.47)	1.00 (0.0)	-	1.00 (0.0)	.49 (.50)	-	.52 (.50)	-	-
1971-1977	.32 (.47)	-	.33 (.47)	-	.51 (.50)	-	-	-	-
1978-1982	-	-	.35 (.48)	-	-	1.00 (0.0)	-	-	-
1983-1991	.35 (.48)	-	.32 (.47)	-	-	-	.48 (.50)	1.00 (0.0)	.50 (.50)
1992-1993	-	-	-	-	-	-	-	-	.50 (.50)

Table 8.2 (continued)

	Yugoslavia	East Germany	Bulgaria	Czechoslovakia	The Czech Republic	Slovakia	Hungary	Poland	Russia
Paid work in hours per week	31.02 (30.19)	26.14 (31.48)	38.13 (25.96)	33.32 (30.34)	51.53 (19.92)	57.50 (23.59)	35.91 (26.82)	35.59 (26.50)	43.35 (18.11)
Married	.78 (.41)	.85 (.36)	.83 (.38)	.83 (.38)	.71 (.45)	.74 (.44)	.78 (.41)	.75 (.43)	.66 (.48)
Children									
no (young) children	.28 (.45)	.22 (.42)	.54 (.50)	.25 (.43)	.58 (.49)	.53 (.50)	.49 (.50)	.36 (.48)	.51 (.50)
youngest child < 5 years of age	.20 (.40)	.36 (.48)	.18 (.38)	.18 (.38)	.10 (.30)	.15 (.35)	.15 (.35)	.18 (.39)	.13 (.34)
youngest child 5-14 years of age	.52 (.50)	.42 (.49)	.28 (.45)	.51 (.50)	.32 (.47)	.33 (.47)	.36 (.48)	.46 (.50)	.36 (.48)
Age	38.01 (9.88)	35.12 (9.59)	40.13 (10.48)	38.99 (10.67)	40.15 (9.93)	39.34 (10.17)	39.54 (10.64)	38.40 (10.27)	38.94 (10.44)
Education									
uncompleted secondary or less	.61 (.49)	.89 (.31)	.31 (.46)	.57 (.50)	.55 (.50)	.47 (.49)	.41 (.49)	.49 (.50)	.17 (.37)
completed secondary	.32 (.47)	.11 (.31)	.45 (.50)	.29 (.45)	.32 (.47)	.36 (.48)	.47 (.50)	.33 (.47)	.48 (.50)
secondary plus	.05 (.23)	.00 (.00)	.20 (.40)	.05 (.22)	.12 (.33)	.13 (.34)	.11 (.31)	.16 (.37)	.31 (.46)
Period (time of survey)									
1961-1970	1.00 (0.0)	1.00 (0.0)	-	1.00 (0.0)	-	-	.34 (.47)	.55 (.50)	-
1971-1977	-	-	-	-	-	-	.35 (.48)	-	-
1978-1982	-	-	-	-	-	-	-	-	-
1983-1991	-	-	.50 (.50)	-	-	-	-	-	-
1992-1993	-	-	.50 (.50)	-	1.00 (0.0)	1.00 (0.0)	-	.44 (.50)	1.00 (0.0)

Source: Multinational Time Budget Archive, Survey 'Social Stratification in Eastern Europe'

Weighing process

In order to make the selected national samples comparable, the data have to be reweighed. As a first step for the Multinational Time Budget Archive data, each sample is made representative of the country and year in which it is held, because it is highly probable that, though carefully designed and completely random, the samples could be distorted by high non-response rates, which is a common weakness of time budget surveys. For this stage of the reweighing process gender, age, and employment status are used, data on which are published by the ILO. The data from the 'Social Stratification in Eastern Europe' Survey are also reweighed to make them representative of the country (Treiman & Szelenyi 1993). Secondly, for the Multinational Time Budget Archive, the samples are reweighed by days of the week, so as to ensure that all days are represented equally. In the 'Social Stratification in Eastern Europe' Survey days of the week are not distinguished, so it is not possible to perform this weighing step.

8.4   RESULTS

In order to analyse to what extent women's individual characteristics influence their paid labour in the respective countries, I have first estimated separate regression analyses for each. The results of OLS regression analyses of paid work of women in 18 European countries are given in table 8.3. What stands out in these analyses is the different influence of all individual characteristics per country. The explained variance (given in R-square) for paid work is much higher in the western part of Europe, than in Scandinavian countries and Eastern European countries. This implies that individual characteristics do not explain much of women's paid work in Scandinavian countries and Eastern Europe.

Table 8.3 *Results of regression analyses of paid work of women aged 20 to 59: 18 European countries*

	United Kingdom	Belgium	Netherlands	West Germany	France	Italy	Denmark	Sweden	Finland	Yugoslavia
Unstandardised regression coefficients of paid work of women[1] (standard errors)										
Marital status										
single	-	-	-	-	-	-	-	-	-	-
married	-.18	-9.61**	-5.74**	-17.71**	-14.76**	-[3]	-11.11**	-2.67	-.13	-12.08**
Children										
no (young) children										
youngest child < 5 years of age	-25.78**	-19.61**	-12.36**	-14.12**	-14.82**	-7.85**	-3.22	-7.12**	-7.39**	-4.56
youngest child 5-14 years of age	-9.55**	-11.91**	-6.37**	-6.80**	-7.97**	-3.42	.31	2.75	3.46*	-1.25
Age	-.55**	-.42**	-.34**	-.44**	-.31**	-.41**	.03	.09	-.10	-.64**
Education										
uncompleted secondary or less	-	-	-	-	-	-	-	-	-	-
completed secondary	-.75	7.18**	3.16**	-3.38**	5.62**	4.84*	4.05**	1.72	1.75	8.73**
secondary plus	3.54	1.19	4.43**	-[2]	5.22*	1.33	3.96	2.43	-.22	-.46
Period (time of survey)										
1961-1970	-	-	-	-	-	-	-	-	-	-
1971-1977	1.81									
1978-1982			-1.15		-3.84**					
1983-1991	.41		5.04**				10.20**		-1.26	
1992-1993										
Constant	47.16**	49.92**	26.19**	53.22**	50.22**	34.81**	21.14**	21.24**	32.77**	63.51**
R-square	.24	.13	.20	.15	.12	.03	.09	.02	.01	.09
Number of cases	1603	1009	2661	1087	2042	1050	2027	1003	2048	1132

Table 8.3 (continued)

	Unstandardised regression coefficients of paid work of women[1] (standard errors)							
	East Germany	Bulgaria	Czecho-slovakia	The Czech Republic	Slovakia	Hungary	Poland	Russia
Marital status								
single	-	-	-	-	-	-	-	-
married	-12.70**	-.30	-6.71**	4.47**	2.03	-5.32**	-8.63**	2.40*
Children								
no (young) children	-	-	-	-	-	-	-	-
youngest child < 5 years of age	-8.63**	-5.50**	-7.92**	3.61	3.01	-12.32**	-6.47**	-4.98**
youngest child 5-14 years of age	.87	3.72*	1.60	-1.89**	4.12*	.54	-1.25	3.98**
Age	-.01	-.03	-.15	.01	.16	-.28**	-.32**	.16**
Education								
uncompleted secondary or less	-	-	-	-	-	-	-	-
completed secondary	-3.41	-.41	6.14**	-.30	-1.75	3.30**	3.50**	1.03
secondary plus	-[2]	-1.45	4.69	-1.72	-5.29*	8.69**	-.98	-.79
Period (time of survey)								
1961-1970		-	-	-		-		
1971-1977								
1978-1982	-					-4.19**		
1983-1991			-				-	
1992-1993		9.87**				5.25**	6.30**	
Constant	38.94**	34.44**	43.10**	48.40**	49.08**	50.32**	52.13**	34.55**
R-square	.04	.05	.02	.01	.01	.08	.06	.04
Number of cases	1214	2007	1075	1021	959	3085	2060	1155

1. ** significant on the 1%-level; * significant on the 5%-level
2. No information on high education for West Germany is available
3. No information on marital status is available for Italy

Source: Multinational Time Budget Archive, Survey 'Social Stratification in Eastern Europe'

In terms of individual effects it is most obvious that the effect of children differs between countries. As expected, in almost all countries, children under five restrict the opportunities to work on the labour market, but this effect seems to be stronger in the western part of Europe than in Scandinavia and Eastern Europe. Women in the United Kingdom, for example, with a child under five spend 26 hours less on the labour market than women without children; for Denmark and the Czech Republic this figure is 3 to 4 hours. This seems to be due partly to the availability of childcare facilities. In the Czech Republic and Denmark, childcare services are much more extensive than in the United Kingdom, and differences in working hours between women with and without children are therefore small. This implies an interaction effect of child care: the more childcare facilities there are in a country, the less the presence of children influences paid work. A youngest child in the five to 14 age group has a significant negative effect on women's paid labour in the western part of Europe, but the effect is not great in Scandinavian countries.

The effect of marital status is also mixed. It was expected that married women spend less time on paid labour than single women, but this hypothesis is not confirmed for all countries. In the Czech Republic, married women work more hours per week than their single counterparts, which could imply that the average income level per household in this country is too low to maintain a family. The effect of age is more visible in the western part of Europe than in Scandinavia or Eastern Europe, with the exception of Hungary and Poland. As expected, the older generations in the western part of Europe adhere to a more strict division of tasks, the domestic component of which is likely to fall to women and the paid work to men. However, this is not the case in Scandinavian countries or in some Eastern European countries. The hypothesis on the influence of human capital on paid work is also confirmed for a few countries only. In many European countries women with a higher education spend more time on paid labour, but this result does not apply for the UK, Sweden, Finland, Eastern Germany, Bulgaria, The Czech Republic and Russia. The last variable in the analyses is period of time as more points of time were available for some countries. However, the number of periods and duration differ to a large extent between the countries, so no conclusions can be drawn from this variable.

The general picture emerging from these analyses is that individual characteristics explain much more of the paid working time of women in the western part of Europe than in Scandinavian countries and Eastern Europe.

To show the effect of institutional characteristics on paid work of women in a multivariate way, this section concludes with a 'multi-level model'. This kind of model can distinguish between individual and country levels. Based on findings given above, a distinction is made between Scandinavia, other Western European countries and Eastern Europe. Model 1 includes the variables on an individual level, namely: marital status, presence of youngest child, age, educational level and period of survey. Model 2 adds a variable on a country level, i.e. which group the

Table 8.4 Results of multi-level analyses of paid work of women aged 20 to 59: 17 European countries

	Model 1	Model 2
Fixed part		
Individual effects		
Marital status		
single	-	-
married	-5.59** (.30)[23]	-5.59** (.30)
Children		
no (young) children	-	-
youngest child < 5 yrs of age	-9.88** (.37)	-9.88** (.37)
youngest child 5-14 yrs of age	-2.60** (.29)	-2.60** (.29)
Age	-.19** (.01)	-.19** (.01)
Education		
uncompleted secondary or less	-	-
completed secondary	3.02** (.28)	3.02** (.28)
secondary plus	1.92** (.43)	1.92** (.43)
Period (time of survey)		
1961-1970	-	-
1971-1977	2.37** (.59)	2.37** (.59)
1978-1982	6.17** (.94)	6.17** (.94)
1983-1991	6.08** (.68)	6.08** (.68)
1992-1993	10.66** (.75)	10.66** (.75)
Country Effect		
Europe in three regions		
Scandinavian countries		
Other Western Eur. countries		4.92 (3.98)
Eastern Europe		-
		17.20** (3.06)
Random part		
individual	647.57	647.57
intercept (group)	94.08	31.24
R-square individual	4.27	4.27
R-square intercept	40.77	66.79
Deviance	410152.25	410133.54
Difference in deviance	1931.12	18.71
Df	7	8
Number of cases	44039	44039

1. As no information on marital status is available for Italy, this country has been omitted from the analysis
2. Unstandardised regression coefficients of paid work of women (standard errors)
3. ** significant on the 1%-level; * significant on the 5%-level
4. As the weighing process is performed in the multi-level analysis itself, we provide here the original N

Source: Multinational Time Budget Archive, Survey 'Social Stratification in Eastern Europe'

country belongs to - Scandinavia, other Western European countries or Eastern Europe. In table 8.4 the fixed part is given with individual effects and country effects.

These effects are the same as the unstandardised coefficients in a regression analysis. The standard errors are given between brackets. The random part in the table gives the variance to be explained at individual and country level. The R-square can be calculated from this random part. The R-square is the same as the one in regression analyses. Furthermore, the deviance of the model is given and the degrees of freedom which together indicate which model has the best fit.

In model 1 the individual characteristics do not explain much of the variance of paid work at an individual level (4.27%), but they do explain much of the variance of paid work of women at a country level (40.77%). It means that more than 40% of the variance between countries is explained by national differences in the composition of women with respect to these individual characteristics. The R-square for the country level increases in model 2 to 66.79%, which implies that 26% of the variance in women's paid work between countries is explained by a variable which indicates in which part of Europe women live. The unstandardised regression coefficients can be interpreted as follows. If a child under five is present in a household, its mother works 10 hours a week less compared to a childless woman whose situation is alike in all other respects. This difference applies to all countries.

I will not discuss the individual effects here but concentrate solely on the variable at a country level. What stands out is that women in Eastern Europe spend significantly more - on average 17 hours more - time on paid labour than women in the western part of Europe. The effect of living in Scandinavian countries is not significant, which indicates that the hours spent on paid work might differ between Scandinavian countries and other Western European countries, but not significantly when controlled for other characteristics at an individual level.

The next step in the research described here is a specification of the relevant institutional constraints and an analysis of the relative weight of institutional and individual characteristics. For the analysis of the institutional context, I use information provided by researchers on the welfare state and its implications for women. The debate currently ongoing among feminist social scientists is based on more or less precise descriptions of specific national institutional constraints (e.g. Plantenga & Van Doorne-Huiskes 1992; Lewis 1993). In this debate, although criticised, the Esping-Andersen typology of welfare state regimes plays an important role. Using national data-sets, this kind of international comparative research clarifies the different patterns of women's labour market participation in Europe by describing specific institutional arrangements in each country.

8.5 CONCLUSION

In this study an attempt has been made to explain women's paid labour patterns in Eastern and Western European countries. In Eastern Europe, the activity rate is high and almost everyone works full time. In the Scandinavian countries, women's participation in the labour force today is as high as in Eastern Europe, but many women work parttime.

A basic assumption in the explanation is that women's paid labour is influenced by individual characteristics, such as family situation and human capital stock, and the institutional context. Examples of the latter are political socialisation, the availability of childcare facilities and tax system.

The results show that individual characteristics explain far more of the amount of women's paid working time in the western part of Europe than in Scandinavia and Eastern Europe. As expected in almost all countries, children under five restrict opportunities to work on the labour market, but this effect seems to be stronger in the western part of Europe than in the Scandinavian countries and Eastern Europe. Married women perform less paid labour than single women, younger women perform more paid labour than older women, and well educated women work more hours per week than less-well educated women only in the western part of Europe.

In future research I will focus both on the elaboration and operationalisation of institutional conditions as well as on individual data. I will analyse relevant institutional conditions of countries and bring them in as measurable variables in statistical models. These models, based on theoretical assumptions of human behaviour under constraints, will be applied on the international data-sets which contain data on the individual level. Not only, however, will these kind of models be tested in a abstract way. It is important as well to describe the specific socio-economic and cultural arrangements in the Western and Eastern European countries and their impact on the labour force situation of women. This kind of information is a meaningful and necessary supplement on statistical models, since these models do not reveal the complex institutional situation in countries and their influence on paid labour of women.

REFERENCES

Andorka, R. 1987: Time budgets and their uses, *Annual Review of Sociology*, 13, 149-164.
Andorka, R. & Harcsa, I. 1992: The income of the population, in: Andorka, R., Kolosi, T. & Vukovich G. (eds), *Social Report*. Budapest: Tarki.
Arber, S. & Gilbert, N. (Eds.). 1992: *Women and Working Lives: Divisions and Change*. University of Surrey. New York: St. Martin's Press.

Becker, G.S. 1975: *Human capital*. New York: Columbia University Press, for the National Bureau of Economic Research. 2nd edition.

Blossfeld, H. 1987: Labor market entry and the social segregation of career in the Federal Republic of Germany, *American Journal of Sociology*, 93, 89-118.

Chatab, J., Van Doorne-Huiskes J. & Ultee, W.C. 1987: Ongelijkheden tussen mannen en vrouwen; enige verklaringen van verschillen tussen geïndustrialiseerde landen getoetst, *Sociale Wetenschappen*, 30, 279-300.

Coverman, S. 1985: Explaining husband's participation in domestic labour, *The Sociological Quarterly*, 26, 81-97.

Einhorn, B. 1993: *Cinderella Goes to Market: Citizenship, Gender and Women's Movements in East Central Europe*. London, New York: Verso.

Ferber, M.A. 1982: Labor market participation of young married women: causes and effects, *Journal of Marriage and the Family*, 44, 457-468.

Funk, N. & Mueller, M. (eds.) 1993: *Gender Politics and Post Communism: Reflections from Eastern Europe and the Former Soviet Union*. New York: Routledge.

Geerken, M. & Gove, W.R. 1983: *At home and at work: the family's allocation of labor*. Beverly Hills: Sage Publications.

Gershuny, J., Jones, S. & Baert, P. 1991: *The time economy or the economy of time: an essay on the interdependence of living and working conditions*. European Foundation for the Improvement of Living and Working Conditions. Oxford.

Gronau, R. 1986: Home production: a survey, in: Ashenfelter, O.C. & Layard, R. (eds.), *Handbook of labor economics, vol. 1*. New York: North-Holland.

Hagenaars, A.J.M. & S.R. Wunderink-van Veen. 1990: '*Soo gewonne soo verteert: economie van de huishoudelijke sector*'. Leiden/Antwerpen: Stenfert Kroese.

International Labour Office. 1984: *World labour report 1. Employment, incomes, social protection, new information technology*. New York: Oxford University Press.

International Labour Office. 1985: *World labour report 2. Labour relations, international labour standards, training, conditions of work, women at work*. New York: Oxford University Press.

International Labour Office. 1987: *World labour report 3. Incomes from work: between equity and efficiency*. New York: Oxford University Press.

Jenson, J., Hagen, E. & Reddy, C. (Eds.). 1988: *Feminization of the Labour Force*. Padstow: Polity Press.

Juster, F.T. & Stafford, F.P. 1991: The allocation of time: empirical findings, behavioral models, and problems of measurement, *Journal of Economic Literature*, 29, 471-522.

Knulst, W.P. & Van Beek, P. 1990: *Tijd komt met de jaren: onderzoek naar tegenstellingen en veranderingen in dagelijkse bezigheden van Nederlanders op basis van tijdbudgetonderzoek*. Rijswijk/Den Haag: Sociaal en Cultureel Planbureau/VUGA (Sociale en Culturele Studies nr. 14).

Lewis, J. (Ed.). 1993: *Women and Social Policies in Europe*. Edward Elgar. Hants England.

Multinational Time Budget Archive. University of Bath, UK.

OECD. 1990: *Employment outlook*. Paris: OECD publications.

Plantenga, J. & Van Doorne-Huiskes, J. 1992. *Gender, citizenship and welfare: An European Perspective*. Paper presented at the first European Conference on Sociology. Vienna, 26 - 29 August.

Robinson, J.P., Converse, P.E. & Szalai, A. 1972: Everyday life in twelve countries, in: Szalai, A. (ed), *The use of time: daily activities of urban and suburban populations in twelve countries*. The Haque/Paris: Mouton.

Siegers, J.J. 1992: Interdisciplinary economics, *De Economist*, 140, 531-547.

Statistics Finland. *Finnish time use surveys 1979, 1987/1988*, transformed by the Multinational Longitudinal Time Budget Archive.

Statistics Sweden. *Swedish time use surveys 1991*: transformed by the Multinational Longitudinal Time Budget Archive.

Treiman, D.J. & I. Szelenyi. 1993: *Social Stratification in Eastern Europe after 1989: General Population Survey* (machine readable file). Los Angeles: University of California.

Van der Lippe, T. & Niphuis-Nell, M. 1994: *Ontwikkelingen in de verdeling van onbetaalde arbeid over vrouwen en mannen, 1975-1990*. Rijswijk: Sociaal en Cultureel Planbureau.

Van der Lippe, T. & Siegers, J.J. 1994: Division of household and paid labour between partners: effects of relative wage rates and social norms, *KYKLOS*, 47, 109-136.

Van der Lippe, T. 1995: *Scarcity of time of women in European Union countries*. Study for the European Union. Utrecht: University of Utrecht.

Van Doorne-Huiskes, J. 1979: *Vrouwen en beroepsparticipatie: een onderzoek onder gehuwde vrouwelijke academici*. Proefschrift Universiteit Utrecht.

Van Doorne-Huiskes, J., Van Hoof, J. & Roelofs, E. (Eds.). 1995: *Women in the European Labour Markets*. London: Paul Chapman.

ACKNOWLEDGEMENTS

The author would like to thank Anneke Van Doorne-Huiskes, Harry Ganzeboom, Jacques Siegers, and Matthijs Kalmijn for their valuable comments on a earlier version of this paper. The research underlying this particular article was subsidised by the Netherlands Organisation for Scientific Research (NWO-grant no. 510-79-609).

The author would like to thank Cora Maas as well for her methodological assistance with the multi-level analyses. Anyone interested in a methodological description of multi-level models can contact the author.

BIOGRAPHICAL NOTE

Dr. Ir. Tanja van der Lippe (1963) is assistant professor of sociology at Utrecht University in the Netherlands, as well as research fellow financed by the Netherlands Organisation for Scientific Research. Her main research interests are division of paid and household labour, labour market positions of men and women in Eastern and Western Europe, and gender stratification issues.

Part III

Time Allocation and Institutional Arrangements

9   Work-family arrangements in organisations

Laura den Dulk
Chantal Remery

9.1   INTRODUCTION

In most Western countries, the participation of women in the labour market is increasing (Plantenga, 1995; Sainsbury, 1996). As a result, the number of families in which both parents are in paid work is also increasing. This brings into question how employees deal with the combination of paid work and household and caring responsibilities. Working parents need, for example, childcare arrangements during the hours they are at work. As it is expected that women's labour market participation will continue to increase, the need for facilities that support the combination of paid and unpaid work will probably increase too. The importance of such facilities for employees is widely recognised nowadays by organisations such as the European Union and the Organisation for Economic Co-operation and Development (OECD). For example, the OECD (1991) advocates enhancing the compatibility between domestic and employment responsibilities. This raises the issue of who should provide the necessary facilities.

In this chapter we address the role of employers in combining paid and unpaid work. Employers can support their employees by providing arrangements which have become known as work-family arrangements. Research suggests that work-family arrangements are not wide-spread among employers. Moreover, there seem to be differences between employers: some introduce work-family arrangements, while others do not. This raises the question why employers would introduce such arrangements. Until now, this issue has received relatively little theoretical attention. In this chapter we will present a theoretical model which attempts to explain this question. The model will be illustrated with results from empirical research. Finally, we will discuss implications of the model with regard to future developments in work-family arrangements by employers.

Time allocation and gender, Kea Tijdens, Anneke van Doorne-Huiskes & Tineke Willemsen (eds.), Tilburg University Press, 1997, © Laura den Dulk & Chantal Remery

9.2   WORK-FAMILY ARRANGEMENTS: A DEFINITION

In most literature an operational definition of work-family arrangements is used. Moss (1990) makes a distinction between fringe benefits for working parents (leave arrangements) and childcare. Kingston (1990) states that the concept of work-family arrangements generally refers to two main types of personnel policy; on the one hand, additions to fringe benefits, such as childcare arrangements or parental leave, and on the other hand, modifications in typical work schedules, such as flexitime, part-time work, or job-sharing. One can also distinguish between direct and indirect policies. Direct policies are explicitly developed to facilitate the combination of paid and unpaid work, whereas indirect policies may or may not have been initiated with this goal in mind, but their effects support this combination (Hayghe, 1988).

We define work-family arrangements as facilities that intentionally as well as unintentionally support the combination of paid work and family responsibilities. We distinguish four types of arrangements: flexible working patterns, leave arrangements, care provisions and supportive arrangements. Examples of flexible working patterns are part-time work, flexible working hours and job sharing. This kind of arrangement allows workers to choose either to reduce their working hours or adjust these to caring tasks. Leaves, such as parental and paternity, enable parents to take (temporary) care of their young children. Provisions like childcare or care for the elderly mean that care functions are performed by others during the time employees are at work. Supportive measures such as distribution of information or management training can increase the awareness of work-family issues within the organisation. In figure 9.1 the different types of work-family arrangements are summarised.

Figure 9.1 Work-family arrangements

I Flexible working patterns	II Leaves
- part-time work - flexitime (flexible working hours) - job sharing - flexplace (teleworking/homeworking) - term time working - buying/selling/saving time	- maternity leave - parental leave - paternity leave - leave for family reasons - career break schemes - adoption leave
III Care provisions	IV Supportive arrangements
- workplace nursery - after school care - holiday play scheme - childcare resource and referral - financial assistance - vouchers - elderly care resource and referral	- work-family management training - employee counselling/assistance programmes - work-family co-ordinator - supply of information

Work-family arrangements can either be formal, written policies or informal arrangements within the organisation. In the case of informal policies the implementation is in most cases at the discretion of the manager (Wolcott, 1991). The manager, not the employee, decides whether an arrangement can be used. In some cases work-family arrangements are only available to certain groups of employees, for example employees with a permanent labour contract or female employees.[1]
Therefore, company arrangements can raise questions about equality of access. Work-family arrangements also differ in the level of costs involved, both organisational and financial. A career break, for example, is in most cases quite easy to arrange, whereas a workplace nursery needs a substantial investment.

9.3   THEORETICAL MODEL

9.3.1   Introduction

The question why some employers introduce work-family arrangements while others do not has until now received relatively little theoretical attention. If a theoretical framework is used, this is based on institutional theories. Institutional theorists emphasise the influence of the environment on organisational structures and practices (e.g. DiMaggio & Powell, 1983; Scott, 1995). With regard to work-family arrangements regulative and normative aspects of the environment are seen as exerting pressure on employers to implement such arrangements (Goodstein, 1994; Ingram & Simons, 1995). The regulative aspect refers to the legal system and state regulations. To the extent that these have incorporated work-family issues, such as the right to take a certain period of maternity leave, employers have to conform to these regulations. The normative aspect consists of norms and values in society. As a result of the increasing participation of women in the labour force and the increasing number of dual-earner families in most Western countries, the issue of combining work and family has come to public attention. This creates increasing pressure on employers to deal with this issue.
Institutional theory has been criticised for considering employers as passive actors. The assumption is that they will conform to institutional pressures. The theory lacks attention to the various ways in which employers can deal with this pressure. However, employers can be considered as decision-making actors who have different options on how to deal with this pressure. Oliver (1991) acknowledges part of this critique by introducing the concept of strategic choice in institutional theory. The concept of strategic choice refers to the assumption that employers can respond in different ways to their institutional environment. Five strategies are distinguished, varying from acquiescence (conformity) to manipulation. The strat-

---

[1] According to European Union directives, it is illegal to exclude certain groups (i.e. men) from arrangements. However, when an employer can show that women are in an unequal position, measures are allowed to eliminate this inequality. In that case employers can restrict the provision of work-family arrangements to women.

egy eventually chosen by employers, is dependent on conditions such as the content of the pressure and the nature of institutional control. In studies on the subject of work-family arrangements in organisations, this framework is used by Goodstein (1994) and Ingram & Simons (1995). Based on this framework they formulate hypotheses on the type of organisations that are more likely to introduce (different sorts of) work-family arrangements.

These authors seem right in their assumption that employers have various ways of responding to their institutional environment. Employers are capable of making decisions and, though it is a factor that has to be taken into account, they are not entirely at the mercy of their environment. However, the starting point in their theoretical analyses remains the institutional environment. In contrast, we will relate the institutional environments more explicitly to the assumption that employers make choices on introduction of work-family arrangements.

9.3.2   Employers as decision-making actors

To answer the question why employers introduce work-family arrangements, we used a behavioural theory. In this theory, also known as rational choice theory, it is assumed that actors strive for the maximum realisation of their goals. As a result of constraints, they have to make choices. According to the theory, actors will choose the alternative with the lowest costs and/or the highest benefits. The costs and benefits of alternatives vary depending on the constraints facing an actor. Examples of constraints are available resources, such as time and money. Constraints also refer to structural and institutional conditions, such as social norms and laws. It is assumed that actors are striving after similar general goals. As a result of different constraints, actors can vary in the alternatives they choose even if they are striving after similar goals (Coleman, 1990).

This general model can be applied to the behaviour of employers with regard to the introduction of work-family arrangements. Whether these arrangements are introduced or not, is the result of a decision taken by the employer. We expect employers to introduce work-family arrangements when they consider the benefits of such arrangements higher than the costs. As employers are confronted with different constraints, the costs and benefits of these arrangements will vary from employer to employer. By specifying relevant constraints, we can explain why some employers are more likely to introduce work-family arrangements than others.

Firstly, we have to determine the goals of employers. Traditionally, neo-classical economic theory considers the maximum realisation of profit as the ultimate goal of employers. In sociological, organisational and psychological theory different goals are distinguished. For example, according to institutional theories employers strive for legitimacy and resources in order to survive (Meyer & Rowan, 1991). Van der Burg et al. (1989, p. 314) assume that actors strive for maximum realisa-

150

tion of their goals and that four arguments contribute to this: income, status, secure position, and harmonious relations. In Van der Burg et al.'s model these goals are related to individuals. We will apply the assumption of multiple goals to the employer as the general actor.[2] This means that we assume that employers strive for maximum realisation of their goals. The more income, the more status and the more the organisation's position is secure, the more an employer achieves his goals. With regard to the fourth argument one can expect employers to try to avoid conflicts.

For employers in the private sector the income argument refers to profit. We are also interested in employers in the public sector. The income argument in terms of profit does not fit for these employers. In public choice literature, the assumption is that public employers strive for budget maximisation (for example McLean, 1987). Therefore, we define the income argument not only in terms of profit, but also in terms of budgets.

Introduction of work-family arrangements can contribute to each of the four goals. Women still carry the main responsibility for household and caring tasks (for example Van der Lippe, 1993). Work-family arrangements make it easier for women to combine paid work with household tasks. Therefore, provision of those arrangements can raise the productivity of women (especially women with small children) and/or reduce absenteeism and turnover (Galinsky, 1991; Glass & Fujimoto, 1995). Higher productivity leads to a higher profit. Reduction of absenteeism and turnover lowers the costs of replacement and/or recruitment. As a result this can contribute to a higher profit.

Status refers to the image of an organisation. One can expect that, in general, a positive image is important to employers for several reasons. A good image attracts customers, but also adequate labour supply. If an employer is known for excellent working conditions, the expectation is it will attract more and/or better qualified personnel. As a result the employer has more choice when vacancies arise. Provision of work-family arrangements can increase the (social) image and, as such, the status of an organisation, because the employer shows awareness of the fact that employees have caring tasks and that working parents need facilities.

For commercial organisations the third goal, the organisation's secure position, is related to market-share. The larger the market-share and/or the more stable that share is, the more secure the position of an organisation. A secure position is also related to profit: reduction of profit endangers the position of an organisation. For public organisations a secure position is related to (political) legitimacy. Loss of legitimacy endangers the survival of public organisations. If work-family arrange-

---

[2] We realise that in decision-making processes in organisations different actors are involved, such as shareholders, managers and employee-representatives. For the sake of simplicity we will use the term employer as general actor representing organisations.

ments increase productivity, the provision of these arrangements contributes to a secure position. However, when an organisation is in an insecure position, the employer is less likely to introduce work-family arrangements because of the costs involved.

The last goal is harmonious relations. Introduction of work-family arrangements can reduce the chance for conflicts. When (female) employees or labour unions request the provision of these arrangements, the employer risks conflicts if he does not meet this request.

The importance of the four goals can differ between organisations. Status can, for example, be of special importance for an organisation which delivers services. A technical company which operates on a highly competitive market will probably attach more value to a secure position. For public organisations it can be expected that a secure position, in terms of political legitimacy, and a good image are the most important goals.

We have described what the expected benefits of work-family arrangements are and how provision of these arrangements can contribute to the realisation of employers' goals. However, work-family arrangements also have costs, both financial and organisational. Provision of childcare arrangements, for example, costs money. When an employer offers paternal leave, employees who take this leave have to be replaced. This leads to organisational costs. As stated before, costs and benefits vary with the constraints faced by employers. Relevant constraints are the institutional environment and organisational characteristics. In the next section we will specify how these constraints influence the costs and benefits of work-family arrangements.

9.3.3 Institutional constraints

We distinguish the following institutional constraints: governmental policy, the cultural context, the influence of trade unions and collective agreements and the situation on the labour market.

Governments have several measures to influence the behaviour of employers. Examples are legislation and stimulatory measures such as subsidisation and recommendations. These measures vary according to levels of pressure. Legislation is compulsory; employers have to comply with the law. In the case of subsidisation it is up to the employers to use it or not. Recommendations can be seen as the weakest form of pressure. The measures taken by governments to promote work-family arrangements will depend on assumptions about the responsibilities of governments and employers. These assumptions can vary by country. Consequently, governments will differ in the extent to which they take measures on work-family arrangements and to which they pressure organisations to develop these arrangements. This will result in differences between countries in the extent to which employers provide arrangements.

Organisations can respond differently to existing governmental pressure. Even if this pressure is high, one can expect that some employers are more responsive than others. Relevant factors are if an organisation belongs to the private or public sector, and the size of an organisation. Firstly, one can expect that public organisations are more likely to respond to governmental pressure than private sector companies (Goodstein, 1994). The main task of public organisations is to execute governmental policy. If this policy states that employers should implement work-family arrangements, this creates normative pressure on public organisations to conform. Public organisations are more often subject to public attention and they are more likely to be evaluated according to governmental standards and norms. The costs of not responding to this pressure are therefore higher for public than for private organisations. A second factor that renders organisations more sensitive to governmental pressure is size. Larger organisations are more often the subject of public discussion, for example in the media, than smaller ones. When the government stimulates the development of work-family arrangements, the introduction of such facilities could benefit the image and social status of the employer, whereas resistance could result in public disapproval.

The cultural context is another constraint which has to be taken into account. This context refers to norms and values on the combination of work and caring tasks. Social norms can dominate which state that one parent, probably the mother, should stay at home to care for the children. If this is the case, a family in which both parents had a paid job would face disapproval. Social norms can also reflect the idea that each individual should be able to combine a paid job with caring tasks. If such norms dominate one can expect that there will be more societal pressure on employers to support this combination by providing work-family arrangements.

Another constraint refers to trade unions. Work-family arrangements can be part of collective bargaining agreements. When this is the case, one can expect employers to be more inclined to provide these arrangements. If employers do not implement the agreed arrangements, they risk a conflict with trade unions. The costs and benefits of such a decision depend, among other things, on the strength of the trade unions and the importance they attach to work-family arrangements.

Finally, the situation on the labour market is included as a constraint. In the case of high unemployment the pressure to develop work-family arrangements is less for employers because it is easier to replace and to recruit employees. When the labour market is tight, there is more competition among employers to retain and recruit personnel. If work-family arrangements attract qualified employees or help retain personnel, which saves costs of replacement, the costs of these arrangements are probably less than the benefits of keeping a qualified work force.

9.3.4 Organisational constraints

Besides institutional constraints, organisational characteristics can also influence the costs and benefits of work-family arrangements. Existing research suggests that work-family arrangements are more common among large than small organisations (Kamerman & Kahn, 1987; Morgan & Milliken, 1992; Goodstein, 1994; Ingram & Simons, 1995). Apart from reasons of visibility and public attention, as noted above, large organisations often have a specialised human resource staff. Such a staff is more likely to notice increasing demands for work-family arrangements and has more expertise in reacting to these developments (Morgan & Milliken, 1992). Moreover, it is easier for large organisations with more staff and financial resources to develop work-family arrangements than for small companies. Large organisations have larger economies of scale, which result in relatively lower costs per employee. For small organisations it could be too expensive to introduce work-family arrangements.

Demographic characteristics of the work force are also important constraints. Since women continue to bear the main caring responsibility, they will benefit most from the presence of work-family arrangements. Consequently, the effects of work-family arrangements on productivity, absenteeism and turnover can be significant when the organisation employs a high proportion of women. However, a high proportion of female employees can lead to a high demand for facilities, which would increase costs for the employer. This can be a reason to decide not to develop arrangements. In addition, it can be a strategy of employers to employ women with caring responsibilities only in occupations and positions within the organisation where productivity losses and turnover costs are low (Glass & Fujimoto, 1995). In this way, the costs of work-family arrangements are avoided.

The position of female employees within the organisation seems of more importance. An organisation with a relatively high proportion of women in managerial positions will probably strive towards retention of these employees. Loss of these women means loss of human capital and results in costs for the organisation. In general, one can expect that the more an employer invests in personnel, the more efforts will be made to retain them. The introduction of work-family arrangements can make the organisation attractive as employer and, as such, contribute to retention of personnel. Furthermore, women in management positions have more power to stimulate the development of work-family arrangements within the organisation. The absence of arrangements can provoke a conflict more easily. Assuming that employers want to avoid conflicts, one can expect a positive relationship between the number of women in higher positions and the existence of work-family arrangements in organisations.

The degree of flexibilisation is another constraint. Flexible employees are mostly deployed in jobs with low replacement costs and in most cases are not entitled to use facilities provided by the organisation. Hence, the presence of a high proportion of flexible employees will decrease the likelihood of employers' involvement in work-family arrangements.

When the economic position of an employer is better, there are more possibilities to take risks and make investments. Consequently, an organisation will have more resources to develop work-family arrangements. Therefore, we expect a positive relation between the economic position and implementation of these arrangements. The economic position of an organisation depends largely on the situation of the industry in which it operates.

According to Auerbach (1990), organisations which have relatively 'progressive' organisational cultures become more involved in childcare. When work and family life are viewed as two separate worlds and traditional male and female roles are dominant within the organisation, it is unlikely that the increasing number of employees who combine work and caring tasks will be seen as a relevant development for the organisation (Morgan & Milliken, 1992). In that case it is also unlikely that the benefits of work-family arrangements are recognised by the employer. Consequently, less arrangements are expected in organisations with a more traditional culture.

We have presented a theoretical model to address the question of why some employers implement work-family arrangements and others do not. In figure 9.2 the model is summarised. The model is based on the assumption that employers are decision-making actors. They have the choice to implement work-family arrangements, or not. We assume that employers will implement these arrangements if the benefits exceed the costs. The alternative chosen by employers will depend on constraints faced by them. As a result of constraints, the costs and benefits of work-family arrangements vary. By specifying relevant constraints, such as institutional pressure, the size of an organisation and demographic characteristics of the work-force, we are able to formulate hypotheses on the type of organisations which are more likely to introduce work-family arrangements. For example, larger organisations are more likely to develop arrangements than smaller organisations. In the next section we will discuss results from empirical research on work-family arrangements within organisations. As hardly any international comparative studies are available, we are not able to show results on institutional constraints. Therefore, we will focus on the role of organisational characteristics.

Figure 9.2 Basis structure of the explanation of work-family arrangements in organisations

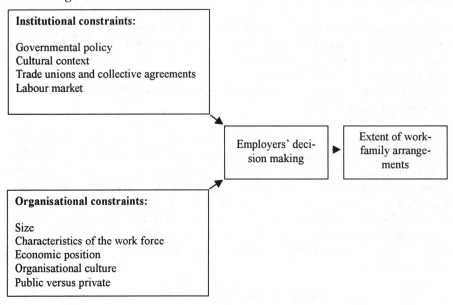

Institutional constraints:

Governmental policy
Cultural context
Trade unions and collective agreements
Labour market

Employers' decision making

Extent of work-family arrangements

Organisational constraints:

Size
Characteristics of the work force
Economic position
Organisational culture
Public versus private

9.4 EMPIRICAL RESULTS

9.4.1 Work-family arrangements within organisations in the United States

Generally, little systematic research is done on work-family arrangements within organisations. The United States of America is the only country for which a few systematic studies on implementation conditions for work-family arrangements are available. We will discuss the results briefly.

Most research shows that large organisations are more likely to provide work-family arrangements than small organisations (Auerbach, 1990; Morgan & Milliken, 1992; Galinsky, 1991; Ingram & Simons, 1995; Goodstein, 1994). The proportion of female employees also seems relevant, though different results are found. In some research the proportion of women has a positive relationship to the existence of work-family arrangements (Auerbach, 1990; Goodstein, 1994), in other studies this relationship is not found (Ingram & Simons, 1995; Morgan & Milliken, 1992; Glass & Fujimoto, 1995). The suggestion is that the position of women within the labour force is of importance. Organisations with a relatively large share of women in higher, managerial positions seem to provide work-family arrangements more often than organisations where female employment consists mainly of lower skilled jobs (Ingram & Simons, 1995; Glass & Fujimoto, 1995).

Furthermore, there are differences between industries. Public organisations are more likely to develop work-family arrangements than private sector companies. Within the private sector, arrangements are more common in the services and finance industry compared to the construction and manufacturing industry (Auerbach, 1990; Morgan & Milliken, 1992; Galinsky, 1991).

The degree of unionisation is often included in analyses. In most cases more work-family arrangements are found in non-unionised organisations (Auerbach, 1990; Galinsky, 1991; Glass & Fujimoto, 1995). This could be explained by the fact that these arrangements are mostly found in growth sectors of the economy. These sectors are traditionally not highly organised. Sometimes it is suggested that employers implement arrangements to avoid unionisation. However, there is no evidence that supports this hypothesis (Auerbach, 1990; Kamerman & Kahn, 1987). It is possible that a survey in the Netherlands would show different results, because of the different role of trade unions.

Limited attention is paid to the role of organisational culture. According to Auerbach (1990), companies that have relatively progressive employment policies and philosophies are more likely to develop work-family arrangements. Morgan & Milliken (1992) include the perception of managers in their research and ask whether the respondents consider work-family issues as a relevant development for their organisation. When work-family issues are considered relevant, the organisation has developed more facilities for workers with caring tasks. However, a more elaborate investigation on the role of organisation culture is lacking.

According to Glass & Fujimoto (1995) the influence of organisational characteristics can vary across different types of work-family arrangements. For instance, they found a positive relationship between firm size and the number of leave and childcare benefits, but a negative one with flexible working patterns. They also noted that childcare arrangements appear to be institutionalised more than work schedule policies. Glass & Fujimoto state that the different types of work-family arrangements vary in their consequences for employers. In most cases childcare arrangements imply that the care of children is performed by others than the parents. As such, these arrangements help to increase the availability of working parents in the workplace. In this way, childcare arrangements increase labour supply. Flexible working patterns, however, have the potential to decrease labour supply. Such patterns offer employees the possibility of reducing their working hours or adjusting these to their family situation. Moreover, flexible working schedules can lead to an increase of employee control and a decrease in the ability of managers to monitor hours and productivity directly. A reason for not developing flexible working patterns can be that employers do not want to lose managerial control (Glass & Fujimoto, 1995).

157

9.4.2 Work-family arrangements within organisations in the Netherlands

Before describing empirical findings on work-family arrangements in Dutch organisations, we will present a few general numbers. Compared to other West-European countries, the participation of Dutch women in the labour market was quite low until fairly recently, but is now increasing. In 1980, 30 percent of women aged 15-64 had a paid job of at least 12 hours per week, whereas in 1994 this percentage was 42 (SZW, 1995). A striking characteristic of the Dutch labour market is that a large number of women work part-time. Almost 70 percent of working women have a job of less than 35 hours (CBS, 1996). In Europe, the Netherlands has the largest share of (female as well as male) part-time workers in the labour force (Plantenga, 1995). The possibility of working part-time facilitates the combination of paid work with family tasks. One can state that this arrangement is widespread in the Netherlands. However, the possibility of working part-time is often limited to employees in non-managerial jobs.

Are other arrangements that support the combination of paid and unpaid work offered by Dutch organisations? Based on 14 case-studies of organisations known as 'family-friendly', Van Stigt (1994) suggests that work-family arrangements are often rather marginal. Most of these organisations provide childcare. Furthermore, in the Netherlands, employees are entitled to take parental leave during a certain period of time. In about half of the organisations the legal entitlement is increased. However, in some cases both childcare and extended parental leave are only available to female employees. Other arrangements are hardly provided. In some cases informal arrangements for leave for family reasons exist, but there is no guarantee that employees can take up this leave. As already stated, part-time work is quite common in the Netherlands. However, this arrangement is often limited to employees in non-managerial jobs. This is also the case for most of the organisations in Van Stigt's study: requests from employees in higher/management positions for part-time work are seldom honoured.

The results of other studies correspond to those of Van Stigt. A representative study on firms with more than 100 employees in the private sector shows that in 1990 less than one-fifth of these firms had an arrangement for childcare or leave benefits. The possibility of taking a short period of leave for sudden family problems was a facility in 35 percent of the firms. The results indicate that work-family arrangements are more common in larger firms (with more than 500 employees) than in smaller ones (100-500 employees). The chance that an organisation offers work-family arrangements also increases when these are part of the collective agreement that applies to the firm (SZW, 1992).[3] Research on organisations in the north of the Netherlands shows that organisations with a relatively highly qualified workforce provide childcare arrangements more often than organisations in which the employees' average level of education is lower. Secondly, larger organisations provide childcare more often than smaller organisations (CMK, 1995).

The available evidence suggests that work-family arrangements are not widespread among employers. The same conclusion applies to collective agreements. In the 1990s, several research projects focused on the provision of work-family arrangements within collective agreements (SZW, 1992; DCA, 1993; DCA, 1994; Tijdens & Lieon, 1993). The most recent study analyses collective agreements made in 1994 (Sloep, 1996). Provisions on part-time work are the most common work-family arrangements: 48 percent of the agreements include a concrete measure. In most cases these measures involve equal treatment between full-timers and part-timers, or the right to work part-time if this is not in conflict with organisational interests. Measures on childcare are part of 38 percent of the analysed agreements. However, the scope and degree of the measures vary from financial support to providing information about childcare options. Leave for family reasons is not very common, only a few collective agreements offer time off for sudden caring problems at home (12 percent). About 36 percent of the agreements supplement the right to parental leave. In most cases this means that social security entitlements continue during this leave. Only one collective agreement offers a (partly) paid leave.

In general, the trade union takes the initiative to include work-family issues in the negotiations. Although emancipation is part of the policy of trade unions, work-family arrangements are not high priority. When agreement is reached about the main issues of the negotiation, work-family arrangements often disappear from the agenda (Sloep, 1996).

9.5   NEW FINDINGS

Relatively little is known about the extent in which Dutch organisations are dealing with their employees' care responsibilities. Therefore, new data were collected. Information from two sources was used as an indicator of the presence of work-family arrangements: social-annual reports and personnel advertisements. Social-annual reports provide information on the social policy of an organisation. Personnel advertisements often provide information on conditions of employment. We are aware that these sources are not completely reliable: when no information is given on work-family arrangements, this does not necessarily mean these are not

---

[3] It is striking that a considerable number of organisations has not implemented the work-family arrangements which are part of the collective agreement which applies to the organisation. One reason is that some organisations do not know the content of the collective agreements. Other organisations do not provide arrangements despite the fact that they are aware of the collective agreement. The reason remains unclear (SZW, 1992).

available. However, it can be argued that subjects in social reports reflect issues which are of importance to the organisation. Also, if conditions with regard to work-family arrangements are stated in advertisements, this indicates the organisation recognises the importance of such conditions to (some) employees. Therefore, these sources are interesting in defining differences between organisations.

Social annual reports
Every year FEM, a Dutch financial economic magazine, publishes the top 100 firms with highest net turnover (Hers, 1995). We phoned the 1994 top 100 and asked each one if it publishes a social annual report. If not, or if it was not made public we asked if any information on the organisation's social policy was provided in the financial annual report. [4], In most reports, however, this was not the case. One organisation could not be traced, so the total number of firms we approached was 99. We also took a sample of three of the 25 largest banks and three of the 25 largest insurance companies (according to Dun & Bradstreet International, 1995). This was done because banks and insurance companies are excluded from the FEM top 100. The total sample consisted of 105 organisations. Of these organisations, 53 published a social annual report. Eventually, 41 of the 53 organisations which publish a social annual report sent one, a response rate of 77 percent.[5] Each report was analysed with regard to information on work-family arrangements. In 21 of the 41 reports, information is found about such arrangements (51 percent); in 20 reports no information was given. Table 9.1 shows how many social reports provide information on work-family arrangements, classified by industry. Half of the organisations in the manufacturing and transport/trade sector which publish a social annual report provide information on work-family arrangements. Five of the six reports analysed in the service industry do so, whereas organisations in the construction industry provide no information at all.

Table 9.1 Work-family arrangements in social annual reports across industries (n=41)

industry	information on work-family arrangements	no information
manufacturing	13	12
transport/trade	3	3
construction industry	0	4
services	5	1
total	21	20

---

[4] Though works councils have a right to be informed about the social policy, organisations are not obliged to publish a social annual report.

[5] Of the remaining 12 organisations, the report was no longer available in one case and in two cases, the report was still in press. Nine organisations promised to send the report but did not.

Most of the 21 organisations which provide information on work-family arrangements in their social-annual reports describe only one arrangement (12). Five organisations describe two arrangements, and four organisations provide information on three different arrangements. It appears that most of the information is on the provision of childcare (16 reports) and policy on part-time work (nine reports). Three organisations have introduced a form of flexibilisation with regard to days off. Employees can save days in order to take a longer (possibly parental) leave or they can buy or sell a few extra days. Two reports contain information on parental leave. They present figures about the use of this leave. Finally, four arrangements are mentioned only once; career-break[6], job-sharing, shortening of the overall working week, and flexible working hours. Table 9.2 summarises the types of arrangements on which social reports across different industries provided information.

Table 9.2 Type of work-family arrangements in social annual reports across industries (n=41)[7]

industry	part-time work	childcare	cafeteria Plan	parental leave	other
manufacturing	7	9	1	1	0
transport/trade	0	2	2	0	2
construction industry	0	0	0	0	0
services	2	5	0	1	2
total	9	16	3	2	4

It must be stated that it often remains unclear whether the arrangements are meant to facilitate the combination of work and family responsibilities and whether the arrangements are structural. Sometimes arrangements are meant to serve other goals. In particular, the possibility of working part-time is not always related to work-family issues; a few organisations use part-time work to reallocate employment *within* the organisation.

To conclude, the number of arrangements which organisations offer is limited. No information at all is given on arrangements such as flexible working hours and possibilities for working at home. This does not necessarily mean that these arrangements do not exist. If they do, one can ask whether they are part of a formal policy. Compared to other subjects, such as pension schemes, sick leave or sav-

---

[6] The report mentions maternity leave but did not clarify the exact meaning. We assume that this leave is a form of career break in which the mother stops working temporarily, but has the right to return to the job.
[7] Social annual reports can contain information on more than one arrangement.

ings-account arrangements, work-family arrangements are less frequently mentioned.

Personnel advertisements
A second indicator for the extent to which organisations deal with work-family issues is the information in personnel advertisements, in particular the information on conditions of employment. Advertisements were taken from two different newspapers, *Intermediair* and the *Volkskrant*. *Intermediair* is a free weekly magazine for people with higher vocational or university training. The jobs offered in this magazine are mostly technical, economic and commercial. Two editions from the month of September 1995 were analysed. The *Volkskrant* is a national, daily newspaper. Most of the personnel advertisements are published on Saturday. This newspaper was chosen because it contains a lot of advertisements from the health and welfare sectors, so it supplements those in *Intermediair*. Two (Saturday) editions were analysed. The dates corresponded to those of *Intermediair*.

Most of the personnel advertisements offer higher-level positions, so the sample is not representative. We assume that organisations use other recruitment channels for lower-level jobs. It is also the case that advertisements in which lower-level jobs are offered contain little information on conditions of employment.

All the advertisements were numbered and checked with regard to appearance in both newspapers. The advertisements were analysed according to a checklist. In total, 746 advertisements were analysed; 363 from *Intermediair* (48.7 percent) and 383 from *Volkskrant* (51.3 percent). The number of organisations offering the jobs could not be determined precisely. Not all organisations do their own recruiting but make use of recruitment agencies. This was the case in 156 of the 746 advertisements (20.9 percent). In nearly half of the cases the customer, i.e. the organisation, is mentioned but in 77 advertisements the employer remains unknown. Leaving the unknown organisations aside and controlling for the fact that some organisations published more than one advertisement, 570 organisations were counted.

What conditions of employment do organisations offer in personnel advertisements? As is shown in the following table, 44 percent of the organisations do not mention any conditions, 24 percent state that the conditions of employment are according to collective agreements, 11 percent simply state that the conditions are good/excellent, while 21 percent specifies them. Overall, it can be stated that organisations hardly specify conditions of employment.

Table 9.3 Conditions of employment stated in personnel advertisements (as percentage of the total number of organisations) (n=570)

conditions of employment	number of organisations
no conditions	252 (44)
good/excellent	60 (11)
according to collective agreement	137 (24)
specified conditions	121 (21)
total	570 (100)

On average the 121 organisations that specify conditions of employment in their advertisements mention two conditions. Table 9.4 summarises these conditions. The types of conditions mentioned are diverse. Most relate to financial issues (7). Only four relate to conditions that facilitate the combination of paid and unpaid work. It is striking that the provision of childcare is the most frequently mentioned condition.

Table 9.4 Specified conditions of employment in personnel advertisements (as percentage of the total number of organisations that specified conditions of employment; n=121)[8]

conditions of employment	number of organisations
good salary	33 (27.3)
good training possibilities	25 (20.7)
good career opportunities	22 (18.2)
attractive pension plan	17 (14.0)
pleasant working climate	21 (17.4)
company car	17 (14.0)
expense account	10 (8.3)
additional insurance	4 (3.3)
attractive savings arrangement	6 (5.0)
additional payments[9]	16 (13.2)
provision of childcare	35 (28.9)
possibility of working part-time	9 (7.4)
parental leave	9 (7.4)
flexible working hours	4 (3.3)
other conditions	15 (12.4)

[8] Organisations could mention more than one condition.

[9] Examples of additional payments are profit-sharing, bonuses, and payment of an additional month's salary (13th month).

As is shown in the following tables, the types of conditions mentioned by organisations differ across industries.

Table 9.5 *Work-family arrangements in personnel advertisements classified by industry*

industry	conditions			
	childcare	part-time work	parental leave	flex. hours
public adm.	11	3	2	2
education	7	3	6	1
welfare/health	10	1	1	1
services	7	2	0	0
total	35	9	9	4

Only organisations in public administration, education and the welfare/health sector mention work-family arrangements in their personnel advertisements. These sectors all employ a relatively high percentage of women. Organisations in the manufacturing industry only seem to provide information on conditions that relate to financial issues and career opportunities, as can be seen in table 9.6. Organisations in the service industry tend to mention both types of conditions.

Table 9.6 *Financial and career conditions in personnel advertisements classified by industry*

industry	conditions			
	good salary	training/educ.	career opp.	add. payments
manufacturing	19	6	13	4
services	13	15	7	12
education	1	0	0	0
public adm.	0	2	1	0
welfare/health	0	2	1	0
total	33	25	22	16

Work-family arrangements can be part of an equal opportunities policy in the organisation. Thirty organisations mention such a policy in their advertisements. However, no systematic relation is found with the presence of work-family arrangements.

In general, it can be stated that it is not common practice to mention conditions of employment in personnel advertisements. It is noticeable that if conditions of employment are specified, facilities that support the combination of paid and unpaid labour occur relatively frequently. This is especially the case for the provision of childcare. However, this occurrence is limited to certain industries (services, public administration, education and welfare and health). Furthermore, the selection of facilities is limited; only four different types of work-family arrangements are mentioned.

9.6   CONCLUSIONS

As far as relevant empirical results are available, the theoretical model presented in section 3 seems to be supported. Empirical research shows, for example, differences between organisations in terms of size and industry. Large organisations are more likely to introduce work-family arrangements than smaller ones, and arrangements are more common among public than private sector organisations. Data from the analysis of social annual reports and personnel advertisements confirms the differences between industries. In future research other hypotheses can be drawn from the model and should be tested empirically.

With regard to the Netherlands, research shows that work-family arrangements are not widespread. The data also suggest that part-time work and child-care arrangements are the most common types of arrangements among Dutch employers. Is it reasonable to expect that the development of work-family arrangements by Dutch employers will increase in the near future?

According to the theoretical model, besides organisational characteristics, institutional constraints, such as governmental intervention, collective agreements, and the cultural context also influence the introduction of work-family arrangements within organisations. In the Netherlands the development of work-family arrangements is seen as a shared responsibility between the government, employers and employees. The government has developed a few minimum entitlements, such as maternity and parental leave, but its policy primarily consists of recommendations and subsidies (TK, 1994-1995). As such, it can be characterised as stimulatory, leaving social partners and organisations relatively free in their decision to implement work-family arrangements. Hence, governmental pressure on employers in the Netherlands to increase the number of work-family arrangements can be considered weak.

Trade unions seem willing to include work-family arrangements in negotiations on collective agreements. In some cases this results in concrete measures. However, in most cases the scope of these measures is limited to part-time work and childcare. Other types of work-family arrangements (see figure 9.1) receive little attention. Moreover, it should be noted that a high number of organisations is still

165

without a collective agreement or has an agreement that does not include work-family arrangements.

The cultural context can also put pressure on employers. Social norms on the division of paid and unpaid labour between men and women have changed in recent decades. It has become more common for women to have a paid job too. However, the social norm which states that children should be cared for within the family is still stringent (Van Dijk, 1994). This is reflected in the high number of women working part-time. Besides the opportunity to work part-time, employers may take the view that it is not necessary to provide other arrangements. The problem is that these processes can reinforce each other. Women continue to work part-time, even if they would prefer more hours, because of the lack of facilities, whereas employers do not provide work-family arrangements because they do not see the need.

For several years there has been concern for future labour shortages of qualified employees (male and female) due to demographic developments. The birth rate is expected to remain low, which, in combination with an ageing population, would lead to a shortage of young educated people. In the United Kingdom, at the end of the 1980s, this demographic forecast was an argument for a considerable number of companies to implement work-family arrangements in order to attract and retain female personnel (Lewis et al., 1996). For the Netherlands it is expected that a shortage of labour will occur within ten to 15 years (Van Hoof & Van Doorne-Huiskes, 1995). This development could create a stimulus for employers to implement work-family arrangements in order to retain and to recruit qualified personnel. Following our theoretical model, however, we expect that this argument will be especially relevant for organisations with a large share of highly qualified personnel. This type of organisation competes on quality of goods and services. There are also employers that compete on price rather than quality. This kind of organisation often has a large share of lower-skilled jobs, which need little on-the-job training and whose turnover costs are low. Flexible use of employees can increase the competitiveness of these organisations. We have argued that the presence of a high proportion of flexible employees and/or lower skilled employees will decrease the likelihood of employers' involvement in work-family arrangements. As a result inequality in access to work-family arrangements between workers can arise: some workers have access to a wide range of facilities, whereas others have hardly any entitlements. Given the emphasis on equality in the emancipation policy of the Dutch government, one can ask if this situation is desirable.

REFERENCES

Auerbach, J.D. 1990: Employer-supported childcare as a women-responsive policy. In: *Journal of Family Issues*, 11/4, pp. 384-400.

Burg, B.I. van der, J. van Doorne-Huiskes, J.J. Schippers & J.J. Siegers. 1989: Loopbaanverschillen tussen mannen en vrouwen binnen arbeidsorganisaties. Een structureel-individualistisch verklaringsschema. In: *Sociologische gids*, 5, p. 312-323.

CBS. 1996: *Statistisch Jaarboek 1996*. Voorburg/Heerlen: CBS.

CMK. 1995: *De marktgerichte kinderopvang in Noord-Nederland, bouwstenen voor een strategische benadering*. Groningen: Centraal Meldpunt Kinderopvang voor bedrijven.

Coleman J.S. 1990: *Foundations of Social Theory*. Cambridge: Harvard University Press.

DCA. 1993: *Verlof in CAO's, een onderzoek naar de omvang van in cao's voorkomende vormen van verlof*. Den Haag: Ministerie van Sociale Zaken en Werkgelegenheid/Dienst Collectieve Arbeidsvoorwaarden (DCA).

DCA. 1994: *CAO-afspraken 1993*. Den Haag: Ministerie van Sociale Zaken en Werkgelegenheid/Dienst Collectieve Arbeidsvoorwaarden (DCA).

DiMaggio P.J. & W.W. Powell. 1983: The Iron Cage Revisited: Institutional Isomorphism and Collective Rationality in Organisational Fields. In: *American Sociological Review*, 48, pp. 147-160.

Dijk, L. van. 1994: *Choices in childcare*. Amsterdam: Thesis Publishers.

Galinsky, E. & D.E. Friedman, C.A. Hernandez. 1991: *The Corporate Reference Guide to Work-Family Programs*. New York: Families and Work Institute.

Glass, J. & T. Fujimoto. 1995: Employer characteristics and the provision of family responsive policies. In: *Work and Occupation*, 22/4, pp. 380-411.

Goodstein J.D. 1994: Institutional Pressures and Strategic Responsiveness: Employer Involvement in Work-Family Issues. In: *Academy of Management Journal*, 37/2, pp. 350-382.

Hayghe, H.V. 1988: Employers and Childcare: what roles do they play? In: *Monthly Labour Review*, september, pp. 38-44.

Hers, F. 1995: Het jaar van tien miljard. In: *Financieel Economisch Magazine* (FEM), September 1995, p. 24-34.

Hoof, J. van & A. van Doorne-Huiskes. 1995: Epilogue: emancipation at the crossroads. In: A. van Doorne-Huiskes, J. van Hoof, E. Roelofs (eds.), *Women and the European Labour Markets*. London: Paul Chapman Publishing.

Ingram P. & T. Simons. 1995: Institutional and Resource Dependence Determinants of Responsiveness to Work-family Issues. In: *Academy of Management Journal*, 38/5, pp. 1466-1482.

Kamerman, S.B. & A.J. Kahn. 1987: *The Responsive Workplace, Employers and a Changing Labor Force*. New York: Colombia University Press.

Kingston, P.W. 1990: Illusions and ignorance about the family-responsive workplace. In: *Journal of Family Issues*, 11/4, pp. 439-453.

Lewis, S. et al. 1996: Developing and implementing policies: Midland Bank's Experience. In: Lewis, S. & J. Lewis (eds.). *The work-family challenge. Rethinking employment*. London: Sage.

Lippe, T. van der. 1993: *Arbeidsverdeling tussen mannen en vrouwen*. Amsterdam: Thesis Publishers.

McLean, I. 1987: *Public Choice; an introduction.* Oxford: Basis Blackwells.

Meyer, J.W. & B. Rowan. 1991: Institutionalized Organizations: Formal Structure as Myth and Ceremony. In: W.W. Powell & P.J. DiMaggio, *The new institutionalism in organizational analysis.* Chicago: The University of Chicago Press.

Morgan H. & F.J. Milliken. 1992: Keys to Action: Understanding Differences in Organizations' Responsiveness to Work-and-Family Issues. In: *Human Resource Management,* Fall 1992, 31/3, pp. 227-248.

Moss, P. 1990: *Kinderopvang en -verzorging in de Europese gemeenschap 1985 - 1990.* Brussel: Europese Commissie/Netwerk kinderopvang.

OECD. 1991: *Shaping structural changes. The role of women.* Parijs: Organisation for Economic Co-operation and Development.

Oliver. 1991: Strategic responses to institutional processes. In: *Academy of management review,* 16, pp. 145-179.

Plantenga J. 1995: Labour-Market Participation of Women in the European Union. In: A. van Doorne-Huiskes, J. van Hoof & E. Roelofs (eds.), *Women and the European Labour Markets.* London: Paul Chapman Publishing.

Scott W.R. 1995: *Institutions and Organizations.* Thousand Oaks: Sage Publications.

Sloep, M. 1996: *Het primaat van een mannenbolwerk. Emancipatie in cao-onderhandelingen.* Den Haag: Emancipatieraad.

Stigt, J. van. 1994: *Zorgende werknemers, werkgevers een zorg.* Den Haag: Emancipatieraad.

SZW. 1992: *Emancipatie in arbeidsorganisaties.* Den Haag: Ministerie van Sociale Zaken en Werkgelegenheid.

SZW. 1995: *Women in the Netherlands 1995. Facts and figures.* Centraal Bureau voor de Statistiek en het Ministerie voor Sociale Zaken en Werkgelegenheid, Den Haag.

Tijdens, K. & S. Lieon (red.). 1993: *Kinderopvang in Nederland - organisatie en financiering.* Utrecht: Van Arkel.

TK. 1994-1995: *Combineerbaarheid van betaalde arbeid met andere verantwoordelijkheden.* Nota om de kwaliteit van arbeid en zorg: investeren in verlof. Tweede Kamer, vergaderjaar 1994-1995, 24 332, nr. 1.

Wolcott, I. 1991: *Work and Family. Employers' Views.* Melbourne: Australian Institute of Family Studies.

ACKNOWLEDGEMENTS

We would like to thank Catherine Hakim and Anneke van Doorne-Huiskes for their valuable comments on an earlier version of this paper.

BIOGRAPHICAL NOTE

Laura den Dulk studied at the Erasmus University Rotterdam. She is presently a PhD student at the Netherlands School for Social and Economic Policy Research (AWSB). Her current research is an international comparison of work-family arrangements in Europe which is partly funded by the Netherlands Organisation of Scientific Research (NWO).

Chantal Remery studied sociology at Utrecht University. She is completing her PhD at the Erasmus University Rotterdam. Subject of the thesis is the impact of equal opportunity policies in Dutch organisations. Publications include articles on job evaluation systems, women's labour force participation, and sociology of science.

10 Are part-time and full-time jobs really so different?

Explaining women's working time from family, housework, individual and work characteristics

Kea Tijdens

10.1 INTRODUCTION

Part-time jobs are strongly associated with female labour. In the European Union, four out of five part-timers are women, and the majority of these women perform part-time work because of their domestic responsibilities (McRae, 1995; Hakim, 1996). Part-time work is increasing. In the ten oldest EU countries the share of part-timers in the female labour force grew from 27% in 1983 to 31% in 1991 (Plantenga, 1995).

Part-time work is said to cause a segmentation in the female labour force, because it is associated with job insecurity, awkward working hours, and restrictions on movement to full-time work (Meulders et al, 1991). It has been argued that segregation processes differ between the full-time and the part-time segments in the female labour force, resulting in higher levels of segregation in part-time employment (Hakim, 1993). In general, part-time work would reinforce women's disadvantaged position at work. Some of these issues have been questioned by Fagan and Rubery (1996). For the Netherlands, the dichotomy between part-timers and full-timers will be questioned in this paper.

The key issue here is the nature of part-time employment. Are part-time jobs a management imperative or are they created because women request reductions in their working hours in order to cope with their domestic responsibilities? McRae (1995) distinguishes between a corporate strategy where employers introduce part-time work for economic or organisational reasons and an individual strategy, where they agree to accommodate the requests of individual workers who prefer reduced working hours. Establishments that follow a corporate strategy are very likely to recruit part-timers on the external labour market, whereas establishments that follow the individual strategy are likely to employ former full-time employees in part-time jobs. A survey in eight countries of the European Union shows that part-time jobs are introduced because of management needs (41%), employees' wishes (36%), or both reasons of equal importance (22%) (Delsen, 1995).

Time allocation and gender, Kea Tijdens, Anneke van Doorne-Huiskes & Tineke Willemsen (eds.), Tilburg University Press, 1997, © Kea G. Tijdens

The Netherlands is well-known for the highest part-time rate among female workers in the European Union (OECD, 1994). This has been steadily increasing since the late 1970s. In 1995, almost three out of every five working women worked between 12 to 34 hours a week (58%), whereas in 1988 this percentage was 50%. It is less well-known that in the Netherlands full-time and part-time jobs hardly differ in terms of pay levels and working conditions (Plantenga and Van Velzen, 1993). Their findings will be supported in this article.

By stressing the dichotomy between full-time and part-time work the dispersion of working hours in the female work force slowed down. This article aims to explain women's working hours from family, housework, individual and work characteristics. Section 2 sketches briefly the development of part-time work during the 1980s and 1990s. Previous studies are reviewed in section 3. In section 4, four models of factors which may explain women's working time are discussed, covering both supply and demand characteristics. Research methodology and data are provided in section 5. In section 6 the descriptive statistics are presented. Section 7 contains the results of regression analyses explaining women's working time as well as the results of logistic regressions which are used to predict who is working in short, medium-sized, and long part-time jobs and who is working full-time. Conclusions are drawn in section 8.

10.2 PART-TIME WORK IN THE NETHERLANDS

During the post-war period women were supposed to contribute to the rebuilding of society by setting up a family, and many of them did, as the baby boom in the late 1940s and early 1950s shows (this section is based on Bernasco, 1994; Tijdens, 1995). The vast majority of women left the labour market on the day of their marriage to become full-time, permanent housewives. The breadwinner system was set up in industrial relations, in wage policies as well as in general attitudes towards gender roles; male workers were supposed to earn the family wage. By the 1950s, the breadwinner system had become the dominant pattern. Yet, in the 1960s, the very rapid growth of the manufacturing and service sectors generated an increasing demand for labour in the female-dominated occupations. To overcome labour shortage, employers recruited housewives with grown children for part-time work, though married women's participation stayed below 10%. By the 1970s women's labour supply behaviour had changed. Increasingly, women preferred to remain in the labour market until they gave birth to their first child. These women mostly had changed their full-time job into a part-time job, in order to have time for household duties.

At the turn of the 1970s, women who gave birth increasingly preferred to continue working on condition that their working hours would be reduced. There may be three reasons for this. Firstly, high unemployment levels at the time reduced women's chances of re-entering the workforce with a comparable job.

Secondly, an increasing share of the female work force performed skilled jobs. Thus, the opportunity costs of a homemaker career increased. Thirdly, periods away from the labour force would cause loss of skills and thus depreciation of human capital, which would depress women's wage levels at re-entry. In growing numbers female workers succeeded in requesting employers to reduce working hours. Childcare was realised, but only informally. It was not until the late 1980s that political pressure led to the establishment of day-care centres.

In the 1970s and 1980s, growing numbers of housewives with grown children desired to re-enter the labour force. These women preferred part-time jobs over full-time jobs for three reasons. Firstly, in general, breadwinners' wages were sufficient for family needs, although from the late 1980s the breadwinner system has been under pressure. Secondly, the absence of extended families, a highly cultivated motherhood culture, insufficient childcare facilities for children over 4 years, and the absence of domestic help influenced women's preferences to work part-time instead of full-time. Thirdly, part-time jobs became increasingly available.

Increasingly, employers have adapted to women's requests for reduced working hours, and the majority of these women remained in the job they already had (Tijdens, 1997a, 1997b). In the early 1980s, some employers allowed a reduction in the individual's working time as their main strategy against union demands for a shorter working week. Then, increasingly, employers preferred skilled female employees to remain working part-time rather than not working at all because of their investments in women's training and qualifications. From the late 1980s, employers were pressed by the unions who in turn came under pressure from their own women's groups. In collective bargaining agreements were increasingly reached on the principle of reducing individual working hours when requested. In the early 1990s, some categories of employers were eager to bring staffing levels in line with the supply of work; part-time jobs fitted this strategy perfectly. Yet nowadays, particularly in health care and education, the number of part-timers has grown so much that the organisational span of control limits further growth in part-time work. Finally, to fight unemployment, government put pressure on employers to create part-time jobs. Nowadays, the dominant strategy of Dutch working women wanting to have a baby is the part-time strategy: three out of four prefer to continue their job, but the vast majority of them only want to continue if they can reduce working hours, usually by half (Tijdens et al., 1994). Furthermore, women who received reduced hours before are now requesting an expansion in working hours.

Thus, part-time jobs are decreasingly introduced because of an employment strategy and employees' wishes. For example, in the banking sector because of part-time work was predominantly key-entry, whereas nowadays it can be found in nearly all jobs. Among the employees asking for reduced hours, skilled women are over represented. Nowadays, part-time jobs are no longer the marginalised jobs they once were, nor is part-time work increasing predominantly in low-paid and low-status female-dominated occupations. Indeed, the evidence shows the contrary. Part-time work enables lifetime employment with the same employer and thus to tenure benefits. If women are in a disadvantaged position because of domestic responsibilities, part-time work reduces the need to seek a new job after a spell out of the labour market. For the female work force, hourly wages and job security hardly differ between part-timers and full-timers, although between sectors some differences may be found.

The acceptance of the reduction of working hours did not happen simultaneously in all industries and occupations. Part-time work was accepted in health care and education at a very early stage, whereas in the manufacturing industry and in secretarial work it was accepted later. The latter is perhaps best explained by managers' strong preferences for their secretary to be present full-time. Therefore, we expect variation in women's working hours between sectors and occupations.

10.3   EXPLAINING WOMEN'S WORKING TIME IN PREVIOUS STUDIES

Reviewing the literature on working hours results in the conclusion that many studies present descriptive statistics based on labour force surveys. Some describe developments over time, for example concerning part-time work or statutory working hours, others present recent cross-sectional data. Few studies focus on instantaneous time use, i.e. hours during the day (Hamermesh, 1996).

In the literature that aims to explain women's working hours, economic models are used to explain households' working time based on wage rates, leisure time and non-market time, whereas empirical findings explain women's working time from household-related characteristics. Research has clearly established that women's weekly working hours are negatively related to the presence of young children, according to Hamermesh (1996). For the US, Shelton (1992) finds that marital status has a negative impact on women's working time, and so has the number of children and the presence of children aged 0 to 4. Furthermore, a curvilinear relationship exists between age and working time: up to a certain age working time decreases with age, from that point it increases with age. Women's education had a positive impact on working time.

As part-time rates vary substantially between the EU countries, it is assumed that the variables influencing women's working also hours do. We will focus on Dutch studies. Henkens et al. (1994) based their findings on several large, cross-sectional housing-need studies. Weekly working hours were influenced negatively by the number of children present in the household. Furthermore, the younger the children, the fewer hours of paid work. Other effects were measured as well, but the findings varied slightly between the years studied. Neither wage rate nor the net remaining household income had the same effects in all studies.

They differed for example between married and cohabiting women, leading to the conclusion that cohabiting female employees behave with more economic independence than their married female counterparts. Furthermore, the impact of age was not the same. A study by Bernasco (1993), based on working history data, found a high possibility of working-hour reduction in households with at least one child under five and a high possibility of working-hour increase if the youngest child is over five. For Belgium, Henkens et al. (1992) found the number of children had a negative influence on married women's working time, but the children's age did not influence working time. Women's wage rates also had a negative impact on their working time, whereas the remaining household income had no impact.

To conclude, the empirical findings show that women's working time might be influenced by different variables. Yet, the impact of the number of children is negative in all analyses and so is the impact of young children. The impact of women's wage rates varies between studies. Some findings indicate a negative influence, some show a positive, and others reveal no influence at all. Work characteristics such as sector or occupation are not used to explain individual working time, which is surprising considering it is so important in the discussion on the part-time / full-time divide.

10.4   MODEL AND UNDERLYING ASSUMPTIONS

A model with four clusters of explanatory variables will be used to explain women's working hours. It will be discussed here, but first some remarks will be made about a major determining factor, i.e. unpaid household time. The dependent variable is working time. This variable will be defined in section 5.

Household time as such is not considered as an independent variable for two reasons. Firstly, we are not sure whether paid working time depends on unpaid working time; the reverse relationship might also be true. Secondly, in housework, both task performance and task frequency are not set like they are in business; there is neither supervision nor job-related training. This means that household time can vary substantially, depending very much on individual performance criteria. Therefore, instead of household time we will use its indicators, which lie predominantly in the family cycle. By doing so, for each phase in the cycle we assume a given burden of household tasks, which can be relieved by various factors, such as domestic help.

Cluster 1 incorporates the family cycle. The underlying idea is that a woman's paid working time is what remains from the time she needs for her household duties which are assumed to depend upon family cycle. If she cares for a husband or for children, her household duties will increase. If the children grow older, household duties per child will decrease. Therefore, the independent variables in-

175

clude partner (0=no, 1=yes), number of children and a dummy variable for the presence of a youngest child in a particular age group, i.e. youngest child aged between 0 and 3 (0=no, 1=yes), youngest child aged between 4 and 12 (0=no, 1=yes), no children and youngest child 13 years and over being the reference categories.

Cluster 2 incorporates strategies which may reduce time spent on household work, therefore leaving more time for paid work. In this cluster the independent variables include the help of a cleaning lady (0=no, 1=yes) and substantial help of a partner (0=no, 1=yes, when the husbands' help is 25% or over of the total time spent on household duties). Single women are coded 0 for partners' time spent on household duties. The size and characteristics of the house will influence the time spent on household work, i.e. to clean a ten-room residence takes more time than to clean a one-room apartment. Therefore, it is assumed that women will spend less household time when living in an apartment (0=no, 1=yes). One more variable is taken into account, which we will call a woman's attitude towards household work: it can be assumed that women who have worked continuously perform their household work more efficiently or that they minimise their household work compared to women who have re-entered the labour force. Therefore, we include a variable 'worked continuously' (0=no, 1=yes).

Cluster 3 incorporates the individual characteristics. The underlying idea is that women's working hours also depend upon individual preferences. Here we will consider the independent variables including age (age and age square/100), and the highest grade of formal schooling completed, ranging from 0 to 18 years. Naturally, individual preferences do include the household income. Two independent variables are used. Firstly, has the partner an income which is sufficient for a reasonable standard of living? A variable is used indicating a monthly additional net income of at least NLG 2,000 in the household (0=no, 1=yes). Secondly, a woman's wage rate is assumed to influence working hours. Its impact is not unambiguous. A high wage rate might go along with many working hours, because it might indicate job satisfaction. A low wage rate also might go along with many hours because of financial needs.

Cluster 4 incorporates demand characteristics. It is assumed that employment strategies vary both between sectors and between occupations. The independent variables include dummies for the sectors, i.e. manufacturing industry (0=no, 1=yes), commercial services (0=no, 1=yes), banking and insurance (0=no, 1=yes), the health sector (0=no, 1=yes), with agriculture/building industry/public sector as the reference category. This cluster also includes dummy variables for occupation. In the survey, the occupations have been classified according to the two-digit level of the International Standard Classification of Occupations (ISCO-1968), in which over 80 occupational classes are distinguished. The largest classes for female employment have been clustered into four groups, i.e.

176

nursing occupations (0=no, 1=yes), clerical workers (0=no, 1=yes), shop assistants and cashiers (0=no, 1=yes), caring and cleaning occupations (0=no, 1=yes), with the remaining occupations as the reference category.

The partners' working time is not incorporated into the model. Of course, it can be argued that the couple's total number of working hours determines their family income and, therefore, the two of them will aim for household equivalence. This argument has been used by economists in household production models (see e.g. Becker, 1979), as well as by the women's movement, arguing that if the male partner would spend less time on paid work, he could spend more time on household work. Yet, several studies have shown that this 'theory of communicating vessels' does not hold (Van der Lippe, 1993). Furthermore, incorporating the partners' working time causes problems because the upper tier of the distribution of working hours is limited by statutory regulations, i.e. about 95% of the male employees have a contractual full-time working week and the remaining 5% work part-time, mainly because they are students. Thus, men's working hours show very little variance. Among the full-time male employees a growing group, mainly in high-level jobs, works more than 40 hours a week, but is not paid overtime. It is assumed that they do so because of high work commitment or because they see the extra working hours as career investments. Finally, women themselves do not consider their partner's working time to be negotiable. If women prefer their partner to work fewer hours, it is not because they themselves wish to work more hours, but because they think their partner works too hard, according to the answers given in the Labour and Care survey used in this article.

10.5   RESEARCH METHOD AND CONCEPTS

For this study, a survey called Labour and Care was conducted. With a random dial technique a random sample was drawn from a very large data base containing telephone numbers provided by Dutch Telecom. Altogether, 6,292 telephone numbers were dialled. In 2,741 cases the interviewers could not get through due to closed numbers, faxes, no reply or because the number was engaged on three occasions. In 3,551 cases the interviewer was able to speak to someone. 35% of the calls found no woman aged 25 to 45 living in the home or a possible respondent was unable to speak Dutch. This left 2,297 telephone calls in the targeted group, of which 38% refused the interview. In the end, 1,420 women aged 25 to 45 were interviewed, of whom two out of three had a job (N=899). This group is used for the analyses. On average, the telephone call lasted around 15 minutes. Additional information about the survey can be found in Tijdens et al. (1994).
The choice of a survey among women aged 25-45 is based on the assumption that this generation, born in the first two decades after World War II, has taken different decisions about withdrawing from and re-entering the labour force, compared to the women who were born one or two generations before. The double-earner family is found more frequently among women aged 25-45, whereas

the single-earner family is mainly to be found among the 45 to 65 age group. Therefore, women aged 25-45 are more likely to develop time saving strategies to combine paid labour and care much more often than older women.

In the survey, detailed questions were posed about household composition, time spent on household duties, domestic help, etc. The working women were questioned about their working hours, overtime, occupation, net monthly income, and why they were satisfied with their actual working time or, if they preferred other working hours, why they were not satisfied. Furthermore, questions were posed about the partners' time allocation pattern, including a partner's help in the household.

There are several problems concerning the measurement of working time. The first problem is that for the weekly working time we have to distinguish between actual working time in the previous week and contractual working time. By asking about actual working time, the employed women, the self-employed women and the co-operating wives can be included in the analyses. By asking about contractual time, only employed persons were able to answer. For this article the contractual time for women workers and the actual time for self-employed and co-operating women were used.

The second problem is that the full-time working week is shifting due to working hour reductions in collective bargaining agreements. For decades the working week was 40 hours with a few exceptions, for example shift work. When the survey was held, a full-time working week could vary between 36 and 40 hours. This makes it difficult to identify who works part-time. Statistics Netherlands uses two definitions. Firstly, full-time or part-time work can be self-defined. Secondly, part-time work is considered less than 35 hours per week, according to contractual working time. In this chapter full-time jobs are defined as jobs of 36 hours or more per week. Long part-time jobs are between 24-35 hours a week, medium-sized part-time jobs are 16-23 hours and short part-time jobs are 16 hours or less.

10.6   DESCRIBING WOMEN'S WORKING TIME

First of all, descriptive findings will be reported, regression results will be presented in section 7. Tables 10.1 and 10.2 show that the number of working hours vary substantially for working women aged 25-45. On average, they work 27 hours per week. Women without a partner and without children work on average 38 hours a week, whereas women with a partner but no children work 34 hours. Women with children under four work only 20 hours, while working hours increase when the youngest children are older. Table 10.2 shows that, compared to the group without children or with adult children, the group with a youngest child under 13 is unlikely to work full-time, whereas they are more likely to work in a

178

short part-time job. These differences are significant at the 1% level. From these tables, it is indicated that family cycle is important when predicting working hours.

Cluster 2 incorporates strategies that might reduce household time. Four variables are examined. Women with domestic help work on average nearly six hours more than women who perform most of their household duties themselves. Women whose partners perform quite a substantial part of the household duties work on average nearly three more hours than women whose partners do not. Women who live in an apartment work seven more hours compared to women living in a larger house. Women who have worked continuously work on average nine more hours than re-entrant women, who are assumed not to have an efficiency attitude towards household work. Therefore, the results indicate that this group of variables also might have explanatory power.

Cluster 3 incorporates individual preferences: age, education, wage rate and additional income in the family. As expected, age shows a curvilinear relationship to working hours. Nearly half of the women aged 25-29 can be found in the full-time category, whereas women aged 30-34 are over represented in the category of jobs under 15 hours a week. Regarding education, the tables show that the longer the education, the more working hours. This relationship is particularly striking in the category of short part-time jobs. Women with little education are more likely to work more in short part-time jobs, whereas women with medium-term levels of education are over represented in the longer part-time category, and women with most education are more likely to work in full-time jobs. Women who do not have an additional income in the family of at least NLG 2,000 work on average three hours more than women who do have a sufficient additional income in the family. Women's average net hourly wage is NLG 15.13 (s.d. 4.83). From the part-time / full-time segmentation thesis significant wage differentials could be expected. Yet, although the women in the shortest part-time category earn the least on average (NLG 14.84) and the women in the longest part-time category the most (NLG 15.48), the differences are not significant. To conclude, within this cluster we will examine age, age square, education and additional family income for its explanatory power.

Cluster 4 incorporates sector and occupation. Regarding sectoral differences, the average working time does not vary substantially between the sectors, but substantial differences emerge in the distribution over working time categories. In the manufacturing and cleaning industry both the shortest part-time and full-time categories are over represented. The highest share of full-timers is to be found in the banking and insurance sector. In the health sector and in the public service, most women work in the long part-time category. These differences are significant at a 5% level. Turning to the occupational classes, the average working hours differ substantially. In the caring and cleaning occupations women work 18 hours a week, whereas the clerical workers do 28 hours and the miscellaneous group works as many as 29 hours. The caring and cleaning occupations are most

179

likely to be found in the short part-time category. The clerical workers and the miscellaneous group are found predominantly in the full-time category, working hardly at all in the short part-time jobs. Both the nursing and the teaching occupations can be found predominantly in the longest part-time category. The differences are significant at a 0.1% level. We conclude that sectoral and occupational differences contribute to the explanation of working hours.

Before continuing the statistical results, the reasons given by women to interviewers for their satisfaction or dissatisfaction with current working time will be sketched briefly. Two out of three women were satisfied with their current working time. Working hours do not differ significantly between the satisfied and the dissatisfied women. Although satisfaction does not differ between women with and without children, the reasons given for their satisfaction did differ. Four out of every five satisfied women without children said they were satisfied with their working hours because they matched the income they needed; slightly over half said their actual working time left them sufficient time for household duties. The satisfied women with children gave various reasons. More than nine out of ten women said their current working time left them enough time to care for their children and seven out of ten said that enough time was left for household duties. Only half of them stated their current working time was in accordance with their need for an income. For women without children, the optimal number of working hours for income is the major argument, whereas the major argument for women with children is household time, including childcare.

One out of three women was not satisfied with her current working time, preferring either less or more working hours. Those who prefer more hours on average have a working week of nearly 17 hours, and those who prefer less, work on average 36 hours. It appears that the re-entrant women particularly prefer more working hours, whereas the women without children and the women who have worked continuously, prefer less hours. One can conclude that it is the current variance in working hours that does not satisfy the 25-45 age group. They prefer to work less in short part-time jobs and less in full-time jobs. Women's preferences converge at part-time jobs between 16 and 35 hours a week.

Table10.1 Average working hours, standard deviation, distribution, F or T-value (N=899)

	Mean	SD	Distribution	F- or T-value
Cluster 1 Family cycle				
No partner, no children	37.6	7.8	9.5%	
Partner, no children	34.3	8.8	24.9%	
Youngest child ≤ 3 year	20.3	13.5	19.4%	
Youngest child 4-12 year	21.5	11.5	30.0%	
Youngest child ≥ 13 year	25.6	12.4	16.2%	74.8***

	Mean	SD	Distribution	F- or T-value

Cluster 2 Reducing household time
Cleaning lady

	Mean	SD	Distribution	F- or T-value
No	25.2	12.7	74.7%	
Yes	31.0	12.5	25.3%	-6.0***

Partner's help > 25%

No	25.6	13.7	59.7%	
Yes	28.2	11.4	40.3%	-3.0**

Living in an apartment

No	25.9	12.9	89.2%	
Yes	33.2	10.8	10.8%	-5.3***

Continuously worked

No	20.2	12.2	29.4%	
Yes	29.3	12.2	70.6%	-10.2***

Cluster 3 Individual characteristics

Age 25-30 year	30.8	11.9	28.1%	
Age 31-35 year	24.4	13.5	23.5%	
Age 36-40 year	24.8	13.0	23.9%	
Age 41-45 year	25.9	12.2	24.5%	13.2***

Education

Low	24.6	13.5	34.3%	
Medium	26.8	12.9	39.9%	
High	29.7	11.3	25.8%	10.4***

Partner's income > NLG 2000

No	30.0	9.2	6.1%	
Yes	26.4	13.1	93.9%	2.7**

Women's net hourly wages

1st quartile ($\leq$ NLG 11.99)	26.5	12.1	25%	
2nd quartile (11.99 - 14.53)	28.5	10.5	25%	
3rd quartile(14.53 - 17.44)	27.6	10.0	25%	
4th quartile ($\geq$ 17.44)	27.5	11.1	25%	1.0 ns

Cluster 4 Sector and occupational class

manufacturing/cleaning services	26.9	12.6	6.5%	
commercial services	28.7	14.7	15.0%	
banking and insurance	28.6	13.1	10.8%	
health sector	25.3	12.1	37.3%	
other sectors	26.6	12.8	30.6%	2.4*

Occupation

nursing	26.1	11.4	15.7%	
caring/cleaning	17.7	11.4	14.0%	
clerical	28.4	10.6	25.1%	
teaching	26.0	14.2	9.1%	
miscellaneous	29.3	14.2	36.0%	21.5***
All	26.7	12.89	100%	

*** p<.001, **p<.01, *p<.05, ns is not significant

181

Table 10.2 Distribution over four working time categories in percentages (N=899)

	≤15 hrs	16-23 hrs	24-35 hrs	≥36 hrs
Cluster 1 Family cycle		Row percentages		
No partner, no children	2	3	21	73
Partner, no children	2	8	38	52
Youngest child ≤ 3 year	34	30	25	11
Youngest child 4-12 year	29	32	26	13
Youngest child ≥ 13 year	20	25	30	26
Cluster 2 Help in the household				
Domestic help				
No	23	22	28	27
Yes	8	20	32	40
Partner's help > 25%				
No	22	23	25	29
Yes	15	19	34	32
Living in an apartment				
No	20	23	29	27
Yes	8	9	27	55
Continuously worked				
No	38	26	22	14
Yes	11	20	32	37
Cluster 3 Individual characteristics				
Age 25-30 year	12	13	28	47
Age 31-35 year	25	26	27	21
Age 36-40 year	20	27	28	24
Age 41-45 year	21	22	32	26
Education				
Low	27	22	24	27
Medium	20	21	30	29
High	8	22	33	37
Additional income > NLG 2000				
No	9	15	41	35
Yes	20	22	28	30
Women's net hourly wages				
1st quartile (≤ NLG 11.99)	20	25	21	33
2nd quartile (11.99 - 14.53)	12	20	36	32
3rd quartile(14.53 - 17.44)	11	24	36	28
4th quartile (≥ 17.44)	16	22	33	29

	≤15 hrs	16-23 hrs	24-35 hrs	≥36 hrs
Cluster 4 Sector and occupational class				
manufacturing/cleaning industry	25	17	21	37
trade	18	18	26	38
banking and insurance	18	21	20	41
health sector	21	23	32	23
other sectors	16	23	32	30
Occupation				
nursing	17	22	36	25
caring/cleaning	48	24	18	10
clerical	10	24	31	35
teaching	18	19	36	28
miscellaneous	15	20	27	38
All	19.1%	21.7%	29.0%	30.3%

10.7   EXPLAINING WOMEN'S WORKING TIME

The explanatory power of the model was tested by regression analysis (table 10.3). Not surprisingly, family cycle is dominant in the explanation of the working hours of women aged 25 to 45. This supports the findings reported in the literature review. A partner, the number of children, a youngest child aged 0-3 years, and a youngest child aged 4-12 contribute negatively to women's working hours. A child aged 0-3 years has the largest negative impact: having a young child reduces the working week by more than six hours compared to that of women who do not have a child in this age group; all other things remain equal. In the model the impact of the family cycle on women's working time remains solid.

Cluster 2 includes strategies that might reduce time spent on household work, and therefore leave more time for paid work. Indeed, a domestic help contributes considerably to women's working hours: women with domestic help work six hours more than women who have no help. Partner's help also contributes considerably: by more than three hours. Our assumption on the efficiency attitude of those who stayed in the labour force is supported, because these women work three hours more than re-entrant women; all other things remain equal. The assumption about an apartment rather than a large house reducing household time and thus enabling women to work more hours does not hold in any of the models. However, women are able to reduce their household time by delegating household labour to other persons, i.e. a cleaning lady or the partner, and by developing an efficiency attitude. This conclusion holds for all models.

Cluster 3 incorporates individual characteristics. Surprisingly, neither age/age square nor education contributes to the explanation of working hours, but income does. Having a partner with an additional household income of at least NLG

2,000 contributes substantially to the explanation. Women who do not have an additional family income of this kind work nearly four hours more than women who have.

In cluster 4, an impact was assumed for sectors and occupations, because sectors and occupations would subsequently adapt to suit women's part-time requests in the 1980s and 1990s. However, none of the sectors contribute to the explanation, except one. Women working in the caring and cleaning occupations have a working week which is six hours less than women working in other occupations; all other things remain equal. This is consistent with the descriptive findings. Mean working hours are very low in this occupation and workers are heavily concentrated in the shortest working time category. Altogether this model explains 37% of the variance in working time.

Table 10.3 Non-standardised regression results for women's working hours, four models (t-values in brackets, N=899)

Variable	Model 1	Model 2	Model 3	Model 4
Cluster 1 Family cycle				
Partner	-3.50***	-4.93***	-4.97***	-4.78***
	(-3.14)	(-4.35)	(-4.32)	(-4.16)
Number of children	-3.76***	-2.85***	-2.78***	-2.49***
	(-8.87)	(-6.30)	(-6.08)	(-5.50)
Youngest child ≤ 3 year	-6.56***	-7.80***	-7.62***	-7.96***
	(-5.88)	(-7.23)	(-7.02)	(-7.47)
Youngest child 4-12	-4.18***	-4.41***	-4.54***	-4.77***
	(-3.88)	(-4.30)	(-4.39)	(-4.70)
Cluster 2 Help in the household				
Domestic help		6.65***	6.78***	6.02**
		(8.20)	(8.31)	(7.46)
Partner's help > 25%		3.08***	2.78***	2.30**
		(3.98)	(3.56)	(3.00)
Apartment		.04	.03	.03
		(1.21)	(1.03)	(1.19)
Worked continuously		3.49***	3.42***	3.04**
		(3.77)	(3.66)	(3.32)
Cluster 3 Individual characteristics				
Age			-.03	-.03
			(-.73)	(-.95)
Age SQU/100			-.02	-.03
			(-.61)	(-.83)
Education			.05	.03
			(1.70)	(1.10)
Additional income > 2000			-3.76*	-4.12**
			(-2.52)	(-2.82)

Variable	Model 1	Model 2	Model 3	Model 4
Cluster 4 Sector and occupational class				
Manufacturing/cleaning				.05
				(1.74)
Trade				.05
				(1.66)
Banking and insurance				-.02
				(-.57)
Health sector				-.02
				(-.80)
Nursing occupations				-.05
				(-1.68)
Caring/cleaning occupations				-6.44***
				(-6.21)
Clerical occupations				-.03
				(-1.22)
Teaching occupations				-0.04
				(-1.64)
(Constant)	37.19***	32.13***	35.81***	37.26***
	(36.65)	(24.59)	(18.36)	(19.37)
R square	27%	34%	34%	37%

10.8 CONCLUSIONS

Does part-time work divide the female labour force? Do part-time jobs reinforce women's disadvantaged position at work? The Netherlands is known for its high part-time employment rate within the EU. Yet, for this country, the thesis that part-time jobs are marginalised compared to full-time jobs cannot be supported. We found no substantial wage differentials between four working time categories. With one exception, we also did not find any impact of a woman's sectoral or occupational category on her working time. This indicates that women's working time is predominantly introduced because of employees' wishes and not because of management needs. Furthermore, focusing on the full-time / part-time divide distracts from differences within the part-time labour force.

We argued that the female part-time workforce consists of two groups of women. The first group consists of women working in part-time jobs that were created as an employer strategy and are likely to be marginalised, i.e. have lower wages and a disproportionate amount of temporary work. Less well-educated women are likely to be over represented. The second group consists of women working in part-time jobs that used to be full-time, but these women have successfully requested reduction in their working hours due to family responsibilities. Highly skilled women are likely to be over represented in this category. While the former group has been decreasing over the past decades, the latter group has been increasing.

Women's working hours were analysed, based on the Labour and Care survey among 1,420 women aged 25-45. Four explanatory clusters were distinguished, relating to the family cycle, to household time reduction strategies, to individual characteristics and to sectoral and occupational differences. According to our expectations, the major findings are that women's working time relates strongly to the family cycle, the presence of a partner, the number of children, a youngest child aged 0-3 years and a youngest child aged 4-12. Furthermore, working time depends positively on contributions to household work from the partner or a domestic help and on a continuous working career. Working time does not relate to individual characteristics such as age and education, but it depends negatively on a partner's income when this is above the minimum standard of living. Finally, working time does not depend on sector or occupation, with the exception of the caring and cleaning occupations, which are found more often in the shortest part-time category.

In the Netherlands, the part-time and the full-time female labour forces differ substantially regarding characteristics such as family phase and women's household time-reducing strategies. Whereas the full-time workforce consists disproportionately of women in their twenties, the part-time workforce consists disproportionately of women in their thirties and forties. Women in their fifties are found disproportionately among housewives.

When starting a family in the 1990s, well-educated women are more likely to request a reduction in working hours and thus benefit from tenure, whereas low-skilled women are more likely to have a period out of the labour force. They will re-enter the labour market with a part-time job, presumably in a caring or cleaning occupation. Thus, it can be concluded that the well-educated group in the part-time workforce counterbalances the less-educated group. This results in a part-time workforce which is about equal to the full-time work force in terms of work-related characteristics such as wage or employment status.

REFERENCES

Becker, G. 1981: *A Treatise on the Family*. Cambridge (MA), Harvard University Press.
Bernasco, W. 1994: *Coupled careers. The effects of Spouse's Resources on Success at Work*. Amsterdam, Thesis Publishers.
Delsen, L. 1995: *Atypical Employment: an International Perspective. Causes, Consequences and Policy*. Groningen, Wolters-Noordhoff.
Fagan, C., Rubery J. 1996: *The Salience of the Part-time Divide in the European Union*. European Sociological Review, 12/3, 227-250.
Hakim, C. 1993: *Segregated and Integrated Occupations: A New Framework for Analysing Social Change*. European Sociological Review, 9: 28-314.

Hakim, C. 1996: *Key Issues in Women's Work*. London, The Athlone Press.

Hamermesh, D.S. 1996: *Workdays, Workhours and Work Schedules. Evidence for the United States and Germany*. Michigan (Kalamazoo), W.E. Upjohn Institute for Employment Research.

Henkens, C.J.I.M., Siegers, J.J, Meijer, K.A. (1994*): Het arbeidsaanbod van gehuwde vrouwen en ongehuwd samenwonende vrouwen in Nederland: 1981-1989*. Sociaal Maandblad Arbeid, 49/5, p. 289-296.

Henkens, C.J.I.M., Siegers, J.J., Van den Bosch, K. 1992: Het arbeidsaanbod van gehuwde vrouwen in België en Nederland: een vergelijkende studie. *Tijdschrift voor Arbeidsvraagstukken, 8/1, p. 56-68*.

Lippe, T. van der 1993: Arbeidsverdeling tussen mannen en vrouwen. Amsterdam, Thesis Publishers.

McRae, S. 1995: *Part-Time Work in the European Union: The Gender Dimension*. Dublin, European Foundation for the Improvement of Living and Working Conditions.

OECD 1994: *Employment Outlook*. Paris, Organisation for economic co-operation and development.

Plantenga J., Velzen S. van 1993: *Wage determination and sex segregation in employment: The case of the Netherlands*. Report for the Network of Experts on the Situation of Women in the Labour Market in Manchester.

Plantenga J. 1995: Labour-Market Participation of Women in the European Union. In Jacques van Hoof & Anneke van Doorne-Huiskes (eds.): *Women on the European labour market*. London, Paul Chapman Publishing, pp. 1-14.

Rubery, J., Fagan C. 1995: Comparative industrial relations research: towards reversing the gender bias. *British Journal of Industrial Relations*, 33: 209-236.

Shelton, B.A. 1992: *Women, Men and Time. Gender Differences in Paid Work, Housework and Leisure*. Westport, Greenwood Press.

Tijdens, K.G., Maassen van den Brink, H., Groot, W., Noom, M. 1994: Arbeid en zorg. Effecten van strategieën van de combinatie van betaalde en onbetaalde arbeid. The Hague, *Organisatie voor Strategisch Arbeidsmarktbeleid*, W-124, 132 p.

Tijdens, K.G. 1995: Verdwijnt de huisvrouw? *Sociaal Maandblad Arbeid*, 50, (3), 161-170.

Tijdens, K.G. 1997a: Allocation of jobs: personnel policies and women's paid working hours in banks. Forthcoming in Tijdens, K.G., A. van Doorne-Huiskes & T.M. Willemsen (eds.) *Time Allocation and Gender. The Relationship between Paid Labour and Household Labour*. Tilburg, Tilburg University Press

Tijdens, K.G. 1997b: Gender and labour market flexibility. Forthcoming in T. Wilthagen (ed.). *Advancing theory in labour law and industrial relations in a global context*. Amsterdam, North Holland, in co-operation with The Netherlands Academy of Arts and Sciences.

ACKNOWLEDGEMENTS

This paper is based on a survey commissioned by the Organisation for Strategic Labour Market Research (OSA), The Hague. The report has been published as OSA working document 124 (Tijdens et al., 1994). The research underlying this particular article was subsidised by the Netherlands Organisation for Scientific Research (NWO-grant no. 759-717-603). An earlier draft of the paper was presented at the 1996 WESWA Conference at Utrecht University, The Netherlands.

BIOGRAPHICAL NOTE

Kea Tijdens (PhD) is a sociologist and senior research fellow at the Department of Economics, University of Amsterdam, The Netherlands. Her recent papers include time allocation in households, gender and employment, and working-time issues in collective bargaining. She has published articles and books on internal labour markets, developments in office technology, occupational segregation, and ageing and careering in banking. Current research topics concern working-time reduction, expansion of opening hours and employers' staffing policies.

11 Job allocation: personnel policies and women's working hours in the banking sector

Kea Tijdens

11.1 INTRODUCTION

A century ago, wage labour used to be part-time labour, i.e. workers were hired by the hour and work was paid by the hour. Seasonal labour used to be a very common pattern, for example in agriculture and in the docks. In the first half of this century, the working time patterns of most workers changed to full-time and all year round. After World War II, the vast majority of jobs were full-time. Now, part-time work is increasing again, especially in female employment. In Western Europe, four out of five part-timers are women.

Among the Western European countries, the Netherlands are known for the highest part-time rate among female and male workers (OECD, 1994). In the ten older EU countries, the share of part-timers in the female labour force grew from 27% in 1983 to 31% in 1991 (Plantenga, 1995). In the Netherlands, this percentage grew from 40% in 1973 and 50% in 1983 to almost 60% in 1993. Two reasons can be given for this growth (Tijdens et al., 1994). Firstly, housewives have re-entered the labour force increasingly. The vast majority of them preferred a part-time job because they wanted time for their household duties. Secondly, growing numbers of women do not leave the labour market after giving birth. Quitting was the dominant pattern in the 1950s and 1960s, but after the 1970s, this pattern started to change. From the 1880s onwards, the dominant strategy of Dutch women was to request a substantial reduction in working hours when having a baby. They prefer working part-time to not working at all because re-entrance is usually coupled to downgrading and because women increasingly face high opportunity costs as well as low returns on their high human capital investments. As a result of insufficient childcare facilities, absence of extended families, and, most of all, a highly cultivated motherhood ideology, these women prefer part-time to full-time work. The Labour Force Statistics show that the main reason women work part-time is their household work.

Creating part-time jobs must be a management imperative, otherwise why would employers accommodate women's requests for working hour reductions? And

Time allocation and gender, Kea Tijdens, Anneke van Doorne-Huiskes & Tineke Willemsen (eds.), Tilburg University Press, 1997, © Kea G. Tijdens

189

how many working hours do women request? In this chapter we will examine employers' strategies and women's preferences in working hours over a time span of 30 years, focusing on the Dutch banking sector. In section 2, theories on supply and demand mechanisms in part-time work will be discussed. Section 3 presents research methodology. In section 4, employers' strategies and women's preferences for working hours are analysed. Finally, conclusions will be drawn on whether part-time jobs reinforce women's generally disadvantaged position at work.

11.2 THEORIES ON PART-TIME WORK

11.2.1 The supply-side of the labour market

Regarding the supply-side of the labour market, the empirical findings show that over time women's working time might be influenced by different variables (Bernasco, 1993; Henkes et al.; 1992, Henkes et al.; 1994; Shelton, 1991; Tijdens, 1997b). The impact of the number of children is negative in all analyses, regardless of country or period. The impact of young children varies between countries, but it is negative for the Netherlands in all years studied. The impact of women's wage rates is not unanimous. Some findings indicate a negative and some a positive influence, while others reveal no influence at all. Surprisingly, work characteristics, such as sector or occupation, are not used to explain individual working time. Assuming that part-time work is a management imperative, one would expect a woman's sector and occupation to have a large impact on working hours.

Several studies indicate that women's actual and preferred hours differ considerably (Renes, 1991; Van der Putte & Pelzer; 1993, Maassen van den Brink, 1994; Tijdens et al., 1994). According to Renes, about half of married women do not work preferred hours. Some prefer a shorter working week, others prefer a longer one. Of the full-time working women who are married, no less than 70 per cent claim to work more hours than desired. Yet, they prefer working to not working at all. For the majority of women whose actual and preferred hours per week differ, the difference is less than 8 hours. We assume that women will try to adjust their actual time to their preferred one.

The women who prefer to reduce working hours are women who work full time or nearly full time, are married, have worked continuously, want to have a baby, or have a youngest child of 4 or under (Tijdens et al., 1994). The women who prefer to increase their working hours have usually had a discontinuous career, they work 20 hours or less and their youngest child is aged from 4 to 12 years. The study also reveals that the working women who want a baby predominantly want to continue working in a job of about 20 hours. These women do have two other preferences: they need day care and they want their partner to be involved

190

in the child minding. If they do not succeed in realising these preferences, they will withdraw from the labour market.

Housewives aiming to re-enter the labour market have strong preferences as far as their working hours are concerned. On average, they prefer a job of 21 hours. According to Renes (1991), these women face a relative scarcity of part-time jobs, because vacancy duration is shorter for part-time jobs than for full-time jobs. Yet, the re-entrant women underestimate their chances of finding a job. Re-entrance, especially in a part-time job, is coupled to change of occupation, according to Dex (1987). Women who worked full-time before interruption and part-time after re-entrance, face downward occupational mobility. However, Tijdens et al. (1994) show that opportunities to reduce working hours or to re-enter in a part-time job vary between occupations. Occupations in which workers are relatively equally distributed over working hours allow both for continuous careers and for re-entrancy. Occupations in which full-time workers are employed relatively often seem to have an over-representation of unmarried women. In these occupations women will not be able to reduce working hours, nor will they be able to re-enter. In occupations in which a relatively high percentage of the workers work only a few hours, re-entrant women appear to be over-represented. The female dominated professional occupations appear to have substantial numbers of both full-time and part-time workers, whereas this is not the case in female dominated unskilled occupations. In nursing and teaching especially, both of which are major occupations for the female labour force, women are able to change back and forth to their preferred working hours during their working life cycle.

11.2.2 The demand-side of the labour market

There is little empirical evidence on why employers want part-time work. Yet, it has been shown empirically that both the labour market and organisations are highly segregated by gender (Bielby & Baron, 1984, 1986; Jonung, 1984; Hakim, 1996; Kalleberg et al., 1996). Therefore, we assume there is no substitution of male and female labour and that the demand for part-time labour is considered part of the demand for female labour. To examine employers' strategies we will assume five factors which influence the demand for part-time workers.

The first assumption is that for economic and organisational reasons employers do not prefer female part-time workers at all. The economic reason is that part-time workers are perceived as less productive or because they are associated with higher costs due to recruitment, training, and the fixed costs. The organisational argument is that the most efficient span of control in organisational units will be reached with full-time employees and not with part-time employees.

191

A second factor is the need to bring manpower levels in line with supply of work. This will be called the organisational need. Traditionally, firms whose workload is concentrated on only a few hours a day, for example restaurants or cinemas, or which experience other forms of fluctuations in the workload, either per day, per week, per month or per year, are likely to employ part-time or seasonal workers. The same applies for work with a high workload; if resting-time is not included in the job, the workers are likely to be employed part-time. Women are more likely than men to work in workplaces that experience substantial workload fluctuations per day and per year (McRae, 1995). Increased competition will re-inforce the need for a flexible workforce, which can be achieved by flexible working hours, by increased numbers of part-time workers, by contracting out, or by other means. Recently, the organisational need for part-time jobs has been in-fluenced by flexibilisation strategies (Horrell and Rubery, 1991). Thus, the or-ganisational need to bring manpower levels in line with work supply can be a major variable influencing the demand for part-time workers.

Economic need is the third factor that may influence the demand for part-time workers. According to this strategy, employers will create part-time jobs to en-able recruitment of workers who can be paid low wages and can be offered flexi-ble labour contracts. The degree to which they do so will depend on the skill re-quirements, because this strategy presupposes that jobs can be created for which workers do not need substantial training. Secondary labour market theories state that employers will create secondary segments for which they will recruit secon-dary workers on cheap labour conditions (Craig et al, 1985). This segmentation strategy prevents wage pressure on core workers. In the United States, minority workers and single men are more likely to work part-time (Hamermesh, 1996). In Britain, women are more likely to work part-time, among others, because part-timers have higher leaving rates than full-timers (Hakim, 1995a). Workers with high turnover rates will be attractive for part-time jobs, because tenure is a major determinant of high wages, at least in Western Europe.

A fourth factor influencing the demand for part-time work is scarcity of labour. In this case, employers will recruit among other categories of workers. If full-time female workers are scarce this category could be housewives, who usually have strong working hours preferences. This presupposes that tasks which used to be done full-time can be transformed into part-time jobs. In fact, the reserve labour army theory was based on this explanation. Several scholars assumed that if the shortage of labour lessened, women would be sent back to their kids and kitchens (Beechey, 1978; Bruegel, 1982).

Finally, employers may construct part-time jobs because of pressure from the workforce. This will occur when the firm employs women who want to adjust their actual number of working hours to their preferred ones. The conditions un-der which employers are willing to accommodate these requests will vary over time and between firms. According to Craig et al. (1985), skilled female workers will use their bargaining power as skilled workers to limit their working hours, whereas unskilled women have to adapt their domestic arrangements to the employer's requirements. We will assume that there are two arguments why employers will be willing to accommodate reduction requests from female workers. First is a result of their bargaining power, either based on scarcity of skilled labour or on unionised power. Secondly, employers may prefer female workers to continue part-time work rather than quitting because of returns on previous investment in on-the-job training of these women or because of recruitment costs for new workers.

11.2.3 The characteristics of part-time jobs

Here, two discussions concerning the characteristics of part-time jobs will be highlighted. The first discussion focuses on the issue: do part-time jobs have clustered characteristics such as low pay, bad working conditions and unskilled work, or do part-time workers have clustered characteristics, i.e. unskilled, low commitment, high turnover rates. Hakim (1995a) looks on the one hand, at authors who suggest that the allocation of female workers in jobs with a range of clustered characteristics is attributable to the way jobs are organised. Thus these features are built into the design of jobs by employers. On the other hand, it is argued that the concentration of female workers in jobs with these features is attributable to the characteristics of the workers only. Yet, according to segmented labour market theories such a contrast does not exist because secondary segments recruit exclusively secondary workers. Fagan and Rubery (1996) conclude that the part-time / full-time segmentation in the female labour force differs substantially between the countries in the EU.

The second discussion focuses on the issue of whether part-time jobs are created by employers or at the request of employees. McRae (1995) distinguishes between a 'corporate strategy' where employers introduce part-time work for economic or organisational reasons and an 'individual strategy', where employers agree to accommodate the requests of individual workers who prefer reduced working hours. Establishments that follow a corporate strategy are very likely to recruit part-timers on the external labour market, whereas establishments that follow the individual strategy are likely to employ former full-time employees in part-time jobs. A survey in eight countries of the European Union shows that part-time jobs are introduced because of management needs (41%), because of employees' wishes (36%), or both reasons being equally important (22%) (Delsen, 1995). Involuntary part-time work refers to a worker's inability to find full-time work. Studies by the OECD (1990) indicate that four out of five female part-time workers have to be classified as voluntary part-time workers.

11.3 ASSUMPTIONS, RESEARCH METHODOLOGY AND DATA

Both the figures on the growing part-time workforce and the recent national debates on part-time work suggest that both employers' strategies and women's preferences for part-time work have changed substantially over a period of 30 years. In order to understand the changing nature of part-time work, a long-term study is designed to evaluate critically the assumptions on part-time work discussed in the previous section.

Regarding the supply side of the labour market, we assume that women's working time preferences will depend upon country-wide ideologies on motherhood, on the chance to re-enter the labour force without a substantial search duration or downward occupational mobility, or on the opportunity costs of a spell out of the labour market. Regarding the demand side of the labour market, we will assume that the demand for part-time work will depend upon a general attitude towards part-time work, or on organisational need, economic need, on labour market scarcity or on the adaptation of worker's requests for working time reductions.

As far as the nature of part-time work is concerned, we assume that an employer's strategy based on an organisational need will not necessarily lead to a division between the full-time and the part-time female workforce. Yet, when the strategy is based on an economic need, the assumption is that the female part-time workforce will be characterised by low pay and related characteristics. When the strategy is primarily an adaptation strategy, we assume that the employer adapts to all requests equally. In that case, we will have to analyse the characteristics of the workers who request the reduction.

The focus here is on one sector of the Dutch economy, i.e. the banking sector, for several reasons. The main reason is that a few large banks dominate this sector and that there is one collective bargaining agreement for the whole sector. Thus, only a few employers on the demand-side of the labour market are involved and they can be studied easily. In the mid-1960s there were five large banks. In the mid-1990s three large banks remain, due to mergers. Moreover, the sector is characterised by a coherent and non-competitive employer behaviour resulting from a powerful employers' organisation. A second reason for choosing banks is that working hours rarely include irregular hours. Thus, by choosing the banking sector we have excluded variables that could intervene in the research design.

11.3.1 Research methods

For a long-term study, time series are usually used to analyse changes over time. However, this study includes only a few employers and the data on personnel policies cannot be quantified in order to produce time series analyses. Therefore, multiple ways were used to gather data and descriptive methods were used to explore the relationship between the variables. The period under study is 1965 to 1995. The choice for this period has been guided by the availability of data. Data for one bank were available from the mid-1960s. Subsequently, in the following years, data became available for the other banks as well. From 1977 on, data were available for all banks under study. The latest data available were those for 1995.

To reconstruct employers' strategies we used predominantly the banks' annual social reports (see Appendix 2 for the reports used). Most large Dutch companies publish annual social reports for their employees and their works' councils. These reports usually include information about both the numbers of employees and the major personnel policies. One could assume that social reports are largely public relations exercises, or at least that they do not tell the whole story. The former is inaccurate, because generally the social reports are not for external use; the latter is accurate, of course. Yet, by studying the consecutive reports over three decades, one can see in which years a bank considered a particular topic important. For example, when women started to ask for reduced working hours, all banks wrote about this new phenomena in their social reports. They said: this is new to us, and we have to set up a study. In the next year's report they usually mentioned the results of the study, especially the degree to which women would reduce their working hours. Thus, through careful reading of the annual social reports we reconstructed employers' strategies. Where additional written information was available, this was used too.

The female workers' working hour preferences were reconstructed by secondary analysis of data collected in surveys in the banks, dating from 1980, 1991, 1993, 1994 and 1996 (see appendix 3 for detailed information on these data sets). It should be noted that the term 'preferred hours' has a double meaning, as it may reflect immediate as well as long-term preferences. In the first meaning, a discrepancy between actual and preferred hours exists and women will be dissatisfied with their working hours. The second meaning suggests a future conflict, women may quit if these preferences are not satisfied.

11.3.2 The banking sector

Before turning to the research findings, the banking sector will be sketched briefly here (see appendix 1 for the main figures). In the Netherlands, the banking sector emerged in the second half of the nineteenth century. Until the early 1960s a broad range of types of banks was in existence. Then, retail banking broke through the traditional division of labour between types of banks. It transformed the bank organisation and its processes resulting in expansion of both the number of local branches and the workforce. To finance and manage the large networks of branches as well as to manage the capital generated by retail banking, a rapid concentration resulted in three large listed banks, called ABN,

AMRO and NMB. Furthermore, the banking sector included co-operative banks for the agricultural sector, which in the early 1970s merged into the large RABO bank. The outsider position of the large state-owned Postgirobank changed when it was privatised in the mid-1980s. Finally, ABN and AMRO merged into ABN-AMRO, and NMB joined Postgirobank to become NMB Postbank. RABO remained on its own. These three banks dominate the Dutch banking sector. They have continuously provided more than two-thirds of sectoral employment.

Employment in the banking sector grew steadily from 1965 until 1992 and declined in recent years. Until the early 1990s, the positive effects of the increase of services seemed to outweigh the negative effects of the introduction of new technology. Almost half of the sectoral labour force are women. Compared to other sectors, wage levels in the banking sector are relatively high, especially for male employees, and the gap between men's and women's average hourly wage is largest. Since the mid-1980s, the banking sector uses a job evaluation system. In recent years, cost reduction policies gave way to the expansion of pay systems that reward performance.

11.4 EMPLOYERS' STRATEGIES AND WOMEN'S PREFERENCES ON WORKING HOURS

In this section, the banks' strategies and female banking employees' preferences on working hours are analysed over a period of 30 years. These years can been divided into five periods, characterised by different personnel policies: the 1960s, the 1970s, the early 1980s, the late 1980s and the early 1990s. The same line of reasoning will be followed for each period. Firstly, general employment trends in the Netherlands will be sketched. Secondly, growth rates will be presented for total employment in the banks under study, for women's employment and for the percentage of part-timers (see table 11.1). Thirdly, employers' strategies will be reconstructed. Fourthly, preferences of female employees for working hours will be analysed again. Finally, the characteristics of part-time jobs will be dealt with.

11.4.1 The 1960s (1965-1971)

The rapid rise of the service sector and severe scarcity in the labour market were the main characteristics of the Dutch economy in the 1960s. At that time, the overwhelming majority of families consisted of a male breadwinner and a full-time housewife. On average, women married in their early twenties and gave birth to their first child at age 23. In the service and public sectors, women's labour contracts were automatically terminated on the day of their marriage. This practice dated from the 1930s when a law was passed which prohibited married women from working in the public sector. The service sector followed this policy until the end of the 1960s. The dominant social opinion was that married women should be housewives. The vast majority of married women followed convention, and did not seek jobs. In this decade, women's work was girl's work.

Unfortunately we have only figures for one bank (AMRO) for the1960s. From 1965 to 1970, AMRO's annual employment growth rate was nearly 8%, due to expanding business. The demand for labour was high, especially in the large cities where the bank's offices and branches were mainly located. Turnover rates were high as well, twice as high for women as for men. Annually, 8% of the bank's female workforce left because of marriage. Up to one third of the workforce was recruited annually.

The social reports show that recruitment policies favoured 16 or 17 year-old school-leavers, boys and girls. Their wages were low. Due to their general education they had enough skills to carry out the majority of jobs. Yet, the bank's demand for labour could not be satisfied and led to both vacancies and substantial levels of overtime. Apart from business removals of data-entry departments towards regions with less tightened labour markets, the bank followed two strategies to meet its need for labour. Firstly, data-entry jobs were fragmented into part-time parts to enable the bank to recruit workers it had never recruited before: married women with grown-up children. If these women had children under 16, the bank allowed them unpaid leave in case of children's illness or holidays. Usually, they worked four hours a day, five days a week, on temporary contracts. The vast majority of them was unskilled, but they were given typing courses. Secondly, the female employees who married were asked to stay on. As they had full-time jobs, they were offered part-time work, usually for six hours a day. They left when their babies were born, usually within a year of marriage.

We do not have figures on women's working hour preferences for this decade, but the vast majority of unmarried women had full-time jobs. Although the bank agreed with the general view that women should withdraw at the time of their marriage, the tight labour market forced it to behave differently. The percentage of part-timers in the banks' female labour force rose from 11.3% in 1966 to 24.4% in 1971.

11.4.2 The 1970s (1971-1979)

The 1970s showed a steady increase in the percentage of unemployed persons. Growing numbers of women did not quit when they married, but when they had their first baby (for turnover rates due to marriage and pregnancy at RABO and NMB since 1976, see appendix 4). Due to longer compulsory education, women entered the labour market at an older age and due to later first pregnancies, they also left at a higher age. The female labour force slowly changed from girl's work into adult's work, including young adults and, increasingly, women in their forties. At the same time the notion that married women should be housewives

197

was slowly fading in society, although this did not apply for mothers of young children. In growing numbers, married women with grown-up children wished to re-enter the labour market.[1]

For this decade employment figures are available for three banks, ABN, AMRO and NMB. Due to the merger in the early 1970s, figures for RABO are only available from 1977 onwards. Figures on part-time work are only available for AMRO. Annual average employment growth rates in this decade are 2.4% for both ABN and AMRO and 5.3% for NMB, but these percentages are substantially higher for women only. Turnover rates declined, but women's turnover remained almost twice as high as men's. As the demand for labour decreased and labour supply increased, the number of vacancies as well as overtime declined. At AMRO, part-timers declined from 24.4% in 1971 until 17.2% in 1979.

The social reports showed that recruitment policies had changed. Now, employees started working at 19 or 20, and recruitment aimed at higher educational levels, because the share of unskilled, clerical jobs was diminishing due to computerisation and specialisation. Furthermore, the banks had stopped recruiting part-timers, because the labour market was less tight. Moreover, the part-time clerical workforce was marginalised, e.g. they were seen as synonymous with cleaning ladies, although this occupational group never rose above 30% of female part-timers.[2] In this decade, the collective agreements did not apply to part-timers who worked less than 15 hours.

Full-time female employees now had fixed contracts, although the annual reports of all banks showed that female workers were still expected to withdraw when they married. They were not asked to continue working as their colleagues had been a decade earlier. Their withdrawal was called 'inevitable turnover'. It was stated that "a married woman will be needed for her house work and caring tasks ..... in general, a married woman is less ambitious for pursuing a career".[3] There are no figures for this decade on the preferences of women on their working hours in the banking sector.

To conclude, although the banks' policies changed when the practice of creating 'women's contracts' stopped and social opinions on women's issues changed, female employees in the banks were still expected to withdraw when they married. Employers stopped creating part-time jobs, partly because the labour market was easier in this decade, and partly because of the decreasing share of unskilled work due to the introduction of new technology.

---

[1] See D'Ancona (1973) and M. van Klaveren. 1973. Gehuwde vrouw en arbeidsproces - een vergeten realiteit? In *M&O*, vol. 27, pp. 209-220

[2] See Social Report AMRO 1975

[3] See Social Report ABN 1973

11.4.3   The first half of the 1980s (1979-1985)

Unemployment rose to high levels in the first half of the 1980s. It was higher among women than among men. The percentage of women in the labour force that continued working after marriage and until they gave birth to their first child increased to 80%. The percentage of women that continued working after giving birth was about 25%. In increasing numbers, women re-entered the labour market and they did so when their youngest child was younger, usually when it went to primary school. Well-educated women were more likely both to continue working and to re-enter after a spell out of the labour force.

For this decade we have figures for four banks, ABN, AMRO, NMB and RABO. They show that educational levels of newly recruited employees were steadily increasing. Annual average employment growth rates in the first half of this decade were negative for AMRO (-2.0%) and NMB (-0.5%) and positive for ABN (1.4%) and for RABO (2.2%). In all banks, growth rates for women's employment were higher than for men's. Compared to other years, in 1982, the year of the deepest recession, recruitment and turnover rates were lowest in all banks. Between 1980 and 1985, the percentage of part-timers in the female workforce grew tremendously from 12 - 22% for the four banks to 30 - 40%. As this was mainly due to requests from women, let us look at women's preferences first, and then at the employers' response.

In this period women's requests for reduced working hours increased. A large number of requests came from women who had recently married, wanted to continue working part-time and postponed having children. In 1980, according to a survey held in one bank, nearly one in three female respondents who intended to stop working indicated that they would not do so if they were allowed to work part-time.[4] Our secondary analysis of the 1980 data shows that female employees in the banking sector more often preferred the reduction of working hours than male employees, and that women were willing to accept lower incomes in exchange for shorter working hours. Married women preferred working less hours a day, whereas unmarried women preferred less days a week.[5] Presumably, women's requests for reduced working hours were a response to high unemployment rates, as unemployment reduced their chances for re-entering, increased the chances of having unemployed husbands, and increased uncertainty in general. Obviously, they perceived the bank as a company that did not recruit re-entrant women.

---

[4] See the report by Attie de Jong. 1983. *Gelijke behandeling en het personeelsbeleid.* Kluwer, Deventer

[5] However, these differences are not significant, probably because of the number (49) of women in the sample, of whom 29 are married.

According to the social reports, the banks' managements were uncertain how to respond to requests for reduced working hours. Local management quite often fulfilled women's requests, but the banks' headquarters had no policy on this issue. They began investigations to discover the demand for part-time work.[6] All subsequent studies recognised changes in women's preferences as shifts away from full-time housewife status towards a lifetime career in the bank. In 1981, the employers' association also investigated the issue of part-time work. It concluded part-time jobs should be stimulated for two reasons. Firstly, in collective bargaining, the promotion of part-time work should be the employers' response to unions' pressure for reducing the working week.[7] At that time, the unions did not perceive the promotion of part-time work as a means of achieving a reduced working week, which could also reduce unemployment (ETUI, 1986). Secondly, part-time jobs would allow employers to bring manpower in line with work supply and this could become an important instrument in cost reduction policies in banks. Surveys in local RABO branches showed that the major problems arising from part-time work were insufficient contacts between employees and planning issues, but that these problems were counterbalanced by the fact that part-timers were more productive, easier to use for less attractive tasks, and allowed flexibility because peak hours were 2.5 times more busy.[8] Therefore, the strategy of employers changed in favour of part-time work. In the 1983-84 bargaining agreement, it was agreed that all permanent staff could reduce working hours individually if supported by the immediate supervisor. Requests from workers in complex jobs were less likely to be successful than requests from workers in unskilled jobs.[9] In 1983, a total of 1,476 full-time jobs (about 1% of the banks' total

---

[6] ABN started in 1979, as the government chose this bank for an experiment in which full-time jobs were changed into part-time jobs ('Samenwerken. Het Sociaal Beleid', ABN bank, October 1979). This experiment was aimed at creating new jobs, as unemployment was rising. Furthermore, this experiment favoured women's emancipation. AMRO started an investigation in 1980, because more women than before aspired a longer lasting career (AMRO 1982). At NMB, both the personnel department and the workers council studied the demand for part-time work (NMB, 1981). RABO finishes investigation (RABO, 1982).

[7] The board of directors of AMRO stated that "part-time jobs can be one -albeit an important one- of the forms of a shorter working week" (Social Report AMRO, 1984, p. 3)

[8] In a survey at the RABO (by De Lange, 1981, cited in Vrieze, A.A.M. de Ervaringen bij de Rabobank, in Schilfgaarde, 1984) branch management's experience with part-timers was predominantly positive. Management of 100 local branches listed several advantages of part-timers. They were more productive (productivity was approximately 6% higher for part-timers working 20 hours a week), they can be deployed more easily for less attractive tasks, and part-time jobs allow employers to match manpower and work supply.

[9] One bank, NMB, explicitly follows the policy that reduction of working hours is permitted if the job is routine, if the relationship with clients is not intensive, if the employee is not a major link in the work chain, if the part-time working hours do not lead to disturbances in the work flow. Jobs cannot be done part-time if they score negative on any point in this list (Van den Berg-Wink, A. et al., Deeltijdarbeid bij de Nederlandse Middenstandsbank, in Schilfgaarde (1984)).

workforce) were changed into part-time jobs.[10] In 1985, the employers' organisation again raised the issue of part-time work in response to the union's request for shortening the working week.[11] Reduced working hours usually were found among typists, secretaries, cashiers, clerical workers and tellers.[12] The majority of female part-timers had a working week of 20 to 32 hours. The part-timers' average age, tenure, and turnover rates were higher compared to full-timers.

Apart from the part-time jobs that originated from female workers' requests, employers continued to create part-time jobs for which employees were recruited in the external labour market, although their share in total recruitment had decreased due to the decreasing share of unskilled jobs. This policy related to cleaning and catering jobs as well as unskilled clerical jobs, for which mainly re-entrant women were recruited. The few attempts to recruit school-leavers for newly created part-time jobs were unsuccessful.[13] School-leavers obviously preferred a full-time job.

To conclude, the banks' employment strategies changed in the first half of the 1980s, due to internal and external pressures. Internal pressure increased from workers requesting reduced working hours, presumably because of high unemployment rates and because of the growing number of skilled female workers considering their opportunity costs. Because of the lack of qualified part-time jobs, banks were not perceived as the appropriate workplace to re-enter. The policies of the banks were in favour of women's requests for two reasons. Encouraging part-time jobs could be used in negotiations with unions and such jobs could also be used in strategies to bring manpower in line with work supply.

11.4.4 The second half of the 1980s (1985-1989)

Unemployment steadily declined in the second half of the 1980s. Women increasingly continued working after giving birth, and thus pressured government to arrange day care centres. Until then, the majority of day care was arranged informally - family, neighbours, etc. Housewives were increasingly seeking paid work when their youngest child went to primary school.

---

[10] Het Financieele Dagblad, 17-2-1984

[11] Het Financieele Dagblad, 27-2-1985

[12] Social Report NMB 1983

[13] At RABO the recruitment of part-time school-leavers failed (Social Report 1985). There was no supply of part-time juvenile workers. If they were recruited, it proved that they had a full-time appointment within a year, either at the bank or for another employer. The same applied to ABN (SR 1985). Juvenile employees prefered jobs of 28 to 32 hours to jobs of 20 hours. If they had the opportunity, they tried to get full-time jobs.

For the period under study, figures are available for four banks. Annual average employment growth rates were just under zero for AMRO (-0.2%), just above zero for NMB (0.3%) and ABN (0.5%), and high for RABO (2.6%). Growth rates of the female workforce were again higher than men's rates. Educational levels of newly recruited employees continued to increase.

In this period, the percentage of part-timers in the banks' female workforce declined slightly. The number of requests for reduced working hours declined, probably because the reserve pool had been exhausted in the preceding years. In general, requests were answered positively, although some branches stated that the share of part-timers had reached an organisational maximum.[14] At the same time, the number of requests to increase working hours started to grow. Furthermore, turnover rates remained higher for part-timers than for full-timers, and recruitment on the external labour market for the unskilled part-time jobs declined. The importance of part-time work as an issue in the banks' personnel policies diminished. Now, other personnel policies aimed at female employees attracted attention. In all banks under study arrangements were made for unpaid maternity leave and for the re-entrance of female employees who left the bank to have a baby, usually within five years after this event.[15] These arrangements for re-entrancy allowed former female employees to apply for vacancies that were advertised only internally. The women who had left the bank were sometimes asked to take part in courses or to replace employees in case of sickness. Although the social reports are not clear about the reasons, this policy can be interpreted as a means to increase the returns on investment in female human capital. The banks recruited re-entrant female workers only if they had worked for the bank before. In general, the banks preferred this kind of arrangement to financial support for day care arrangements. One bank that shared a day care centre with a neighbouring hospital in the early 1980s considered terminating this project, but finally decided not to do so due to pressure from employees.[16] Another bank studied the need for financial support for day care arrangements, but concluded that many female employees were uncertain about both the timing of maternity and their preferences for a day care centre or looking after the children themselves.[17]

---

[14] RABO indicated that within the branches the share of part-timers which can be managed by an organisation had been reached (1986). Moreover, the women who wanted to change working hours had done so.

[15] RABO made an arrangement for re-entrant women comparable to the other banks (Social Report 1986). ABN made an arrangement in 1987 (Social Report 1987). NMB offered unpaid maternity leave (Social Report 1987). AMRO also had a leave regulation, which was evaluated in 1989 (Social Report 1989). This regulation proved to contribute to labour market attachment of mothers after having a baby.

[16] NMB

[17] Social Report ABN 1987

As far as demand for working hours is concerned, women intended to leave the labour market to a lesser degree, preferring reduced working hours. A survey held in 1988 showed that the majority of female employees in banks intended to have a continuous working career.[18] On the assumption of downward occupational mobility due to labour market interruption, one women stated: "Where would I earn as much as in this bank. Certainly not as a cashier in a supermarket".[19]

Compared to the part-timers in the 1960s, the part-timers in the 1980s were of the same age, were married to the same extent and were over-represented in lower graded jobs, although to a diminishing degree. However, whereas the part-timers in the 1960s were unskilled, had no experience in clerical work and had never worked in a bank before, the part-timers in the 1980s were skilled women, highly qualified for clerical work, and they usually changed working hours at a tenure of at least 5 years. The part-timers at the end of the 1960s were explicitly recruited for part-time jobs, whereas at the end of the 1980s banks had no recruitment policy for part-time jobs at all.

11.4.5   The first half of the 1990s (1989-1995)

Unemployment was rather low in the first half of the 1990s. Women increasingly continued working after giving birth, the vast majority in a part-time job. More than half of the female workforce was employed part-time, i.e. had a working week between 12 and 35 hours. The government had set up day care centres, and increasingly, collective bargaining included agreements in which employees were supported financially when using day care. In even greater numbers, housewives increasingly were seeking paid work when their youngest child was at primary school. In this decade, for the first time in post-war history, the majority of housewives is 45 years or over.

In 1989, ABN and AMRO merged to become ABNAMRO. Slightly later, NMB merged with Postgirobank into NMB Postbank. Employment growth rates in the first half of this decade were slightly under zero for ABNAMRO (-1.4%), for NMB Postbank (-0.7%), and for RABO (-0.07%). For ABNAMRO and RABO

---

[18] In 1988 the Service Sector Union conducted a written questionnaire for female employees in the banking sector. 350 women replied, of whom one third was a union member. 60% of these women wanted to remain in the labour market until retirement, whereas 40% wanted to withdraw. As far as the age group 25 or under was concerned, 70% intended to withdraw. Only 30% of women over 25 wanted to withdraw. Full-timers were more likely to have the intention to withdraw than part-timers, half versus one-third (Dienstenbond FNV: 'Overzicht van de belangrijkste enquête resultaten', Woerden, October 1988).

[19] This is said by a skilled female employee (encoder) in an interview. She reduced working hours after she had a son. She said that if she could not have had reduced working hours, she definitely would be forced to stop working. Social Report Postbank 1987.

the growth rates for the female workforce were slightly closer to zero than men's rates. For NMB the opposite obtains. Mergers as well as new technology curbed rising employment curves and set in a declining slope that could end up in personnel redundancies. At the same time, the educational level of newly recruited employees went up. In these five years, part-time rates rose a few percentage points. In 1995, at ABNAMRO and RABO nearly 40% of the female workforce was employed part-time. The percentage of part-timers at NMB rose after the merger with Postgirobank, because the percentage in the latter bank was about ten points higher than it used to be at NMB. At NMB Postbank this figure is now 48%.

In this period, personnel policies focused on part-time work in management. One bank explored the possibilities of part-time managerial jobs, because creating part-time work in these jobs was part of the policy to pursue organisational flexibility.[20] All employers continued their policies towards re-entrant women. They reconsidered their policies towards day care arrangements and they were increasingly willing to contribute to the costs of childcare for a fast increasing number of employees.[21] By doing so, they facilitate a continuous working career for women. Although, in all banks, the vast majority of part-timers have been wo-men, in the 1990s the percentage of part-timers in the banks' male labour force is rising, but is still well below 5%.

Secondary analyses of the 1991 survey show that female part-timers can still be found relatively often in clerical jobs, and relatively less in commercial jobs. They are older than full-timers, have longer tenure and work in lower-qualified jobs. However, female employees in higher grade jobs increasingly prefer to work part-time as well. They expect to reduce working hours without negative implications for their careers.[22] The 1993 survey shows that two out of every three 25 to 45-year-old female employees in the banking sector were satisfied with their number of working hours. One in six wanted to reduce working hours by a maximum of eight hours per week, and one in six wanted a reduction of a maximum of 16 hours. Women with children were the most likely group to reduce working hours.

Working time preferences not only include working hours, but also working irregular hours. This must be seen against the background of the banks' aim of longer opening hours in exchange for shortening the working week, as agreed in the collective agreement of 1994. The 1994 and the 1996 survey showed the same gendered patterns as the 1980 survey. Female employees preferred a

---

[20] Sociaal Jaarverslag ABN-AMRO 1993

[21] At NMB Postbank, the number of children of whom the parents applied for financial support of the bank, increased from 283 in 1990 to 820 in 1993. ABNAMRO also arranged childcare. The number of employees applying for support increased from 117 in 1990 to 619 in 1992.

[22] See Social Report ABN-AMRO 1993

shorter working week more often than male employees.[23] Yet, when the 36-hour working week was introduced in 1996, there were no gender differences in the assignment of a reduced working week (Tijdens, 1997c). In 1994 and 1996, men were willing to do evening work significantly more often.[24] In both years, no gender differences were found for Saturday work. No differences can be discovered on the issue of wage reduction. In 1994, women and men alike were prepared to reduce income in exchange for a shorter working week. In 1996, the shorter working week was introduced without income reduction.

To conclude, banks encourage male and female employees to reduce working hours as part of their flexibilisation strategies. An increasing number of women continues to work when they have children. The majority of these women request reduced working hours. The banks support childcare financially. Women with grown children request increased working hours.

11.5   CONCLUSIONS

In section 2 the findings on women's preferences for working hours appeared to be influenced by several factors. The presence of children under six is the most important explanatory factor. Yet, women's actual working hours substantially differ from their preferred ones. Women who have worked continuously and full-time and who are married tend to prefer reduced working hours. Women who have an interrupted working career, and women with a continuous working career and reduced hours tend to increase their working hours.

In terms of the demand-side of the labour market, five factors are assumed to explain the demand for part-time work. Four factors are part of corporate strategy, i.e. no part-time work at all, part-time work to bring manpower levels in line with work supply, part-time work for low-paid jobs in the secondary segment of the workforce, and creating part-time jobs when full-time female workers are scarce. The fifth factor is the individual strategy, i.e. employers agree to accommodate the requests of individual workers who prefer reduced working hours. In table 1, these assumptions are applied to employers' strategies in banks during the 30 years under study. The table shows that the strategies have changed over time. The first assumption of no part-time work at all does not hold true for the banks studied. The second assumption, bringing manpower in line with work supply, holds true from the mid-1980s onwards. In the 1990s this strategy is also applied to the managerial field. The third assumption was that for reasons of low pay employers created part-time jobs for segmented labour. This holds partly true for the 1960s, mainly because of expanding business combined with scarcity on the labour market. The fourth assumption was that employers will create part-time

---

[23] 88% versus 84%, p.<.01

[24] 53% versus 45%, p<.001, in 1994 and 33% versus 25%, p<.001 in 1996

jobs because of scarcity of full-timers on the labour market. This holds true for the 1960s. In the 1970s, when the labour market was less tight, the banks returned to the recruitment of full-time young women. The fifth factor was that employers are willing to fulfil the requests of individual workers who prefer reduced hours. It was assumed that this might depend upon the bargaining power of female workers, either based on the scarcity of their skilled labour or on their unionised power. It might also be based on the assumption of higher returns on investment in education. All of these arguments hold true for the 1980s and 1990s. In the second half of the 1980s, the trade unions changed their views on part-time work, as happened in other European countries (see Hakim, 1995b for the United Kingdom). Since then, unions claim the rights of part-time workers should be on a par with those of full-timers. Skilled female workers also seized bargaining power, partly because of the activities of women's groups in the banks, and partly because employers' (wo)manpower investments had grown so great that accepting requests for reduced working hours represented higher returns on investment than if these skilled female workers would quit. The demand for skilled female workers was high, especially because the number of skilled jobs increased, whereas the number of unskilled jobs decreased. This strengthened their bargaining position. Obviously, in the late 1980s the position of women became so strong that they could even demand longer working hours. To conclude, since the early 1980s, corporate strategy is increasingly dominated by the individual strategy.

Table 11.1 *Four factors in employers' strategies on part-time work in Dutch banks from 1965 until 1995.*

Year	Manpower and supply of work	Segmentation of part-time jobs	Scarcity in the labour market	Reply to re-quests	Share of part-time work
1965	No attention	Segmentation	Scarcity of full-	No requests	Increase
1966	"	of unskilled	time young	"	"
1967	"	clerical	women;	"	"
1968	"	jobs	Recruitment	"	"
1969	"	"	of female mar-	"	"
1970	"	"	ried part-	"	"
1971	"	"	timers	"	"
1972	"	Decline of un-	No scarcity	"	Decrease
1973	"	skilled jobs	"	"	"
1974	"	"	"	"	"
1975	"	"	"	"	"
1976	"	"	"	"	"
1977	"	"	"	Number	"
1978	"	"	"	of requests	"
1979	"	"	"	increases	"
1980	"	Segmentation	"	Studies	Increase
1981	"	of skilled	"	"	"
1982	"	work not	"	Agreement	"
1983	"	possible	"	on requests as	"
1984	"	"	"	part of	"
1985	"	"	"	bargaining	"
1986	Increased	"	"	Requests are	
1987	attention	"	"	granted for	
1988	"	"	"	reducing and	
1989	"	"	"	extending	
1990	"	"	"	hours	
1991	"	"	Scarcity of	Further support	Increase
1992	"	"	skilled	for women	"
1993	"	"	female	having young	"
1994	"	"	workers	children	"
1995	"	"	"	"	"

" means continued

One argument is shown in the table but was not reviewed in section 2. This argument concerns the role part-time work played in collective bargaining in the early 1980s. In this period, working time reduction became a major bargaining issue. Employers in many EU countries saw this as a chance to introduce flexible work and extended operating hours (De Lange, 1995). This was not the case in the Dutch banking sector. Here, employers perceived the shortening of the working week as worse than meeting individual workers' requests for reduced working hours. The main reason for this acceptance was that shortening the working week would supposedly lead to higher average hourly wages, although in most EU countries bargaining for a shorter working week was combined with more moderate wage demands by the unions. Obviously, individual reductions of working times would not lead to higher hourly wages. Essentially, this was a gender conflict. The conflict was won by the female workers - with a little help from the employers.

Obviously, employers were not willing to meet requests for reduced working hours for all jobs. For a long time, managerial jobs were excluded from part-time work, as were head-office positions. Thus, the higher graded jobs could not be part-time. These jobs were highly male dominated, whereas the majority of skilled female workers worked in female dominated jobs, e.g. tellers. In other words, if management allowed part-time work in these jobs, this could be a signal to the male employees that their jobs could be feminised. Managers and staff resisted fiercely any strategies to allow part-time work into their jobs. However, the need for flexibilisation obviously became stronger in the 1990s and employers increasingly ignored the signals. It can be expected that part-time work will soon be regarded by the majority of management and employees as just as normal as full-time work.

REFERENCES

Beechey, Veronica 1978: Women and production: a critical analysis of some sociological theories of women's work. In A. Kuhn & A. Wolpe (eds.): *Feminism and materialism*. Routledge & Kegan Paul, London, pp. 155-197.
Bernasco W. 1994: *Coupled careers. The effects of Spouse's Resources on Success at Work*. Amsterdam, Thesis Publishers.
Bielby, W. T. and James N. Baron 1984 *'A Woman's Place Is With Other Women: Sex Segregation Within Organizations'*. In Barbara F. Reskin (editor). Sex segregation in the Workplace. National Academy Press, Washington D.C., pp. 27-55.
Bielby, William T. and James N. Baron. 1986: Men and Women at Work: Sex Segregation and Statistical Discrimination. *American Journal of Sociology*, 91, nr. 4, p. 759-799.
Bruegel, Irene. 1979: Women as a reserve army of labour: a note on recent British experience. In *Feminist Review*, no. 3, pp. 12 – 23.
Craig, C., E. Garnsey and J. Rubery. 1985. Labour market segmentation and women's employment: A case-study from the United Kingdom. In *International Labour Review*, Vol. 124, no. 3, pp. 267-280.
Delsen, Lei 1995: *Atypical Employment: an International Perspective. Causes, Consequences and Policy*. Groningen, Wolters-Noordhoff (Ph.D. thesis).
Dex, Shirley. 1987: *Women's Occupational Mobility, A Lifetime Perspective*. London: Macmillan Press.
ETUI. 1986: *Flexibility of working time in Western Europe*, European Trade Union Institute, Brussels.
Fagan C, Rubery J. 1996: The Salience of the Part-time Divide in the European Union. *European Sociological Review*, 12/3, 227-250.

Hakim, Catherine. 1995a: *Labour mobility and employment stability: Is there a continuing sex differential in labour market behaviour?* Working Paper no. 1, London School of Economics, Department of Sociology.

Hakim, Catherine. 1995b: Five feminist myths about women's employment. In *British Journal of Sociology, 46:1, 429-455.*

Hakim, C. (1996). *Key Issues in Women's Work.* London, The Athlone Press

Hamermesh D S. 1996: *Workdays, Workhours and Work Schedules. Evidence for the United States and Germany.* Michigan (Kalamazoo), W.E. Upjohn Institute for Employment Research.

Henkens, C.J.I.M., J.J. Siegers & K.A. Meijer. 1994: Het arbeidsaanbod van gehuwde women en ongehuwd samenwonende vrouwen in Nederland: 1981-1989. In *Sociaal Maandblad Arbeid,* 49/5, p. 289-296.

Henkens, Kène, Jacques Siegers & Karel van den Bosch. 1992: Het arbeidsaanbod van gehuwde vrouwen in België en Nederland: een vergelijkende studie. In *Tijdschrift voor Arbeidsvraagstukken,* 8/1, p. 56-68.

Horrell, Sara & Jill Rubery. 1991: *Employee's Working Time Policies and Women's Employment.* London, Equal Opportunities Commission.

Kalleberg, Arne L., Knoke, D., Marsden, P.V. and Spaeth, J.L. 1996: *Organizations in America. Analyzing Their Structures and Human Resources Policies.* Thousand Oaks, Sage.

Lange, Willem de. 1995: Working time and time resource management. In Joris van Ruysseveldt, Rien Huiskamp & Jacques van Hoof (eds.): *Comparative Industrial & Employment Relations.* London, Sage Publications, p. 208-242.

Maassen van den Brink, Henriette 1994: *Female Labour Supply, child care and marital conflict.* Amsterdam University Press (Ph.D. thesis).

McRae, Susan. 1995: *Part-Time Work in the European Union: The Gender Dimension.* Dublin, European Foundation for the Improvement of Living and Working Conditions.

OECD. 1990: *Employment Outlook.* OECD, Paris.

Plantenga, Janneke. 1995: Labour-Market Participation of Women in the European Union. In Jacques van Hoof & Anneke van Doorne-Huiskes (eds.): *Women on the European labour market.* London, Paul Chapman Publishing, pp. 1-14.

Putte, Bas van den & Ans Pelzer. 1993: Wensen, motieven en belemmeringen ten aanzien van de arbeidsduur. In *Sociaal Maandblad Arbeid,* 48/ 7, pp. 487-495.

Renes, Gusta. 1991: *Working women. Their preferences and constraints.* University of Leiden, Leiden (Ph.D. thesis).

Rubery, J. 1995: Internal Labour Markets and Equal Opportunities: Women's Position in Banks in European Countries. In *European Journal of Industrial Relations,* 1: 2, pp. 203-227.

Schippers, J.J.M. 1985: Deeltijdarbeid in het bankbedrijf. In *Bank- en Effectenbedrijf,* January.

Stewart, M.B. & Greenlagh, C.A. 1984: Workhistory patterns and the occupational attainment of women. In *The Economic Journal,* vol. 94, September, pp. 493-519.

Tijdens, K.G., H. Maassen van den Brink, W. Groot & M. Noom. 1994: *Arbeid en zorg. Maatschappelijke effecten van strategieën van the huishoudens om betaalde arbeid en zorg te combineren.* The Hague, Organisatie voor Strategisch Arbeidsmarktbeleid (OSA), W-124.
Tijdens, K.G. 1997a: Gender and labour market flexibility. Forthcoming in T. Wilthagen et al. *Labour Law.* Amsterdam, KNAW.
Tijdens, K.G. 1997b: *Are Part-time and Full-time Jobs really Segmented? Explaining Women's Working Time from Family, Housework, Individual and Work Characteristics.* Belle van Zuylen Institute discussion papers, no. 10, University of Amsterdam.

APPENDIX 1 DATA ON THE BANKING SECTOR

Balance sheet figures	1	ABNAMRO	Dfl. 393 bln.
	2	RABO	Dfl. 202 bln.
	3	NMB-Postbank	Dfl. 174 bln.
Number of branches	1/2	NMB-Postbank	3100
	1/2	RABO	3100, including sessions
	3	ABNAMRO	1900, including foreign offices
Number of employees	1	ABNAMRO	59,634,including employees abroad
	2	RABO	37,850
	3	NMB-Postbank	23,876

Banks according to balance sheet figures, branches and number of employees in 1990.

APPENDIX 2 ANNUAL REPORTS

RABO	1977 until 1995
AMRO	1965 until 1989
ABN	1973 until 1989
ABNAMRO	1990 until 1995
NMB	1970 until 1989
NMB Postbank	1990 until 1995

Annual reports of the banks studied. Postgirobank is not studied until the merger with NMB.

APPENDIX 3 THE SURVEYS

The 1980 survey was a questionnaire, conducted among 1,466 employees, of which 296 were employed in the banking sector, among them 16% female workers (See Buningh, C.A., H.B. Colenbrander & H. Smit-Jongbloed. 1980. *Funktie en beloningsverhoudingen (computerfile)*. Amsterdam, Steinmetzarchive, number P0760).

The 1991 survey was conducted by the Service Sector Union. 9,461 questionnaires of bank employees, of which 4,094 by women, in order to trace their demands for negotiation of collective bargaining agreements (Noten, Han & Jan Warning. 1991. *Zo zit U op de bank. Onderzoeksverslag enquête onder bankpersoneel*. Woerden: Dienstenbond FNV). The questionnaires were sent to all union members in this sector and they were distributed at the buildings. Response rates cannot be given. The percentages of women and full-timers in the sample hardly deviate from the population means, whereas older people are slightly over-represented. In one respect the sample differs from the population: union density is nearly 60% in the sample whereas this is 9% in the population. Regression analyses however showed that union membership hardly attaches the dependent variables. The sample covers 7% of the workforce in the banking sector.

In 1993 a survey called Labour and Care was conducted (Tijdens et al., 1994). With a random dial technique a (pseudo-) a-select sample was drawn from a large data base containing telephone numbers. Altogether 1,420 women aged 25 to 45, of which 95 were employed in the banking sector, were interviewed by telephone. Among others, questions were posed about the household, paid work, working hours and preferred working hours.

In 1994 the service sector union again distributed a questionnaire among their members. Again the response was very high with 2,230 respondents, of which 812 were female. The Service Union was so kind as to give the system file to me.

In 1996 works' councils distributed questionnaires focusing on the 36-hour working week among the bank's workforce. Almost 30,000 questionnaires were sent back (Tijdens, 1997c). Distribution of major samples variables were comparable to those of the population.

APPENDIX 4 TURNOVER BECAUSE OF MARRIAGE AND BECAUSE OF PREGNANCY

Reasons to quit	1976	1980	1983	1986	1989
Turnover because of marriage					
RABO share in female workforce	2.07%	0.96%	0.47%	0.20%	0.16%
share in female turnover	12.29%	6.96%	5.45%	1.76%	1.41%
Turnover because of pregnancy					
RABO share in female workforce	3.85%	4.19%	3.97%	3.75%	2.78%
share in female turnover	25.43%	30.35%	45.75%	33.26%	24.2%
NMB share in female workforce			3.02%	3.79%	1.95%
share in female turnover			15.07%	14.67%	8.77%

Annual turnover because of marriage and because of pregnancy as a percentage of the female workforce and as a percentage of the female turnover at NMB and RABO. Source: Own calculations based on Social Reports NMB and RABO.

ACKNOWLEDGEMENTS

The research underlying this paper was funded by a grant from WVEO/NWO for the NWO-aandachtsgebied Time allocation and gender, no 759-717-603.The author would like to thank Catherine Hakim for her thorough comments on an earlier version of this chapter and Maarten van Klaveren and Anne Lavelle for their kind review of the English language. The author wishes to thank the Dienstenbond FNV for two data sets on bank employees, and the Steinmetzarchive for the 1980 dataset.

BIOGRAPHICAL NOTE

Kea Tijdens (PhD) is a sociologist and senior research fellow at the Department of Economics, University of Amsterdam, The Netherlands. Her recent papers include time allocation in households, gender and employment, and working-time issues in collective bargaining. She has published articles and books on internal labour markets, developments in office technology, occupational segregation, and ageing and careering in banking. Current research topics concern working-time reduction, expansion of opening hours and employer's staffing policies.

12   Time allocation as a major issue

Anneke van Doorne-Huiskes
Tineke Willemsen

12.1   INTRODUCTION

Inequalities in the division of paid and unpaid work between women and men seem to exist at all times and in all places. The Human Development Report 1995, specially written for The Fourth World Conference on Women held in Beijing in September 1995, concludes that, even at the end of the twentieth century, most women's work remains unrecognised, undervalued and unpaid. This not only applies to developing countries, but also to countries in the Western world. In developing countries, more than three-quarters of men's work consists of economic activities which are officially counted. The share of women in these activities is 24%. In the Western world such figures are slightly more equal: men allocate 66% of their time to paid economic activities, for women the figure is 34%. So, worldwide, men receive the lion's share of income and recognition for their economic contributions. In terms of total workload, women in developing countries account for 53% of the total working time spent on all economic activities, both "official" and "unofficial". Men account for 47% of this time. In the Western world, that proportion is 51/49.

For a number of Western countries, table 12.1 (see next page) shows time allocation patterns of women and men, including official and non-official time.

A major part of this so-called unofficial time is spent on household chores. Abstract figures on official and unofficial working hours at a macro level of societies represent a micro world of negotiations and division of tasks in households. In households all over Europe and elsewhere, unpaid domestic work has remained primarily a women's affair. Given the increased participation of women in the labour market in Europe in recent decades, this is a rather remarkable phenomenon. This remarkable phenomenon is the central issue of this chapter.

The main questions that will be addressed here are: How are patterns of paid and unpaid work developing in European countries? What explanations are there for the

Time allocation and gender, Kea Tijdens, Anneke van Doorne-Huiskes & Tineke Willemsen (eds.), Tilburg University Press, 1997, © Anneke van Doorne-Huiskes & Tineke Willemsen

fact that unpaid work still is done primarily by women? Which economic, socio-logical and psychological theories are available to explain current time allocation patterns of women and men? Is a more emancipated time allocation possible and, if so, which conditions have to be fulfilled to create equal time allocation patterns between women and men?

Table 12.1   Time Allocation by Women and Men in 13 Industrial Countries (as a Percentage of Total Working Time)

		Total working time		Female		Male	
	Year	*Official*	*Non official*	*Official*	*Non official*	*Official*	*Non official*
Australia	1992	44	56	28	72	61	39
Austria	1992	49	51	31	69	71	29
Canada	1992	52	48	39	61	65	35
Denmark	1987	68	32	58	42	79	21
Finland	1987-88	51	49	39	61	64	36
France	1985-86	45	55	30	70	62	38
Germany	1991-92	44	56	30	70	61	39
Israel	1991-92	51	49	29	71	74	26
Italy	1988-89	45	55	22	78	77	23
Netherlands	1987	35	65	19	81	52	48
Norway	1990-91	50	50	38	62	64	36
United Kingdom	1985	51	49	37	63	68	32
USA	1985	50	50	37	63	63	37
Average		49	51	34	66	66	34

Source: Human Development Report 1995

The next section presents some international data about time spent on paid and un-paid work. Subsequently, an overview will be given of sociological, economic and psychological explanations for the gender division of paid and unpaid work within the family. In addition to economic explanations based on differences in wages and earning potential between women and men, norms and taken-for-granted values, definitions and social constructions on what is seen as men's and women's respon-sibilities also appear important in current time allocation patterns between women and men. It is interesting to discover how feminist research adds new insights to mainstream theories on division of tasks between men and women. This will briefly be elaborated in the theoretical perspective of gender. At the end of this chapter, the focus will shift to proposals for more emancipated time allocation patterns between men and women.

12.2 TIME SPENT ON HOUSEHOLD WORK

Very little (recent) international comparative data is available on shifts in the amount of time spent on household work. The Irish study Changing Use of Time (1991) indicates how much time women in Canada, Denmark, the Netherlands, Norway, the United Kingdom and the United States spend on unpaid household work. The study splits unpaid work into routine domestic chores, childcare, odd jobs and shopping, and travel. Between 1970 and 1985, in each of the countries investigated, the average amount of time women spent on routine domestic chores appears to have declined by about an hour and a half. This change has been adjusted for so-called "compositional effects". In other words, the decrease in the time spent on domestic work cannot be explained by the fact that women in 1985 were more likely to engage in paid work than in 1970. Neither can the decrease in domestic work time be ascribed to a reduction in family commitments. That means the amount of domestic work has been declining for women, even when we adjust for structural changes in women's employment and family status. At the same time, men's domestic work seems to have increased in this period.
A French study on how women spend their time (1991) also shows that men contributed more to household work in 1986 than in 1975 and that women contributed less. The contribution that women in dual-career households made to "genuine" household work, however, was still almost three times as great as the contribution made by men. Wyatt (1992) observed the same phenomenon in the United Kingdom. The more hours that women work outside, the more unpaid work men do in the home. But men tend to spend their time working on tasks that do not have to be performed every day. Women continue to do the typical routine household work, such as cooking, laundry and cleaning. Van der Lippe (1992) investigated the distribution of paid and unpaid work between men and women in households in the Netherlands. Her analyses also demonstrate that there is a slight redistribution of household tasks between partners when women work (longer hours) outside the home. Her conclusion is an interesting one: partners redistribute the household tasks not so much because men begin to do more inside the home when women increase their working hours outside the home, but because women reduce the amount of time they spend on household tasks when they increase their outside working hours. So the relationships between paid and unpaid work change, without a substantial rise in the overall number of hours spent by men on unpaid work.

One issue in current time budget research in the Netherlands is whether a new type of household is developing in which paid and unpaid work will be equally divided between women and men. Time budget studies (SCP, 1995; Task Force on Future Scenarios Redistribution of Unpaid Work, 1995) show on average that women spend more than two times as many hours on unpaid work at home than men and/or than their husbands. Women spend an average of 32 hours per week on unpaid work, men spend 16 hours per week. For women, the number of unpaid hours varies according to the number of working hours. Women without paid jobs spend about 44 hours per week in the home. If women have jobs of less than 10 hours per week, then the average home work is 41 hours. If women work between 11 and 29 hours outside the home, their working week inside the home is about 34 hours. A significant reduction in unpaid work for women emerges if women have jobs of more than 30 hours per week; these women in general spend 18 hours on household tasks. Regardless of the number of hours worked by their partners, men's contribution varies from only 16 to 17 hours unpaid work per week. So, only when women are working (more or less) full time does there seem to be an equal share of household tasks between husbands and wives. In the Netherlands this pattern applies mainly for households of young couples without children. After children are born, patterns of task specialisation between women and men are very likely. We will return to this point later.

Although labour force participation of women has some redistributive power in relation to unpaid work, the general picture in the Netherlands, and in other countries, seems to be rather traditional. In general, as it turns out at the moment, men are responsible for 70% of all paid working hours and for 30% of the unpaid hours, while the reverse is the case for women. The next section focuses on the continuing dominant role of women in unpaid work, despite the increase in the number of women performing paid work. An overview will be given of economic and sociological arguments. In addition, the gender perspective on time allocation patterns between women and men will be briefly explored.

12.3   A SOCIOLOGICAL PERSPECTIVE

One of the earliest sociological explanations for the gender division of paid and unpaid work within the family is the theory of role differentiation (Parsons and Bales, 1955). Role differentiation in families can be considered as a specific case of the more general patterns of small groups. In this pattern, two roles emerge: that of the adaptive-instrumental leader and that of the integrative-expressive leader (e.g. Hiller, 1989). In family terms, the instrumental leader has to earn money outside the home, while the expressive leader stays home to take care of the members of the household. In the middle of the 20th century, little imagination was needed to answer the question of which person was most suitable for each role. This division of labour was considered efficient, functional and more or less inevitable in the family. Blood and Wolfe (1960) also stressed the efficiency of the division of labour between women and men. Much of the progress of the modern economy, they argued, was due to the increasing specialisation of its division of labour (e.g. Hiller & Philliber 1989). With this argument, they were in line with Becker's proposition for maximising the economic well-being of the family (1965). We will return to Beckler's theory later.

Because of the dominance of this so-called functionalistic thinking, sociological research on time allocation has emphasised norms, values, role expectations and role attributions as behaviour-regulating mechanisms. In this approach, processes of so-

216

cialisation guarantee that the functional prerequisites of societies transform themselves into personal needs of individuals. And if these socialisation processes do not always result in the full transformation of societal needs, there are always - according to socialisation theories - sanctions and other mechanisms of social control to redress deviant behaviour.

Another important approach to the division of paid and unpaid work between the sexes in sociological research is the so-called relative-resources theory (Hiller & Philliber 1989). Blood and Wolfe (1960) stipulated that the partner with greater resources - in terms of education, occupation and income - would have more power in the relationship. Blood and Wolfe's premise was that people would try to avoid unpleasant work and that household work was primarily seen as unpleasant. They contended that the partner with greater power would be more able to minimise his or her contribution to household chores and childcare duties than the partner with less power. Empirical evidence on this relative-resources theory is not convincing. Also, the general assumption that household work is considered unpleasant could be challenged.

12.4   AN ECONOMIC PERSPECTIVE

Economic theories on the division of paid and unpaid work between men and women within households are based predominantly on the so-called new home-economics approach. In this approach, market goods and the time household members spend both at home and in the market are seen as combined to produce household commodities. An example of this type of commodity is the "home", that is, a pleasant place or atmosphere in which family members like to live (e.g. Van der Lippe and Siegers, 1994). A household, according to these authors, can be considered as a "small factory" trying to maximise output, given constraints of time and money. The goal of the family is to maximise utility. It will, therefore, create that division of labour that gives the highest utility, or the most pleasant set of household commodities for the family (e.g. Chapter 5 in this book, van Velzen).

Becker (1965) has argued that households allocate their members' time according to each member's potential contribution, that is, according to the earning power of the partners. If the male partner is relatively more productive as a paid labourer and thus can earn more and is relatively less productive as a household labourer than the female partner, he will specialise in paid labour and she in unpaid labour at home. It could, of course, be the other way round, although this is empirically less probable. The household productive capacity matters as well. If both partners have the same productive capacity in paid work, but both agree - be it voluntarily or not - that the woman will be more productive in domestic tasks, then a specification of tasks along traditional lines will still occur. From a feminist point of view, the expression "agree" is a very interesting one. We come to this when we discuss the gender per-

217

spective. First of all, the empirical evidence of these types of decisions has to be addressed.

Evidence from research shows that decisions on divisions of tasks have accumulating effects (De Jong and De Olde, 1994). If, at a certain time, partners divide their tasks according to a true or false estimation or definition of their household capabilities, this estimation will become reality later on. Specialisation processes transform an expectation or definition at point T1 into reality at point T2. If the female partner reduces her participation in the labour force in order to meet the needs of the family, she will lose some of her professional skills and experience. Moreover, and perhaps even more importantly, she will lose part of her professional self-confidence and identity. These losses, in turn, later legitimise the division of tasks which has developed in the mean-time between male and female partners. In their research on division of household tasks between partners in the Netherlands, De Jong and De Olde (1994) made clear that partners in general do not take these long-term accumulative consequences into account. The aim of their study of 256 male / female couples was to discover how time allocation patterns developed after an important event in the household, namely the birth of a child. The emergence of a traditional pattern appeared to be the most probable case: the male assumed the role of the only or main breadwinner and the female took on the responsibilities of the main care provider. A factor which was not predicted by the economic model, however, was that later on in their marriages, many of these "traditional" women indicated regret about the separate spheres of responsibilities that had emerged between them and their partners in the intervening years. After years of specialisation, however, the division of tasks could hardly be changed.

In terms of policy measures this means that if women and/or men want to share tasks and responsibilities of work at home, they have to prevent traditional patterns from emerging and stabilising. This requires a lot of rational thought at a time when emotions normally have the upper hand, namely after the birth of a child. The - understandable - short-term thinking at this moment seems to provide an explanation for the persistent patterns of unequal division of unpaid work between males and females who share their lives. Of course, this short-term thinking often has a strong foundation in economics: most women do earn less than men, and more women than men find themselves in jobs with low mobility opportunities. But economic rationality is not the whole story as far as task divisions in domestic labour between the sexes are concerned. More subtle mechanisms have been revealed by studies based on the gender perspective. Before discussing this, the psychological perspective will be briefly described.

12.5 A PSYCHOLOGICAL PERSPECTIVE

From a psychological point of view it is important to clarify how preferences, opinions and perceptions influence human behaviour. The assumption of rational choice, which is implied in economic theory, does not always hold in psychology, where individual differences and subjectivities form the domain of study. Time allocation has been studied most extensively in social psychology, the psychological discipline in which the social context is explicitly included.

Psychological theories to explain time allocation in households can be divided in two broad categories. Nearest to economic theories are social exchange theories, in which social interaction, described as a series of transactions between two or more actors, form the central focus of attention (Thibaut and Kelley, 1959). The actors exchange personal resources (e.g. skills) for a desired benefit (e.g. employment). Actors weigh the costs and benefits of available options and decide upon the course of action they consider most beneficial to themselves. Decisions about the division of tasks in households are based on the relative resources of the partners. The more resources one has (e.g. income), the more power (e.g. to refuse to do housework). This economy-inspired model has often been criticised, because it neglects institutional limitations and social norms regarding household tasks (Van der Vinne and Brink, 1997). Brines (1993) argues that the assumption that principles of exchange theory - resources and outcomes - are gender neutral, is not correct. In her study of married couples, the division of household work only follows the rules of exchange theory in the traditional situation, when the husband earns more money than the wife. In that case, the wife will do most of the household tasks, even if she works full time. Where the wife earns more, however, there is a great chance that she also does most of the work at home. Husbands tend to do even less than in the traditional situation. In this way, they still adhere to the prevailing gender norms and so protect their definition of masculinity. So couples are "doing gender", which means that they confirm the traditional norms by their behaviour. Theories of social justice derive from exchange theory the assumption that individuals strive in interaction for a fair division of inputs and outcomes. However, different rules of fairness may be applied. This theory is extensively discussed in Chapter 4 by Van der Vinne.

A second type of psychological explanation is based on individual differences. Two concepts, attitudes and gender identity, have been especially popular in the explanation of gender differences in time allocation. As gender identity is treated elsewhere in this book (Chapter 3, Brink and Willemsen), we restrict ourselves to some comments on attitudes. In general, attitude theory predicts that one's evaluation of a certain object (attitude) predicts the behaviour towards that object and related objects. An attitude therefore can also be defined as a tendency to behave in a certain way. For instance, attitudes towards gender roles influence one's willingness to participate in housework. According to attitude theory, traditional men do not want to spend much time on housework, because they feel this is women's work. The results of attitude research are mixed. These "deep feelings", as Hochschild (1989) has called them, do not always predict how people will divide the work. It seems clear that not only one's own attitude, but also the attitude of the partner is important for the division of work between a couple. Individual concepts cannot fully explain interactional phenomena.

Neither psychological variables, nor economic variables alone can explain the total structure of the gender gap in time allocation. Different theoretical explanations obtain at different levels. We are convinced that only a combination of economic, sociological and psychological viewpoints can lead to a full understanding of what is happening in the time allocation process between the sexes. Moreover, it has become apparent that many theoretical concepts are not as gender neutral as they pretend to be. For instance, men and women may have different perceptions of the fairness of a certain division of tasks. Therefore, a gender perspective should be integrated in mainstream theories, in order to fruitfully study time allocation processes between women and men.

12.6   A GENDER PERSPECTIVE

A central perspective in feminist research on the division of paid and unpaid work between women and men, is that of gender. Gender refers to sex as a socially constructed reality rather than as a biological definition. Gender is seen as a social and normative construction, in which traditional task divisions along the lines of the sexes are considered and defined as natural and taken for granted. Gender, feminist theory claims, is continuously being constructed in the way men and women define themselves and each other. Emphasis is put on social constructions: norms, meanings and definitions about what is "normal" and "natural" behaviour for women and men as moral categories. This emphasis links feminist studies theoretically with sociological insights which have already been formulated by classic sociologists like Thomas and Mead, and which have been elaborated on by, for instance, Berger and Luckmann (1967).

Ferrée (1990) made clear how in many dual-earner families in the United States, the wife's income was defined and qualified as merely supplementary to that of her husband, even if the wife earned her income in a full-time job. Women, in general, do not define themselves as co-providers, but more likely as providers of a supplement to the income of the breadwinner. Husbands are likely to agree. This type of definition prevents men from giving up their privileges as breadwinners and women from easily transferring household duties to their husbands. Many women - as well as men - seem to think that household duties are simply part of a woman's responsibilities, even if the woman contributes substantially to the household income. This is taken for granted which assumption, and the symbolic construction of household work as "women's work" and as an expression of love towards her husband and family, make a sharp articulation of a change in the order of household work rather unlikely. Most women try to prevent conflict over household tasks. The (emotional)

220

costs of this kind of conflicts are high and their effects are, generally speaking, small. Using more formal economic terminology, it could be said that minimalisation of conflicts is a highly important utility function for many women. Conflicts are costly and marital harmony is a valuable aim. In the name of this harmony, many attempts to change the traditional patterns of time allocation are nipped in the bud. This very fact provides a viable explanation for the lasting inequality between women and men in the pattern of the division of domestic labour. It goes beyond economic rationality. This reality of social definitions needs to be taken into account in order to get a more complete insight into the division of tasks between men and women.

12.7   CHANGING TIME ALLOCATION THROUGH WOMEN'S PAID WORK?

We now shift our focus from a theoretical explanation of the gender gap in unpaid work especially to the possibilities of changing this situation. Until recently, policies in the EU aiming to enhance the reconciliation of paid and unpaid work were mainly concerned with paid work. This has resulted in equal opportunities policies, equal pay for equal work, and sometimes in affirmative action. On a European level, this emphasis on paid work is in line with the mainly economic character of the European Union, of which its social policy is a reflection, as many authors have already mentioned (Duncan, 1996; Hoskyns, 1996; Rossilli, 1997).

Notwithstanding this emphasis on paid work, the situation of women and men in this field is still unequal. In spite of significant improvements in women's labour market conditions, in every country in Europe women work less, earn lower hourly wages and have lower positions in the organisational hierarchies than men (Eurostat, 1995; UNHD, 1995; Willemsen & Frinking, 1995). Undoubtedly there have been important changes in the labour force participation of women. However, from the various data on time allocation for unpaid work in relation to paid work, it is clear that the increased labour force participation of women does not automatically lead to enhanced housework participation by men.

Equal opportunity policies have often implicitly or even explicitly assumed that a redistribution of unpaid work would result from changes in paid work. This is in accordance with economic theories such as new home economics and the more psychological exchange theory: if women are going to spend more time on paid work it is predicted that they will diminish the time spent on unpaid work. The assumption is, moreover, that the amount of unpaid work is a fixed quantity and, therefore, if women spend less time on it, men will have to spend more time. As we have seen, however, time allocation, and especially the distribution of tasks among men and women who form a household, does not always follow the courses considered rational in these types of theories. For instance, the total task load of household work seems to be a flexible quantity. Or, men and women do not compare their total workload with each other but compare themselves to their same-sex parent or

221

friends, so that men have male comparison figures and women female comparison figures. Even if spouses do compare their unequal taskloads they are not always dissatisfied (Van der Vinne & Brink, 1997). And even if women are dissatisfied with the division of tasks they often seem to apply a coping strategy instead of a change strategy. So it seems that in real life people find all kinds of ways out of the rational behaviour expected from them by policy makers. They may have in mind other priorities than an equal division, for instance conflict reduction, as discussed above.

European policy documents like the Fourth Action Programme (1996-2000) indicate that there is a growing recognition of this unequal division of tasks between men and women; and an increasing recognition that the growth of women's labour force participation is hindered by a lack of growth in the actual participation of men in unpaid work. Time allocation is a major policy issue, and policies for the redistribution of time are more varied now than they used to be. Also, as we have demonstrated in the previous sections, more sophistication and variation have developed in the theoretical explanations for gender differences in paid and unpaid work, this most persistent gender gap. In the next sections we will present a number of new projects that have been proposed to diminish the gender gap and evaluate them in the framework of the explanations presented in the previous sections. In this way we hope to shed some light on the conditions that are necessary for any solution to be really effective.

12.8   CHANGING TIME ALLOCATION: SOME RECENT EXAMPLES

Approaches aimed at the redistribution of paid and unpaid work among women and men share one common factor: they are very recent. They are all models or solutions that focus not only on the participation of women in paid work, as so many of the older policies do, but are explicitly meant to make the two types of activities, paid work and work in the home including childcare, more compatible.

In the Netherlands the recognition of the insufficiency of traditional policies has led to a systematic reconsideration of the goals of redistribution policies and of the means to reach these, as will be demonstrated in the first example. The second example, from the United Kingdom, demonstrates that there is a tendency towards less state intervention in these matters in many countries of the EU. Governments are redistributing responsibility and leave more to social partners. Some countries will only encourage private initiatives or initiatives from the social partners for the reallocation of time. The Opportunity 2000 initiative is an example of this tendency. Finally, the third example discusses one of the first policies aiming directly at the redistribution of unpaid work among men and women and not indirectly through women's work. The Italian City Time experiment is aimed at giving both men and women possibilities for combining their paid work with family tasks.

12.9 THE NETHERLANDS: FOUR SCENARIOS FOR THE REDISTRIBUTION OF UNPAID WORK

The Dutch government, in a kind of back-to-basics movement, started to study the question: what kind of distribution of paid and unpaid work is desirable and how should these tasks be divided among men and women? In 1994 a Task Force on Future Scenarios Redistribution of Unpaid Work was established with the task of developing four scenarios and in this way evaluate four different options for the future. These four scenarios differed in the degree to which household and care work:

1   are either mainly unpaid and performed by women;
2   are unpaid and performed equally by men and women;
3   are a balanced mix of paid and unpaid work and performed equally by men and women;
4   are mainly in the form of paid work, while the remaining tasks are equally performed by men and women.

For a redistribution of unpaid work the Task Force stipulates that different types of policy measures are necessary. First, the flexibilisation of paid work, for instance through a legal right to part-time work, and various social security measures which encourage rather than discourage workers to combine their jobs with family responsibilities. Next, changing the tax system so that breadwinners' facilities are replaced by individual rights. Also, by enhancing facilities for paid care, such as day care for children, and by facilitating the contracting out of care tasks, for instance through tax benefits.

In their report (1995), for each of the four scenarios, the Task Force considers which combination of policy measures can achieve the stated goal within 15 years, as well as its feasibility and desirability. Not surprisingly, the Task Force considers the third scenario, which they call the Combination Scenario, the most desirable: there is a balance between paid and unpaid work, i.e. about half the work is paid and half is unpaid, and a gender balance exists, i.e. men and women participate equally in both types of work. The normal working week for paid work will be 32 hours at most. In this scenario, men are expected to reduce current hours of paid work, and to spend more time on taking care of their families than they do now. The Task Force thinks this is a feasible scenario because men still will hold a considerable amount of paid work so that they will not have to give up the breadwinnership that is considered so important for their identity. And parents will retain a large share in the care of their children, which is very important in the Dutch cultural value system, as it is in many others.

Although these last remarks imply that the Task Force has given some thought to the implementation of these plans on the level of individuals and households, they nevertheless show an almost naive optimism with regards to the makability of soci-

223

ety through legislation and financial measures. This scenario has to be realised at household level, i.e. within households partners should have an equal division of all tasks. The policy measures which have been proposed, however, are all on a national level and their effects have hardly been tested. As we have seen in the previous paragraphs, however, individuals do not always behave in an economically rational way. The neglect of measures directed at the social and psychological level in this scenario makes it almost unpredictable how the combination of policy measures they propose will work out in practice. To encourage people to behave in the desired way, a well-designed campaign will be necessary to influence attitudes towards work and care, and to make people aware of the assumptions they have always taken for granted, e.g. that women are better suited than men to take care of children.

As a sequel to this study another Task Force was set up, the Task Force on the Daily Timetable, whose assignment is to come up with new and creative ideas for the daily schedule in Dutch society which would facilitate the combination of work and care tasks. Also, the Equal Opportunity Council wrote a recommendation based on this same assumption that a working week of 32 hours, for men and women, should be striven for. To make this possible they advise individualising the social security and tax systems in such a way that men and women are really considered individuals who both have a responsibility for paid work and care tasks (Emancipatieraad, 1996).

So, in contrast with many previous equal opportunity efforts which aimed at making more women work and work more hours, plans have been developed in the Netherlands which aim at men working less in paid work. These are only plans and recommendations, however; daily reality in the Netherlands still lags behind these sometimes rather revolutionary concepts. But then, it seems almost a hallmark of Dutch society that there is a big gap between progressive thinking and traditional practice (Willemsen, 1997).

12.10   UNITED KINGDOM: OPPORTUNITY 2000

In the United Kingdom a program was launched in 1991 by "Business in the Community", to increase the proportion of women in the work force. In 1991, 61 organisations, predominantly from the private sector, took part in this campaign. It has participation from some public organisations, but it is set up by and must be carried out by private initiative. Opportunity 2000, which has a small staff unit, provides its members with workshops and conferences and conducts an annual review of their progress. Companies and organisations are free to join, they have to pay a fee (minimum £1,000) to do so, and they can set their own goals which they then have to monitor. The program's approach is based on the necessity of changes in organisational culture. At first glance, it seems a very realistic program as both its goals and its measures are at the same level, that of organisations. Besides, no measures are enforced, participation in the program is voluntary.

The success of the Opportunity 2000 project is difficult to evaluate. Its success in terms of participation seems to have dwindled. By the end of 1991 it had more than doubled its membership: 150 organisations had joined (Opportunity 2000, 1992). Although membership has steadily increased since then, growth has not been as fast as in this first year. The Fifth Year Report (1996) mentions 305 members. Also, progress towards the goals of more opportunities for women seem to have lost momentum or sometimes even regressed. The percentage of women in top management positions had doubled from 8 percent to 16 percent in 1995; however, in 1996 this percentage decreased to 11 percent. In 1996, 70% of the members offered a short paternity leave; however, in 1994 this was already the case for 67% of the members. Bagilhole (1997) characterises the development of Opportunity 2000 as: "Initial success - then mixed progress?"

Its voluntary nature is a strong point of this programme. It means that the organisations that take part are really committed to equal opportunities for men and women. However, its voluntary membership could also be its weak point. As soon as members do not see the (economic) benefit from their participation, either directly or indirectly through a better public relations standing, there is no incentive left to participate, apart from an ethical one. Government support is totally absent in an economic sense, participants get no extra facilities of any kind. Therefore, the program is probably vulnerable to economic recession.

In the Netherlands, a similar campaign was launched in 1996: "Opportunity in business". In contrast with the British program this initiative stems from, and is supported by the government. The campaign receives a generous starting grant from the government for the first three years and then will have to be self-supporting. As yet, no data are available to evaluate its success.

12.11 ITALY: CITY TIME EXPERIMENT

A very interesting example that is mainly concerned with unpaid work is the City Time experiment in Italy (Bimbi, 1995). The philosophy behind this project is that, if one wants to give both men and women the possibility to work and to take care of others, the opening hours of schools, offices, official city services and shops should be harmonised in such a way that people can indeed perform their caring tasks at different times from their paid work. No fixed model is prescribed, in every city different solutions can be planned. Large organisations may, for instance, have fixed opening hours, while schools are open at the same time and public services will be open after these hours. Or organisations may have flexible working hours in order to allow employees to adapt their working hours to other tasks. In some cities, schools' timetables have been changed. In general, a City Time project also includes streamlining bureaucracy at local level. In many of the larger cities that take part in this project there is a separate office for City Time policies, headed by a woman (Bimbi, 1995).

The City Time experiment forms a good example of literally reallocating time. The program is still rather new, and has not been evaluated formally. Its success in terms of participating cities is clear. Nine regions have approved a law on City Time matters, and at least 80 cities, including some large provincial capitals, have adopted a City Time program (Bimbi, 1995; Trifilletti, 1997). Bimbi (1995) estimates that the experiment will have a good chance of becoming successful in the reallocation of time. Firstly, it stems from theoretical and empirical research done by female researchers and is based on policy initiatives from female policy makers at national as well as local level. Moreover, these experiments concern not only the reconciliation of work and household tasks for women, as is so often implicitly or explicitly the case with other policies, but are also aimed at reallocation of time for men. Trifiletti (1997, personal communication) is less optimistic, however. She fears that in the euphoria of the success of this really high standard of planning and of innovative time management at a city level, the main problem, i.e. the unequal distribution of care tasks among men and women, disappears from view. Also, the project deals only with practical solutions, no efforts are made to change the gender role attitudes and assumptions on which they are based.

Even if no formal evaluation is yet available and in spite of the aforementioned objections, these experiments seem worthwhile to describe because they represent the first large-scale effort to reconcile paid and unpaid work for men and women through a very simple mechanism: by giving people the time to do it! In this way, they mesh very well with a new trend of downshifting, i.e. the phenomenon now propagated by some critical economists - not working so hard, not always wanting better jobs, and working harder but paying more attention, and spending more time, for personal development, leisure, and family matters. One can, however, also be cynical about this latter tendency and consider it an example that as soon as women have found their way in organisations, the rules of the game will change. Women finally succeeded in gaining access to higher positions, to management levels, and as soon as they get there, hard work and long working hours are devalued, depicted as not really worthwhile and leading to much stress, with downshifting as the solution. A more optimistic viewpoint, however, would emphasise that finally women are getting more influence, that the more "feminine" view that there is more to life than work alone and that it is also important to spend more time on your family is acknowledged. The City Time Experiment at least allows people to make their own choices in this respect; they can work hard if they wish to and at the same time they still have the opportunity to fulfil other tasks.

12.12 CONCLUSION

These examples show that in European countries different approaches have been developed to redistribute paid and unpaid work. On the one hand, there is a growing consciousness that changing men's and women's behaviour by policy measures at government level is a hard job. On the other hand, this recognition gives room to very innovative and practical projects of which the Italian City Time Project is an excellent example. What is clear is that changes in time allocation of paid work of women and men do not automatically lead to changes in their division of unpaid work. This redistribution of unpaid work, however, is the very basis of better conditions for women in the labour force. In policy programs at the European level, and at national level in policies, by local authorities, by firms and by the women's movement, and in daily practice of households, this relationship between a fair division of unpaid work and women's opportunities in the labour force is recognised. To realise such a fair division needs commitment and co-operation from all these actors.

The chapters in this book make clear that there is not one all-embracing theory which explains time allocation patterns of women and men. Different mechanisms are at issue: economic rationalities, normative realities and personal identities. In the world of business other, sometimes more rational expectations count often more than within families where normative constructions and assumptions which are taken for granted deeply influence the daily patterns of behaviour of women and men. For researchers this means that multidisciplinary projects, of which this book is an example, are most important. For policy makers the lack of an all-embracing theory implies that diversity in measures, adapted to the cultural context of states, is a condition sine qua non for a fair division of that most precious of all commodities: time.

REFERENCES

Bagilhole, B. 1997: *Recent initiatives with regard to the division of paid and unpaid work between women and men: The role of the social partners in the UK.* Paper prepared for the European Network on Policies and the Division of Unpaid and Paid Work.
Becker, G.S. 1965: A theory of the allocation of time. *The Economic Journal*, 1980 (pp 493-517).
Berger, P.L. and Th. Luckmann. *The social construction of reality.* Doubleday & Company. New York, 1967.
Blood, R.O. and D.M. Wolfe 1960: *Husbands and wives: the dynamics of married living.* Illinois: Free Press of Glencoe.
Bimbi, F. 1995: Gender division of labour and welfare state provisions in Italy. Governmental policies on reconciliation of paid and unpaid work for parents. In T. M. Willemsen & G. A. B. Frinking (Eds.), *Work and family in Europe: The role of policies* (pp 113-127). Tilburg: Tilburg University Press.
Brines, J. 1993: The exchange value of household work. *Rationality and Society, 5*, 302-340.

Commissie Toekomstscenario's Herverdeling Onbetaalde Arbeid 1995: *Onbetaalde zorg gelijk verdeeld* [Unpaid care divided equally]. Den Haag: Ministerie SZW.

Duncan, S. 1996: Obstacles to a successful equal opportunities Policy in the European Union. *European Journal of Women's Studies, 3*, 399-422.

Emancipatieraad 1996: *Met zorg naar nieuwe zekerheid* (With care to a new security). Den Haag: Emancipatieraad. Advies nr. IV/45/96.

European Foudation for the Improvement of Living and Working Conditions. 1991: *The changing use of time: Report from an international workshop.* Loughlinstown House. Skanhill, Co. Dublin.

Eurostat 1995: *Women and men in the European Union.* Luxembourg: Office for Official Publications of the European Communities.

Ferree, M. Marx. 1990: Beyond separate spheres: Feminism and family research. *Journal of Marriage and the Family. 52.* November, 866-884.

Hiller, D.V and W.W. Philliber 1989: *Equal partners: Successful women in marriage.* Newbury Park, CA. Sage Publications.

Jong, A. de and C. de Olde 1994: *Hoe ouders het werk delen* (How parents divide their work). Ministery of Social Affairs. Vuga Uitgeverij B.V. Den Haag.

Opportunity 2000 1992: *Towards a balanced workforce. First year report.* London: Opportunity 2000.

Lippe, T. van der 1992: De verdeling van huishoudelijk en betaald werk in Nederland. (The division of paid and unpaid work in the Netherlands). *Mens en Maatschappij. 67, 2,* pp 128-139.

Lippe, T. van der and J.J. Siegers 1994: Division of household and paid work between partners: effects of relative wage rates and social norms. *Kyklos,* pp. 109-136.

Lippe, T. van der 1995: *Scarcity of time of women in European Countries.* European Union Report.

Opportunity 2000 1996: *Towards a balanced workforce. Fifth year report.* London: Opportunity 2000.

Parsons, T. and R.F. Bales 1959: *Family, Socialization and Interaction Process.* Illinois.

Rossilli, M. 1997: The European Community's policy on the equality of women. From the Treaty of Rome to the present. *European Journal of Women's Studies, 4,* 63-82.

Roy, C. 1991: *Evolution des emplois du temps des citadins en France entre 1975 et 1985.* Institut National de la Statistique et des Etudes Economiques. Insee. Paris Cédex.

Sociaal en Cultureel Planbureau 1995: *Tijdopnamen.* Sociale en Culturele Studies-22. Rijswijk.

Thibaut, J.W., & Kelley, H.H. 1959: *The social psychology of groups.* New York: Wiley.

Trifiletti, R. 1997: *Work-family arrangements in Italy.* Paper presented at the Expert Meeting on Work-Family Arrangements in Europe, Rotterdam, May 1997.

United Nations Development Programme (UNDP) (1995). *Human Development Report 1995*. Oxford: Oxford University Press.

Van der Vinne, H., & Brink, M. 1997: Dilemma or compromise: The division of housework and child care among dual earners. In G. A. B. Frinking & T. M. Willemsen (Eds.), *Dilemmas of modern family life* (pp. 91-111). Amsterdam: Thesis.

Willemsen, T. M. 1997: Dutch women and men between egalitarianism and traditionality. In G. A. B. Frinking & T. M. Willemsen (Eds.), *Dilemmas of modern family life* (pp. 5-16). Amsterdam: Thesis.

Willemsen, T. M., & Frinking, G. A. B. (Eds.) 1995: *Work and family in Europe: The role of policies* (pp 113-127). Tilburg: Tilburg University Press.

Windebank, J. 1996: To what extent can social policy challenge the dominant ideology of mothering? A cross-national comparison of Sweden, France and Britain. *Journal of European Social Policy, 6*, 147-161.

Wyatt, S. 1992: Tijdsregistratie bij huishoudelijk werk: winst en verlies voor vrouwen. *Mens en Maatschappij*. 67, pp. 106-127.

BIOGRAPHICAL NOTE

Anneke van Doorne-Huiskes is a Professor of Women's Studies at the Faculty of Social Sciences of the Erasmus University of Rotterdam. She also works as a consultant for organisational change and equal opportunities policy. She has published books and articles on women's careers, pay differences between men and women and the effects of equal opportunities policies.

Tineke M. Willemsen is a social psychologist. She has had academic positions in Social Psychology at Leiden University, and in Women's Studies in Amsterdam University and Tilburg University, where she now holds the Chair of Women's Studies. Her research interests concern gender stereotypes and gender identity; female managers; and the division of paid and unpaid work in families. She is co-founder and co-ordinator of an international network of researchers that is doing a comparative study on the last topic, The European Network on Policies and the Division of Unpaid and Paid Work.